DO ALL ROADS LEAD TO JERUSALEM?

First Published in 2014 by Manohar Publishers and Distributors

Title ID: 5331070

ISBN-13: 978-1508578376

DO ALL ROADS LEAD TO JERUSALEM?

THE MAKING OF INDIAN RELIGIONS

S.N. BALAGANGADHARA
with DIVYA JHINGRAN

CONTENTS

PREFACE

In 1994, E.J. Brill published *The Heathen in His Blindness...*, whose second Indian edition was published by Manohar in 2005. Ever since the book was first published, a need was felt for bringing out a smaller and more readable version. However, this meant a quasi-total rewriting of the book, a task that I did not feel like undertaking. Until, that is, Divya Jhingran stepped in and took it upon herself to perform this huge task. The result is what you have in your hands: a simpler, slimmer and very readable version of my book. Divya's magnificent effort has taken nearly two years to complete. The end result, in some senses, is a new book: while being faithful to the original, this book also surpasses it in clarity, focus and accessibility. There is no way I can thank her adequately for what can only be termed as an extraordinary feat and a labor of love.

This book brings the central thread of my research and enquiry much more sharply into focus than the original. It cuts out all the digressions and the secondary lines of enquiry that *The Heathen* was forced to pursue for the sake of academic completeness. Consequently, Divya and I have jointly decided to publish this book under a new title, instead of calling it an 'abridged edition' of the original work. By bringing the central thread clearly into focus, this book answers many criticisms made by some of my readers, who missed the key arguments of *The Heathen*. It is my sincere hope that the reader will now be able to follow my investigation better without being distracted by the secondary arguments that the original contained.

Perhaps it would be good to outline my basic argument by elaborating on the title: *Do All Roads Lead to Jerusalem?* If the point of reference that provides meaning to the word 'religion' is taken to be the Semitic religions (Judaism, Christianity, Islam), it is my claim that Indian culture does not have any indigenous religions (like 'Hinduism', 'Buddhism', 'Jainism', etc.). However, for many centuries now, in both academic discourse and in theological debates, one continues to speak about Indian religions. I explain this situation by showing that the discussions about religion are fully trapped within a theological framework that is basically Christian (and Semitic) in nature. In this book, I not only clarify that framework but also show how and why it imprisons all discussions about the existence of religion.

Some of my critics found fault with *The Heathen* because they felt that I defined the word 'religion' the way I wanted to, and that too in the first chapter itself. Nothing is farther from the truth. There is no definition of the word religion for the first seven chapters of the book. This is because a specific definition of the word is not required for outlining the historical and theoretical origins of the contemporary situation with respect to religion. I provide an ostensive definition of religion in chapter eight, and then proceed to develop a hypothesis on what religion is, in chapter nine. A definition is necessary only when one develops an explanatory hypothesis and not before. Of course, many of my critics have missed this crucial point in their haste to criticize without paying adequate attention to the scientific way of investigating a phenomenon. It is my hope that this volume will go some way in solving this problem.

Yet other critics, in their rush to pigeonhole me, have decided that I am a post-colonial thinker and a follower of Edward Said. It is hard to figure out how they came to this conclusion, but it might nevertheless be useful to declare openly that I am neither of the two. While I did read Said's *Orientalism*, it was singularly unsuitable for the task I had at hand. Even though my initial reaction to the way the West portrays the East may have been a conviction similar to that of Said–that these writings are inherently racist, imperialist and sexist–pretty soon this conviction gave way to doubts. It is neither possible nor particularly enlightening to condemn all European authors as being racist or imperialist. Nevertheless, we're still left to grapple with the question: why did they all say pretty much the same things? What lies behind the systematic nature of this western way of talking about the Orient? In other words, surely the more interesting question is "Why is the West orientalist?" Said's plea ends up denying any possibility of understanding cultural differences or indeed why Orientalism came into being, or what sustains it. To say, as the post-colonials do, that the relation between power and knowledge answers this question is to make a mystique of Foucault's idea, as though it explains everything. If such buzzwords do anything at all, they explain why the post-colonials earn a good living: they talk the talk of their employees, and walk the walk of their patrons. This is not to deny that there are genuine and committed people among them, or even to deny that they want to address themselves to genuine and urgent issues. It is only to draw attention to this aspect of post-colonialism.

My quest has been to try and highlight the fact that labeling someone racist, or orientalist, or Eurocentric merely obfuscates the deeper issue, one that is more insidious than any of the above three. Why do these attitudes persist, why do they keep reproducing themselves, and how have they come to infect the social sciences in India and the rest of the world? My research has nothing to do with the post-colonial way of looking at things. In fact, I consider that line of research intellectually pernicious. I do not seek to follow some fad; I seek to begin the process of scientifically investigating cultural and social phenomena with the seriousness that they deserve.

Some others, especially in India, and the defenders of 'political correctness' in the US, have decided that I belong to the 'Hindu Right' and that I am a spokesman of the *Sangh Parivar*. Of course, this charge is entirely baseless. It is a matter of public record that I claim that 'Hinduism' (as a religion) does not exist in India. Consequently, from my writings on the subject, no one can accuse me of supporting a stance that is founded on 'Hinduness' or 'Hindudom' or 'Hinduism', (whether conceived as a religion or called *sanatana dharma*). So, from where could these people have drawn this conclusion? Unfortunately, gossip-mongers do not go by evidence or fact; mendacity and demagoguery provide them with their 'moral' justification.

It is ironic that the so-called secularists in India and their 'Hindu' opponents are mirror-images of each other. Their ideas about religion, their responses to the colonial descriptions of India, the respective paths they have chosen to pursue–all of these are symmetrical and arose amid the same constellation of concerns. If the rise of Hindu nationalism is a major threat to intellectual freedom in the study of India, so is the state of (implicit and explicit) censorship imposed by the secularists. If I criticize the secularists it does not automatically follow that I side with nationalists or fundamentalists of any stripe. Let's assume that, in some of my writings, I happen to reach the same conclusion as some or the other ideologue from Hindutva. The question is: what does that indicate, or prove, or provide evidence for? After all, you may reach the same conclusion as the Hindu Right does when asked about the chemical composition of water. Would this count for evidence that you belong to the Hindu Right?

Any movement that captures the imagination of a people has to have some kind of a narrative. Normally, the crafting of such a narrative involves the labor of intellectuals. The Indian Congress Party used to have a narrative, although it has completely lost it in the last few decades. The Communist parties had a strongly resonant narrative provided by intellectuals from yesterday and today. The Hindu Right has indeed found resonance with a broad cross-section of the people in India and yet they appear to have no distinct narrative of their own. The fact that they are characterized as Fundamentalists, Fascists, or Nationalists indicates that these characterizations have more to do with individual feelings about the above-named movements rather than the story the Hindu Right narrates about itself.

Furthermore, the Hindu Right is hostile to intellectuals. In fact, it is very typical to hear them identify intellectuals with 'secular thinkers'. It is almost as though they think that this social layer, which the intellectuals are, is an alien growth in Indian culture, something that the British created. While it is undoubtedly true that the kind of academic intellectuals we have today are an outgrowth of colonial and post-colonial developments, this situation does not quite explain the hostility of the Hindu right towards intellectuals. Hostility towards knowledge and truth is not native to Indian culture. Knowledge and search for truth have typically been regarded as the most highly prized and deeply revered aspects of Indian culture. Funnily enough, the Hindu right is not hostile to something that is truly alien to Indian culture–Nationalism. I hope these observations can put to rest any misunderstanding about my political leanings.

While these and the other criticisms that this book has met raise important questions about the deplorable state of social science research in India and abroad, it may be more useful to focus on the state of religious studies today. When *The Heathen* first came out, not many were willing to accept the basic thesis of the book: that Indian religions are non-existent and that they were created by the Semitic religious theologies. Today, however, it has become almost orthodox in the field of Religious Studies to proclaim loudly that the Indian religions are 'constructs'. While it is entirely unclear what kind of constructs they are and what it means to speak of 'constructions', it is nevertheless good to note that most scholars in the domain of Religious Studies have moved on from the previously uncritical attitude that was characteristic of their research.

Despite this fact, there is something very disturbing about this state of affairs. The original book is by now well-known and is cited reasonably regularly. There have been reviews published in many academic journals as well. Thus, one is forced to assume that the book did not die out due to lack of notice. Yet none of the scholars has been able to mount a challenge to any of the theses that the book argues for. The hypotheses outlined in my book undercut many of the ideas that are popular in the academia today. Are the intellectuals of today so enamored by themselves that they forget it is their duty to take intellectual challenges seriously? It appears so. Truth and falsity are less important to academics today than fame and popularity. It is my hope that this new book will go some way in contributing to the rectification of this horrifying situation.

I would like to end this short introduction by thanking Divya once again for her herculean effort. This book would simply not exist without her. Many, many thanks. Thanks, too, to Mr. Jain, the vision behind Manohar Publishers, for his willingness to publish this book.

S.N. BALAGANGADHARA

INTRODUCTION

This is a book about western culture. To be more specific, it is about one element that went into the formation of western culture, i.e., religion. Anthropologists generally recognize that people from any given culture use concepts and theories native to their own culture when they describe other cultures. Underneath this fact lies the problem that this book will examine. The problem is: in what way are the beliefs of the people from western culture reflected in their descriptions of other cultures? Or to formulate it more concretely, can we specify, for instance, how much of what the West says about India is rooted in western culture rather than in Indian culture? By examining the way in which people from the West have described religions in India, we can decipher what their portrayal tells us not only about religion but also about their own culture.

Since culture is a broad term, to sharpen the focus, there is a specific guiding theme throughout this book. It is an examination of the claim that *all cultures have religion*. I will argue that this claim about the universality of religion tells us more about western culture than it does about human cultures, and examine why this is the case.

While intellectuals throughout the world generally agree that all cultures have religion, they concede that many people are irreligious, atheists, agnostics, or simply ignorant about religion. So their assertion about the universality of religion is merely a claim that native to each culture is some religion or the other. Religion, they believe, is not only characteristic to cultures, but also one of its constitutive elements. Since religion partly lends identity to a culture, it seems to make sense to believe that differences between cultures can be explained by speaking about differences in their religion.

This commonsense idea rests upon generations of anthropological research and the comparative studies of religion. Most ethnographers put it rather bluntly: Since religion is a universal phenomenon, any study of a society or a culture cannot ignore it. They fill their journals with matters as diverse as the meaning of corn pollens for the Navajo Indians, the role of the guru in India, the evidence for miracles, or the problem of evil and the existence of God. The belief that religion is found in all cultures is not just limited to anthropologists and religious scholars. Philosophers, social scientists, and psychoanalysts share in this belief, while socio-biologists speculate on the genetic basis of religion, or neuroscientists try to figure out the nature of the human brain that creates religion.

Mountains of literature have been generated by these different fields. This has had an enormous impact on the way in which religion has come to be conceptualized all over the world. It has resulted in an accord between scholarly theory and folk knowledge. The intellectual and the man on the street both share the view that religion is a cultural universal. So much so that today it is almost sacrilegious to suggest that there may be cultures that do not have religion. What are the issues that underlie this apparent consensus on the idea that all cultures have religion?

To tackle this problem, we will need to reflect on the following three statements: (i) western culture has been profoundly influenced by Christianity; (ii) people from different cultures experience many aspects of the world differently; and (iii) the theoretical study of culture and religion emerged in the West. The point to note is this: The constitution and identity of western culture is tied to the dynamic of Christianity. Therefore, if people from other cultures experience the world differently, it should be possible to conceptualize their cultures differently from the descriptions generated by western theorizing. It may well be that in some cultures, let's say the Indian culture, there are no indigenous religions at all. Why have such alternate possibilities never been entertained? It is because the belief that all cultures have religion is taken as a starting point for all such studies. It is a *presupposition* that has *never been examined.*

Why have generations of brilliant scholars overlooked this possibility? Why has it been problematic for them to conceive that all cultures need not have religion? To get to the bottom of this mystery we will have to wade through two thousand years of history. In doing so we will establish how the experience of a small segment of humanity in the West has become universalized to describe all of humanity.

We can then proceed to consider the implications of this, not only for the understanding of Indian culture, but also for the field of religious studies, and the social sciences in general.

CHAPTER I

PUZZLES AND PROBLEMS

Apart from the problem relating to the nature of religion as such, the manner in which contemporary authors look at religion in other cultures (i.e., non-western cultures) is a problem in itself. So much so, that some scholars have begun to argue that it may be a good idea to get rid of the concept of religion altogether. This would be a good idea, except that getting rid of the concept will not make religion go away, so the object of study will still remain. This does not mean to imply that the scholars who advocate getting rid of the concept of religion are merely seeking linguistic reform. The questions we confront when studying religion are genuine and the fact that there are no self-evident answers requires further inquiry. The questions and problems remain whether we choose to call the object of our study 'faith', 'cumulative tradition', 'religion', or 'pif-paf'. That is why, in the following discussion, until further notice, the word 'religion' simply refers to our common sense understanding of this word and the way we use it in our daily language.

Modern writings on the subject of religion in other cultures are enough to mystify any reader. On one hand, these writings suggest that it is impossible to say what constitutes religion in these cultures. That is, what these researchers identify as religion in other cultures may not be religion at all. On the other hand, these same scholars are convinced about their belief that what they are studying in these cultures is indeed religion. For example, a specialist in Native American studies notes this:

> ...(I)n terms of my training as a student of religion, I had no text, no canon upon which to base an interpretation of...highly

complex events. There is no written history, no dogma; no written philosophy, no holy book... Our very way of looking at religion is such that these cultures have nothing that we are trained to see as religion. (Gill 1987: 6).

What can we make of this? Either the Native Americans do not have religion, or they do have religion but it cannot be seen because of the way we have been trained. Gill remarks, "Our usual approaches to the study of religion...(are) largely unusable and inadequate." But since he is convinced that the Native Americans do have religion, he tries to develop a theory of religion that will accommodate the Native American practices. He does not even entertain the possibility that what he is seeing is not religion at all but something else.

Sir Moses Finley confronts the same problem with respect to the pagan Greeks. He notes:

(1) Greek religion had no sacred books...no revelation, no creed. It also lacked any central ecclesiastical organization or the support of central political organization...

(2) Although large numbers of men and women were involved in the administration of religion, in the case of temples and altars or sacred sites, in the conduct of festivals and sacrifices, and so forth, and though we call them 'priests' in the modern languages, a priesthood as that vocation is understood in many post-ancient religions simply did not exist. The great majority of the so-called priests were simply public officials whose duties in whole or in part, usually the latter, included some responsibility for some portions of the religious activity of the community. More often than not, they were selected by lot and they held office for only a year or even six months... There was no special training, no sense of vocation. Greek 'priests' in sum were customarily not holy men; they were also not particularly expert or qualified in matters pertaining to their duties in office (1985: xiv-xvi).

In other words, the Greek religion did not look like religion either. But, nevertheless, it needed to be made sense of, thought Sir Finley. Need one add, as a religion?

Another scholar (Gould 1985) decided to help Sir Finley out and suggested that it would be easier to understand the Greeks if we studied the Dinka religion–the religion of a tribal people in southern Sudan. Needless to say, this did not solve the problem, since the Dinka religion, according to Reinhardt, a scholar who studied it, did not look very much like religion either.

The data of Greek religion did "not fit into any given category" according to yet another scholar. Yet we are to assume that they fit into the category of religion! So we are left with puzzles regarding the identity of the subject matter. Which phenomenon is being described here? Is it one phenomenon (the Greek religion) or sets of phenomena unrelated to each other? If the former, why is it difficult to say what the Greek religion is? If the latter, how are we supposed to understand religion better by studying what does not look like religion at all?

An Indian scholar, Dandekar, in talking about Hinduism, says:

> Hinduism can hardly be called a religion in the popularly understood sense of the term. Unlike most religions, Hinduism does not regard the concept of god as being central to it... Hinduism does not venerate any particular person as its sole prophet or as its founder. It does not...recognize any particular book as its absolutely authoritative scripture. (1969: 237).

In spite of these observations, Dandekar claims that "Hinduism has persisted through the centuries as a distinct religious entity", and goes on to talk at great length about 'Hinduism' without showing how or why it is a distinct religious entity.

Similar accounts are given by other scholars:

> Hinduism displays few of the characteristics that are generally expected of a religion. It has no founder, nor is it prophetic. It is not creedal, nor is any particular doctrine, dogma or practice held to be essential to it. It is not a system of theology, nor a single moral code, and the concept of god is not central to it. There is no specific scripture or work regarded as being uniquely authoritative and, finally it is not sustained by an ecclesiastical organization. Thus it is difficult to categorize Hinduism as 'religion' using normally accepted criteria.
>
> It is then possible to find groups of Hindus whose respective faiths have almost nothing in common with one another, and it is also impossible to identify any universal belief or practice

that is common to all Hindus. Confronted with such diversity, what is it that makes Hinduism a single religious tradition and not a loose confederation of many different traditions? (Weightman: 1984: 191-192).

A very good question, indeed. Weightman provides us with an answer to his own question by noting the "crucial" fact that Hinduism can be regarded as one single religion because Hindus affirm that it is one. But if Hinduism is a religion because Hindus say so, are we allowed to conclude that it is not a religion if Hindus don't call it one? The fact of the matter is that the question "Are you a Hindu?" does not make sense to most Indians. The following interview conducted in a village in Tamil Nadu by a Belgian, Thierry Verhelst, illustrates this point. He records the following question and answer:

Q. Are you still a Hindu?

A. No, I grew critical of it because of Casteism... Actually, you should not ask to people if they are Hindu. *This does not mean much.* If you ask them what their religion is, they will say, "I belong to this caste". (1985: 9; emphasis added).

This is interesting for two reasons. First, the interviewer is told that he should not ask Hindus what their religion is, since it is a meaningless question. His stance, incidentally, is normal and not something exceptional. Second, this Hindu says he has ceased being one because he is critical of casteism. He pretty much identifies 'Hinduism', a so-called religion, with caste. How absurd would it be if we came across writings that said "Casteism, Judaism, Christianity and Islam are major world religions"! This is a strange situation indeed. Weightman's answer depends upon what a majority of people say as if an opinion poll could help solve the problem. Yet he does not bother to provide us with any data about precisely how many Hindus call Hinduism a religion.

Another scholar complained that his European Christian heritage made it difficult for him to understand non-Christian religions. He identified three presuppositions, which he believed got in the way:

(1) Our Western Christian thinking is qualified in its deepest philosophical and methodological ideas by a personalistic idea of God. This concept makes it particularly difficult to understand the fundamental disposition of Buddhism, which

knows of no personalistic idea of God... It is difficult for a Westerner to comprehend the specifically Buddhist form of the approach to the transcendent...*the basic difference between the two is not of one abstract theological concepts. It goes deeper than that.*

(2) Hindu and Shinto polytheism confronted me with still another problem. I simply felt incapable of understanding why a believer preferred just one god or goddess among the vast pantheons... Christian theology itself has screened the Christian doctrine of trinity, sometimes interpreted in a polytheistic sense*, in such a way that an understanding of genuine polytheism was no longer possible.*

(3) The third point is that Hinduism, like Buddhism and Shintoism, lacks one other distinction that is so fundamental for our Christian thinking: the basic essential difference between creation and Creator. For our Western Christian thought this absolute discontinuity between Creator and creation is normative, but it does not exist in Buddhism and Shintoism (Benz 1959: 120-124; emphasis added).

It appears from the above that the difference between Christianity and other religions lies deeper than at the level of abstract concepts. The above citation highlights at least one consequence of this fact. If a 'genuine' understanding of polytheism is not possible, then are we safe in presuming that no understanding of polytheism is possible? If an understanding of polytheism is not possible by people from a certain culture, on what basis can they go about calling Hinduism polytheistic? How can they say that Shintoism is any kind of theism, bearing in mind the idea of theism that Christian scholars bring with them?

Another scholar tries to evoke a picture of Taoism as it is practiced in China. One of the difficulties that westerners face in understanding this phenomenon, he says, is the religious language and practice of the West.

To begin with, the concept 'religion' as we define it is itself a stumbling block... In our times...it has already reached the state where the good Chinese have learnt that they are Buddhists, or Confucianists, or syncretic or even...quite simply superstitious...

> For a long time, Chinese language did not have a word to express our concept of religion. To translate this concept from foreign texts, there exists a word in modern Chinese, *zongjiao*, which literally means: 'the teaching of the sects'. (Schipper 1982: 12-13).

Are we only talking about a translation problem here? If so, it does not matter much. But if the question is really about the inability of the Chinese language to *refer* to any phenomenon familiar to European culture that goes by the name of religion, then we do have a problem. If the problem were simply about the definition of religion, then another definition should make the problem go away. Having raised all these problems, Schipper ends lamely with a warning note to his reader:

> When we apply this term to China's *own religion*, which wants to be truly a bond between all creatures without doctrines, without creeds, and without dogmas, misunderstandings are inevitable (emphasis added).

It is ironic that Schipper points out all these problems but misses the biggest one of all. The problem that is created when he talks about Taoist Canon, Taoist holy texts, Taoist Liturgy, in an effort to explain a 'religion' that does not have canons, dogmas, or credos!

So we could go on and on with citations from the studies of the peoples of Africa, the Americas, and Asia, but the above sampling should be sufficient to support the point that the writings of these scholars leave us more mystified than enlightened. They try to assure us that Hinduism, Taoism, etc., are examples of different religions. However, unless they are able to find a unifying property that makes them into religions, this is a trivial claim that signifies nothing. They simply state that these are different kinds of religions, but are unable to specify what that difference in kind is. Because they conceive of Hinduism or Shintoism as religions, the general stance is that there must be something common to them, even if it is at the level of our language use.

There are four striking aspects to this situation. The first has to do with the very intelligibility of the enterprise. If the Native Americans, the Hindus and the Ancient Greeks did not have what one could 'properly' call religion, why insist that they did? Why not simply declare that these cultures did not have religion. If Buddhism and Taoism are not 'really' religions, why not simply say so?

The second aspect has to do with the ease with which these authors assume the identity of their subject matter. Despite the fundamental differences between these traditions, we are supposed to believe that they are all members of the same class. The concepts, practices and organization of these traditions are so different from one another that it would be more justifiable to believe that they are not members of the same class. To believe that Buddhism, Hinduism and Shintoism are also religions we need compelling arguments rather than simple assertions because at first sight they do not look like religions.

The third aspect relates to the authors themselves rather than to the object of their study. Clearly each of these authors is working with some notion of the 'religious'. They point out the absence of creeds, prophets, scriptures, and the notion of God in some traditions in order to say that 'properly speaking' these are not religions. But this does not mean that when these authors talk about other traditions, they use a definition that lays down the necessary and sufficient conditions for calling something a religion. If they did have such a definition, it would be easy for them to say, "according to this definition, the Native Americans, the Hindus and the Greeks have or don't have religions." Instead, their statements have this characteristic form: "Some traditions have neither X, nor Y, nor Z, but they are religions nonetheless."

The fourth striking aspect is related to the above point. These authors make it appear as though they do have a notion of what it means for something to be a religion, and what the criteria are for distinguishing religion from other phenomena. Otherwise, why not just go ahead and call Hinduism 'psycho-therapy', 'philosophy', 'magic', or 'proto-science'? But they call it religion nonetheless and all they have to offer in support of their claim is that whatever makes Christianity into a religion is not what makes Hinduism into a religion.

Here is where this strange situation becomes even stranger. The Hindus, the Native Americans, and the Greeks have (had) a set of traditions that lacked creeds, belief in God, scriptures and churches. Despite this, so claim the scholars, these were religious traditions which were distinguishable from one another. So far so good. Now, let's see how this argument holds up if we extend it a little further. If the above-mentioned traditions retain their identity as distinct 'religions' even when they lack some properties, the same should be true for other religions. Now consider a tradition in the Middle East with the following properties: it does not believe in Allah or in Mohammed as His Prophet; it does not have the Koran or the mosques. Could such a tradition be called a religion? Of course it could. Judaism and Christianity lack these properties but they are religions, and distinguishable from one another as religions. In other words, even where traditions do not speak of Allah or Mohammed, they remain distinguishable from each other as religions. The point of this exercise is to demonstrate that whatever properties go into making some tradition into Islam are different from those that go into making Islam into a religion.

Therefore, the question to consider is not what makes some tradition into Islam, Christianity or Judaism, but rather what makes Islam, Christianity or Judaism into religions. Whatever property makes Hinduism a religion must also make Islam a religion. We have seen that creeds, etc. are irrelevant for some traditions to be labeled religions. Suppose we bracket away creeds, belief in God, prophets, existence of scriptures, and churches from Judaism, Christianity and Islam. Would anything be left over? We would not be able to tell the difference between these traditions, let alone distinguish them as distinct entities. We would get an indistinguishable whole that could not be called a religion. Obviously these properties are absolutely necessary for these three religions if they have to remain not just distinct traditions but religious traditions as well.

This confronts us with a glaring inconsistency: (a) the existence of creeds *is a necessary condition* for some traditions to qualify as religions; (b) the existence of creeds *is not* a necessary condition for some other traditions to qualify as religions. Now, the consensus among scholars is that other cultures have religions too. But the conditions under which other cultures are said to have religions are those that make it impossible for the Semitic religions to be perceived as religions. That is to say, if the Semitic religions are what religions are, other cultures do not have religions. If other cultures have religions, then the Semitic religions are not religions. The inconsistency lies in insisting that both statements are true.

What can we make of this inconsistency? We have already seen that these authors could not be working with any definition of religion that lays down the necessary and sufficient conditions for something to qualify as a religion. Perhaps they could just be reporting a consensus of scholars, but surely this is not a matter to be settled by an opinion poll. Moreover, if we simply concede that the existence of creeds, belief in God, etc., are irrelevant for something to qualify as religion, it would be both wrong and inadequate. It would be wrong because the divisions within Judaism, Christianity and Islam have historically and factually turned around prophets, churches, beliefs and creeds. It would be inadequate because it would not make sense of the experience of these traditions. Belief in God, existence of holy books, etc., are so important to Judaism, Christianity and Islam that in their absence it is impossible to recognize them as religions. Consequently, if we are to consider them to be religions at all, we are compelled to accept the idea that God, a holy book, etc., are the central, determining properties without which no phenomenon could be called religion. For the same reason we can assert that Hinduism, Buddhism, etc., are not religions and the ancient Greeks and Native Americans did not know of religion, either.

How could generations of brilliant scholars not see this inconsistency? How can we make their claims appear plausible? Perhaps we could appeal to linguistic practice. We could say that a word like 'religion' is much the same as a word like 'game'. We do not know what is common to games such as chess, football, solitaire, or the Olympics except that there is a 'family resemblance' and we just 'know' that they are all games. But such reasoning does not help. Linguistic practices have a cultural history. This history is the history of a community that has learned to speak this way and not that way. For the West, this cultural history happens to be the history of Christianity. Therefore, the question is this: why are those influenced by this cultural history convinced that other cultures have religion?

To say this is just a language-game misses a crucial point. *Religio* comes from Latin and was first used by the pagan Romans and later appropriated by Christianity. What was the nature of Roman *religio* and how was this 'language-game' appropriated and modified by Christianity? This historical question will enable us to shift the focus from the nature of the subject under investigation to the culture of the investigators. We will then be able to appreciate the conceptual problems underlying the inconsistencies in the reports of these scholars.

PART I

The relation of Christianity to the pagans and heathens must be understood in terms of the internal problems of Christianity. Christianity never understood the pagans and it transformed what it could not comprehend into terms that made sense to itself. It repeated the same feat nearly 1,500 years later in its encounter with the heathens in Asia.

CHAPTER II

"NOT BY ONE AVENUE ALONE . . ."

In the beginning, the Christian Bible tells us, was the Word, that Word was God, and God said... This is a good place to begin this chapter because this idea of the beginning is true. Not because the Genesis is the truth, or Christianity is the true religion, but because our world–our intellectual world–happens to be a Christian world. Whether a Jew, a Dinka, or a Brahmin or whether a theist, an atheist or an agnostic, our questions have a common origin.

Christianity grew within the confines of a Greco-Roman world against the background of the Judaic community in the Roman Empire. By coming to grips with the dynamic of Christianity's relation to its environment we can gain a better understanding of the Christian religion itself, and thus of our own current intellectual world. We can trace the history of our ideas by examining the following questions: (i) What was *religio* to the Romans; (ii) How did the Romans look at Christianity; (iii) What was the attitude of the Christians to Roman *religio*.

The Romans

One of the striking things about the various descriptions of the ancient Roman world is the extraordinary emphasis they placed on a variety of associations, philosophical schools, cults and cultic practices in their social life. Many of these associations were involved in political intrigues; the associations of specific professions regularly supported candidates for political power. The activities of these associations–their ceremonies and ritual practices–often overlapped with those of the cults.

The Roman Empire was made up of city units, plus a considerable number of ethnic groupings labeled 'tribes' or 'client kingdoms'. The divine forces worshipped in each of these units might be seen as similar, analogous, or parallel; one obvious example is the Juno, the cohesive force which gives life to any social unit, whether a family or a city-state. The Romans worshipped not only the Juno who had once belonged to their own kings–Juno Regina–but also the Junones of other states whom the Romans had invited to abandon their original communities and settle at Rome... These Junones were parallel, but not identical, in the same way as the many Jupiters and Zeuses worshipped throughout the empire were parallel but not identical. Each cult honored its own god. (Wiedemann 1990: 69).

This profusion of cults was underpinned by a toleration of differences–a toleration that bordered on indifference about the differences. Even though there were attempts to suppress the activities of this or that cult, a peculiar kind of tolerance permeated the Roman cultural world. One reason for this tolerance was the unanswerable question: who's to say which gods are to be celebrated and which gods not? The many cults, the numerous theories and disputes concerning the nature and existence of gods, the many philosophical schools with their differing theories on Man and Nature pointed to two truths about human beings. First, it is in the very nature of human existence to entertain multiple perspectives; second, because of this diversity is inevitable in human communities.

There is a remarkable document, written around 177 C.E., addressed to the Roman Emperor with a request that Christians be allowed to practice their worship. Although coming from a Christian writer, it begins by noting that diversity is a fact in the Roman Empire.

In your empire...different nations have different customs and laws; and no one is hindered by law or fear of punishment from following his ancestral usages, however ridiculous they may be... In short, among every nation and people, men offer whatever sacrifices and celebrate whatever mysteries they please... And to all of these both you and the laws give permission so to act, deeming, on the one hand, that to believe in no god at all is impious and wicked, and on the other, that it

is necessary for each man to worship the god he prefers...
(Roberts and Donaldson, Eds. n.d., Vol. II: 129).

Amidst all of this diversity, certain practices were zealously
preserved: residents of cities 'had to' participate in the religious
practices and ceremonies celebrating the deities of the cities. There
were those who refused to celebrate the Roman gods–the Jews
early on, and later the Christians. While they were persecuted for
this, as Weidemann notes (1990), these persecutions have to be
seen in the context of the wider problems affecting the city, and the
imperial government's response to the crises. There was no
imperial 'religious policy' divorced from other aspects of imperial
policy.

There is an intriguing paradox to the religious practices of pagan
Rome. There was no dearth of books, tracts, and philosophical
schools denigrating or even dismissing the importance of the gods,
or even denying their existence. Even individuals dared to do it.
Lucian, a satirist, endangered his life when he openly mocked a
particular cult. The danger lay not so much in challenging as in
mocking. Even mockery was welcomed if it was directed at the
overly credulous, as in Plutarch's *On Superstition*. The intriguing
feature here is that many leading intellectuals participated in
religious activities but did not believe in their gods! Cicero is one
prominent example. Almost the entire arsenal of arguments against
religion that was later picked up by the Enlightenment thinkers
comes from Cicero's single work *De Natura Deorum*. Yet Cicero
himself was a priest. Though a skeptic and a critic of augury, he
retained his membership in the Board of Augurs of the Republic.

Cicero was not the only one. Plutarch, the author of the famous
essay against superstition, spent his later life as a priest in Delphi
composing tracts on divine punishment and the evident terrors of
the next world. In Greece, Epicurus, himself a skeptic, urged his
followers to take part in sacrifices; he himself participated in the
religious festivals of Athens. His follower, Lucretius, followed his
master's example in venerating ancestral gods.

How shall we understand this phenomenon of participating in
religious activities and sacrifices while not believing in the gods to
whom such sacrifices were offered? How could one deny the
existence of the gods and yet officiate at religious ceremonials?

Let us first look at what some of the Enlightenment thinkers, who perceived of this as a problem, have to say about it.

To Montesquieu, this disparity had to do with the genius of Roman politics. Rome used rational means to govern irrational masses. There was neither fear nor piety, but a simple recognition of the fact that all societies need religion as a mechanism to govern the masses by taking advantage of their credulity. Perpetuation of cults and the manipulation of myths enabled the enlightened senators and others to control the superstitious masses.

Diderot had a slightly different take. He suggested that Cicero was irreligious but then, in his time,

> The people hardly read at all; they listened to the speeches of their orators, and the speeches were always filled with piety towards the gods; but they did not know what the orator thought and wrote about it in his study. (*Encyclopédie*, "Aius-Locutius", cited in Gay 1973: 156).

Hume was even more explicit, suggesting that the Romans were either downright dishonest, or lived in fear of persecution. Speaking of Cicero, Hume asserts that no matter how skeptic he appeared to be in his philosophical writings, yet in his personal life he took care to avoid any reproach of profaneness:

> Even in his own family, and to his wife Terentia, whom he highly trusted, he was *willing to appear a devout religionist*; and there *remains* a letter, addressed to her, in which he seriously desires her to offer sacrifice to Apollo and Aesculapius, in gratitude for the recovery of his health. (1757: 347; emphasis added).

Gibbon, in his *Decline and Fall of the Roman Empire,* accepts this theme wholeheartedly and talks about the pagan intellectuals as if they were actors in a charade.

> In their writings and conversation, the philosophers of antiquity asserted the independent dignity of reason; but they *resigned their actions to the commands of law and custom.* Viewing, with a smile of pity and indulgence, the various errors of the vulgar, they diligently practiced the ceremonies of their fathers, devoutly frequented the temples of the gods; and sometimes condescending to act a part on the theatre of

superstition, they *concealed the sentiments of an Atheist* under
the sacerdotal robes... It was indifferent to them what shape the
folly of the multitude might choose to assume; and they
approached, *with the same inward contempt, and the same
external reverence,* the altars of the Libyan, the Olympian, or
the Capitoline Jupiter (emphasis added).

Or, again, this time on a lager canvas:

The various modes of worship which prevailed in the Roman
world, were all considered by the people as equally true; by the
philosopher as equally false; and by the magistrate, as equally
useful.

These are not merely the opinions of scholars from the past. Peter
Gay, a contemporary scholar continues along the same vein:

Cicero was urging the Romans to stand fast against new cults
and oriental superstitions, but Cicero did not see, or did not
say, that his policy sanctified practices which he scorned
privately as vulgar and absurd. (1973: 155).

Explanations of the kind cited above make the Greco-Roman
intellectuals seem inauthentic if not downright dishonest in the
manner in which they lived. Even when they did not believe in the
divinity of their deities or in their existence, an Epicurus, a Cicero
and a Plutarch not only participated but actually led religious
practices. Not that the European Enlightenment thinkers called
them inauthentic. On the contrary, Diderot considered Cicero as
the first Roman philosopher and Voltaire thought that *De Natura
Deorum* was "perhaps the best book of all antiquity". With a
unanimity that is rare among the philosophers of the
Enlightenment, all agreed with the assessment of Diderot and
Voltaire.

There is something odd about this situation. The philosophers of
the Greco-Roman period are on a par with, if not better than, their
counterparts of the Enlightenment period in terms of their
theoretical sophistication with respect to the socio-psycho-
epistemic origins of the gods and religion. The Enlightenment
thinkers based most of their arguments against religion on the
works of the Greco-Romans. Yet the striking thing is that the very
same arguments that led the Enlightenment thinkers to shun

religion and veer towards atheism did not have this effect on the pagan philosophers.

If we heed the explanations provided by the Enlightenment thinkers in the above citations, we would have to agree to the wholesale condemnation of an entire culture as inauthentic. This cannot possibly be the case, and, in any case, such a blanket condemnation leaves many people uncomfortable. Therefore, let's focus instead on why the same arguments had such a different effect on people from two different cultures–the pagan culture of the Greco-Romans and the Christian culture of the Enlightenment thinkers, some 1,800 years later.

Here's the crux of the matter. Even though both the pagan intellectuals and the Enlightenment thinkers used the same arguments against religion, they did so in a radically different cultural matrix. Roman *religio* could not have been similar to religion, as the Enlightenment thinkers understood it. No matter what their intellectual inclinations, the Romans did not pitch their philosophical beliefs and doctrines against religious practices. Roman *religio* was such that its practice was indifferent to any fixed set of theological doctrines. Their religious practice was not based on religious beliefs. Thus, the attitude of the Enlightenment thinkers says more about what the European intellectuals thought about religion than it tells us about Roman *religio*.

Today it is well accepted that while trying to understand the texts of a particular culture, we need to come to grips with the period that the texts were written in. Even though this fact is well-understood, there is still a problem because the only route to understanding a period is through the texts that we are trying to understand in the first place. If Plutarch and Cicero write atheistic books and yet officiate in religious ceremonies, what are we to make of this? Or, to shift across time and cultures, how can a contemporary Indian communist actively participate in religious festivals? How can an Indian nuclear scientist start his day off by doing *puja* to a clay god? Labeling this behavior as inauthentic or insincere is not a satisfactory explanation. Thus, any description of Roman religion must lend authenticity to the facts presented. To appear plausible, it must exhibit the facts as *its* facts and not *our* facts. So let's set aside any moral problem about the behavior of the individuals and simply look at this as facts about a culture.

Roman Religio

The facts tell us that Roman culture appears to have allowed for two diverse things: theoretical debate about the gods on one hand and religious practices on the other. This means that religious practice was not dependent upon the status of the gods as real or unreal, or whether they were worthy of veneration or not. How, then, was participation by the people in religious rites ensured? Here is a sample from Cotta, the skeptic, in Cicero's dialog:

> ...when you exhorted me to remember that I am both a Cotta and a pontiff. This no doubt meant that I ought to uphold beliefs about the immortal gods which have *come down to us from our ancestors*, and the rites and ceremonies and duties of religion. For my part, I shall always uphold them and have always done so, and no eloquence of anybody, learned or unlearned shall ever dislodge me from the belief...*which I have inherited from our forefathers...* Balbus...you are a philosopher, and I ought to receive from you a proof of your religion, *whereas I must believe the word of our ancestors even without proof.* (*De Natura Deorum*, III, ii: 290-291; emphasis added).

Two points in the above citation are worth emphasizing. First, some things are retained because they have been transmitted over generations and they require no other legitimization. Second, philosophical argument may be able to establish or prove some opinion, but it is irrelevant to traditional practice. It is important to note how Cotta argues. Balbus feels the need to prove the existence of the gods. Cotta tries to show that his opponent is looking for the wrong thing in the wrong place:

> You did not really feel confident that the doctrine of the divine existence was as self-evident as you could wish, and for that reason you attempted to prove it with a number of arguments. *For my part a simple argument would have sufficed, namely that it has been handed down to us by our forefathers.* But you despise authority and fight your battles with the weapon of reason. (*ibid.* III, iv 295; emphasis added).

Cotta's main point is that our belief about the existence or non-existence of gods is irrelevant to religion because religion is handed down over generations. It is not that religion is transmitted

along with other things, but *that which is transmitted is religion.*
As Plutarch puts it:

> *...you are discussing what should not be discussed at all,* when
> you question the opinion we hold about the gods, and ask
> reason and demonstration about everything. *For the ancient
> and ancestral faith is enough, and no clearer proof could be
> found than itself...*it is a common home and an established
> foundation for all piety; and if in one point *its stable and
> traditional character* be shaken and disturbed, it will be
> undermined and no one will trust it... If you demand proof
> about each of the ancient gods, laying hands on everything
> sacred and bring your sophistry to play on every altar, *you will
> leave nothing free from quibble and cross-examination...* Do
> you see, then, the abyss of atheism at our feet, if we resolve
> each of the gods into a passion or a force or a virtue? (Cited in
> Glover 1909: 76; emphasis added).

Similarly, in *The Octavius*, Caecilius argues his case by
emphasizing that it is better to receive the teaching of the ancestors
and to cultivate the religion of one's forefathers, than to assert an
opinion concerning the deities.

Religion, thus, appears to fall together with the tradition that is
handed down. *Religio* is what *traditio* is all about. There was little
doubt in people's minds that the religious practices of one
generation should be cherished by the next. To be pious, to be
respectable and decent, required the perpetuation of a cult.
Continuing a tradition did not require any reason since what was
being continued was tradition itself. That is to say, *no theoretical
justification was needed* to uphold ancestral customs.

> The primary test of truth in religious matters was custom and
> tradition, the practices of the ancients... In philosophical
> matters one might turn to intellectuals and philosophers, but in
> religious questions one looked to the past, to the accepted
> practices handed down by tradition, and to the guarantors of
> this tradition, the priests (Wilken 1984: 62).

This does not mean to imply that the intellectuals of antiquity were
dogmatic traditionalists. As our history books never tire of telling
us, the Greco-Roman intellectuals pioneered the spirit of scientific
enquiry–the spirit of ruthlessly questioning every belief. They
questioned practices too. Yet there was one sphere, that of religion,

that was not affected by critical questioning and was practiced simply because it was tradition. Pagan rationalism, thus, was never taken to its logical conclusion—a rejection of traditional religious practice.

> Such respect for ancestral authority would assure the continuity of traditional ritual, just as the childhood associations, family tradition, and the peculiar nature of pagan beliefs would tend to preserve traditional mental attitudes (Liebeschuetz 1979:31-32).

People were identifiable by their *traditio* as belonging to a certain city with a language, a culture, and a history. Different groups had different traditions and besides practicing their own, they mostly respected the traditions of the peoples among whom they lived.

By the time Christianity had aggressively come into power, the Romans had to make a plea to continue practicing their traditions. Symmachus, the last pagan prefect of Rome, makes his case in the following moving passage:

> *Grant, I beg you, that what in our youth we took over from our fathers, we may in our old age hand on to posterity. The love of established practice is a powerful sentiment...*

> Everyone has his own customs, his own religious practices; the divine mind has assigned to different cities different religions to be their guardians. Each man is given at birth a separate soul; in the same way each people is given its own special genius to take care of its destiny...If long passage of time lends validity to religious observances, we ought to keep faith with so many centuries, we ought to follow our forefathers who followed their forefathers and were blessed in so doing...

> And so we ask for peace for the gods of our fathers, for the gods of our native land. It is reasonable that whatever each of us worships is really to be considered one and the same. We gaze up at the same stars, the sky covers us all, the same universe compasses us. What does it matter what practical system we adopt in our search for truth? Not by one avenue only can we arrive at so tremendous a secret. (Barrow, Trans., 1973: 37-41; emphasis added).

If we look at tradition, that is, a set of practices handed over from generation to generation, the term seems to convey the same sense as what we intuitively understand by the word culture. For pagan Rome, to have religion was to have culture. Wherever there are a people with a history, identifying themselves as a people, there *traditio* exists too. That is, they have *religio*. This is what the word *religio* appears to have stood for in pagan Rome. The ancient Romans even prided themselves in the superiority of their *religio* that was open to worship of all divinities whereas most foreign people merely had their local gods and national rites.

This respect for different traditions, demonstrated by practicing the tradition of the other, appears to characterize the Roman *religio*. How, then, can we place the persecution of the Jews and later of the Christians in such a context of tolerance? The fundamental objection that the Romans would have had to the Jews and the Christians would have been that Judaism and Christianity are not *religiones*, that is, they are not traditions. They refuse to recognize that the traditions of other peoples and places are valid.

The Jews appear to have met this charge in two ways: Firstly, by showing that the Jews were a people with a history; and secondly, by laying claims to great antiquity. They argued that they were more ancient than the Ancients themselves. They claimed that Greek legislators had actually plagiarized the Mosaic Law and Heraclitus stole his theory of opposites from Moses "like a thief". Perhaps this need to establish the antiquity of Judaism was aimed at showing that Judaism was a *traditio*. The Jews needed to justify that their ancestral practice forbade them from worshipping the various deities that littered the Roman landscape. When it comes to traditions, especially when a group claims exemption from practicing the traditions of others, the most important claim they can make is related to their own antiquity. The Jews could argue that theirs was the most ancient of all traditions, therefore a *religio*, allowing them not to follow the traditions of others in matters of conflicting injunctions. They had to provide a philosophical underpinning to their ancient custom to explain why they would not venerate the ancestral practices of other people. Their explanation centered on their scripture, more precisely, around the truth of their scripture. The uneasy recognition that the Judaic tradition managed to obtain in the Roman Empire can be observed in the way Celsus speaks about the Jews. Even though he supposedly despised many of the Jewish customs, he nevertheless notes:

> The Jews became an individual nation, and made laws according to the custom of their country; and they maintain these laws among themselves at the present day, and *observe a worship which may be very peculiar but is at least traditional.* In this respect they behave like the rest of mankind, because *each nation follows its traditional customs,* whatever kind may happen to be established. This situation seems to have come to pass not only because it came into the head of different people to think differently and because it is necessary to preserve the established social conventions, but also because it is probable that from the beginning the different parts of the earth were allotted to different overseers... In fact, the practices done by each nation are right when they are done in the way that pleases the overseers; and *it is impious to abandon the customs which have existed in the locality from the beginning.* (Origen, 5.25: 283; emphasis added).

The Christian Quandary

The Christians could not follow the route taken by the Jews, even though they had to lay claim to the Judaic tradition. The fact was that they were a people without tradition, and as such, were accused of atheism by the Romans. As the pagans of that period saw it, the early Christians were 'atheists' lacking religion. In a passage that is supposed to derive from Porphyry, Eusebius summarizes the charges thus:

> (H)ow can men fail to be in every way impious and atheistical, who have *apostatized from those ancestral gods* by whom every nation and every state is sustained? ... (They have not adhered) to the God who is honoured among the Jews according to their customary rites, *but (have) cut out for themselves a new kind of track*...that keeps neither the ways of the Greeks nor those of the Jews. (Gifford, Trans., 5-6; emphasis added).

This was the challenge the Christians faced: they were not Jews, nor were they Romans. The Christians could not see themselves as a people with a history, a tradition, a language–they could not trace themselves back to any particular people. The Jews could; the Romans could; even the Egyptians who worshipped "cats, crocodiles, serpents, asps and dogs" could. The Christians alone could not. They had to show that Christianity was a *religio* even though their enemies accused them of not being a *traditio*. They set out to do precisely that.

During its first five centuries, writer after writer tried to establish the antiquity of Christianity. They tried to demonstrate that their philosophy was older than the system of the Greeks, older than Homer, and "the invention of letters". During the second century, Theophilus of Antioch, after a thorough exposition of Biblical chronology, states that:

> one can see the antiquity of the prophetical writings and the divinity of our doctrine, that the doctrine is not recent, nor our tenets mythical and false, as some think, *but very ancient and true.* (*Theophilus to Autolycus*. In Roberts and Donaldson, Eds., n.d., Vol. II: 121; emphasis added).

Such arguments were not limited to one or two names; the roll call reads like a who's who of the early church fathers. Each of them tried to show that Christianity had existed as "the first, most ancient, and most primitive of all religions" and, therefore, "shown not to be modern and strange but, in all conscience, primitive, unique, and true".

There are two things of crucial importance about Christianity's defense regarding its antiquity. The first is the question itself. The pagans challenged the Christians to show that they followed the ancient, and hence venerated, customs and practices of their forefathers. The Jews had met this challenge by arguing not only that Moses was older than Homer, but also that they were faithful to *their ancient custom*. On the contrary, the Christians transformed the very question: Instead of showing that they were true to ancestral practice, they argued that their doctrines were ancient and therefore true.

The second thing of importance is the problem generated by transforming the pagan question. How could *adherence to a doctrine* be equivalent to *following a practice*? Both of these points need to be examined more closely.

When Christianity entered into polemics with the pagan thinkers it regarded itself as having superseded Judaism, as its fulfillment.

The Old and the New Testaments, together, formed the Christian scriptures. Because these were the most ancient of all doctrines, Christianity was also ancient. Their religion was everything the Jews were waiting for. In their dispute with the Jews, the Christians had implicitly severed the age-old tie between being a *traditio* and thus having a *religio*. They argued, instead, that they were the followers of 'true' doctrines and therefore their religion was true.

Now, in their polemic with the pagans, Christians would travel much further down the same path. Their religion was the fulfillment of the expectations of not merely the Jews, but all peoples. All that was good and noble in pagan thought had anticipated the coming of Christ. The Christians were merely announcing the Good Word that the expectations of all nations had been met.

Thus, the process of establishing the antiquity of Christianity took a new turn: many early Christian writers tried to show that Socrates, Plato, Virgil and even the Sibylline Oracles had implicitly anticipated and prepared for the coming of the Gospels. After Christ came in the flesh, this preparatory work was finally finished. Christianity was the religion of all humankind. Such a claim must have been doubly shocking to Roman sensibilities. Firstly, though not a *traditio* of any nation, Christians claimed they had *religio*. Secondly, as *religio* of all peoples, Christians claimed exemption from following the traditions of the pagan cities.

By opposing their *beliefs* to the prevalent *practices*, the Christians brought about a fundamental shift: Religion, which so far had been almost synonymous with tradition, was now countered to tradition. In its polemic with the Jews and pagans alike, the Christian religion counter-posed its doctrines to the prevalent customs. Christianity was ancient not because it was the practice of any nation, but because of its doctrines. It was *religio* precisely because it was not *traditio*.

But again, how could adherence to a doctrine be equivalent to following a practice? The only way this could be was if the practice embodied or expressed the doctrine, that is to say, if the practice of the Christians expressed the teachings that they accepted. If the teachings they accept are true, it follows that their practices are likewise true. *Thus was formed a link between belief and practice.* If we look at the Christian defense in the face of persecutions in the first three centuries, or at Christian criticisms of paganism in the centuries to follow, there is one thing odd and striking: the criticisms are directed against pagan practices but the object of criticism is pagan beliefs.

Now, criticisms of either beliefs or practices were nothing new to the intellectuals of the Roman world. But their criticism did not challenge tradition; it merely restrained superstition. The tradition handed down was not meant to be supplanted by reason but to be held in check whenever practices threatened to run wild. Christianity postulated a link between practices and beliefs, a link of a type that was unknown in Antiquity. By doing this, it reduced Roman *religio* to 'religion' as we understand the term today. *Religio* became a variant of religion, and paganism, as the Christians claimed, was nothing but an expression of false or corrupt beliefs.

The Christians claimed that their religion followed the most ancient of all doctrines and that the Jews as well as all other nations on earth had anticipated the coming of Christ. By saying this, the Christians began the process of constructing the history of humanity. In appropriating the Old Testament, they also appropriated the past of humankind. The Old Testament was not just the past of humanity as the Jews envisaged it, but a true chronicle of events on earth. The real or imaginary framework of the Jews became the framework for describing the history of humanity. As a result, a philosophy of history came into being—not merely in the sense that chronicles that traced and rediscovered the truth of Biblical events on earth were penned, but also in the sense that Christians experienced worldly happenings as the execution of a divine plan. Human history, they claimed, embodied this divine plan. Thus Christianity appropriated the multiple pasts and histories of peoples on earth within the framework of the past of one people.

The simplest version of the story that was to masquerade as nothing less than the history of all humans was this: There was once a religion, the true and universal one, which was the divine gift to all humankind. A sense or spark of divinity was installed in all races and individuals of humanity by the creator God himself.

During the course of human history, this sense was corrupted, and idolatry or devil worship began to prevail. Then God spoke to Abraham, Isaac and Jacob and led their tribe back on to the true path.

Two aspects of this story are important. First, the 'best' among the pagans, by anticipating and preparing for the advent of the Gospels, were now a part of world history as the Christians wrote it. Second, within the broad framework of this history, the *religio* of the pagan Romans became the prototypical false religion. The pagans were seduced by the Devil into accepting false beliefs as true. The Devil and his minions tempt people into worshipping false gods and that is why the true God made his appearance in the Arabian Desert. Consequently, the Roman deities were absorbed into the Christian framework as demons and their worship was nothing but idolatry. That is why, the Christians argued, it was supremely important to follow true doctrine in matters of faith. The antiquity of a practice, in most matters, cloaked erroneous doctrines and seduced men into following false paths. Hence the antiquity of a custom was no authority as far as religion was concerned and all the pagan cults, with their multitude of practices, ceremonies and rituals were examples of false religion–ones that worshipped the Devil.

Because it had no tradition to fall back on, Christianity was forced to emphasize its doctrinal purity from its very inception. Consequently, an extraordinary emphasis was placed on written texts and their correct interpretations.

> This attachment to written texts was remarkable in itself, even if it did not penetrate far down the social scale; *there was little or nothing in Roman culture as a whole to induce such a development*, and many features of this highly traditional society in fact worked against it. (Cameron 1991: 110; emphasis added).

Thus, the Christians met the pagan challenge by arguing that their practices were embodiments of their beliefs. Because their doctrines were true, this implied that their scriptures were not mythical, but factual. This, in turn, implied that the pagan *religio* was false since it was at odds with Christianity. That is why, they claimed, paganism was an expression of false or corrupt beliefs.

If religion has to do with practicing the true doctrine, then there can only be one avenue, because there can be only one true doctrine. Everything that deviates from it can only be false. At least, that is what the Christians maintained. No Greek or Roman thinker had ever defended his theory on the grounds of its antiquity. Neither Plato nor Aristotle, let alone any of the lesser luminaries, ever suggested that their philosophical doctrine ought to be accepted because it was "ancient, most unique, and therefore true". But the Christians, in their battle to establish themselves as *religio,* did precisely that.

Religio and *traditio* had both coexisted in the Roman milieu. With the transformation in both meaning and reference of the word *religio,* the Christians were able to raise questions which must have sounded like nonsense to pagan ears: Is your *religio* true? Is your *traditio* true? A pagan could understand the question: "Are you faithful to your ancestral practice?" However, no pagan could answer the charge that his ancestral practice itself was false. How could tradition be true or false? The Christians nevertheless thought it could. Surely this is an indication of the huge gulf that had come to separate the pagan and the Christian worlds.

CHAPTER III

THE WHORE OF BABYLON

Our story picks up around the sixteenth century when European culture encounters other cultures elsewhere in the world for the second time. The first encounter occurred when the Greeks came into contact with India. Empirical investigations into the universality of religion will have to begin here, if anywhere. As we will see, travel reports of this period simply assume that religion exists in India, except that it is the religion of the heathens, that is to say, a false religion. This is a familiar theme as once again Christianity transforms what it sees but cannot comprehend. The existence of religion in other cultures was never a matter of empirical investigation because it was theoretically so certain that no empirical research seemed necessary. How did the Europeans discover 'Hinduism' and what were the multiple contexts of this discovery? Let's try and retrace their steps.

Imagine a medieval monk or a university student at the turn of the fifteenth century compiling an overview of all the accumulated knowledge about the Asian continent. What would have been its content? The constraints on such a treatise can be identified with a little bit of imagination. The first thread that would have gone into weaving this tapestry would have been about the exotic nature of the far-off lands. Even if there was disagreement about the geographic location of Asia, it was unanimously agreed that Asia was exotic. These authors would have referred to writers from the ancient world–both Greek and Roman–as sources of information. Besides normal creatures and unknown animals, they would write, weird and quixotic monsters live in these parts of the world.

People with one monstrous foot, no head at all but with eyes in their chest... Thus the list of oddities would have gone on.

The second thread in the tapestry would be about the great quantities of wealth available in these countries. Vast amounts of gold and precious stones were easily to be had; ants were trained to recover golden nuggets from the soil; great varieties of spices were to be found, not to mention silk. Again, the list would have been limited only by imagination.

The third aspect of the overview would be about a kingdom in Asia ruled by a devout and pious Christian king. Powerful and mighty, he was ever ready to march towards Europe in order to join his Christian brethren. The 'lost' Christians of Asia had built a peaceful Christian kingdom, where milk and honey flowed on streets paved with gold. In brief, both our monk and the university student would have painted a similar picture of Asia. How could they not? They would have culled their information from the same sources–the writings of the Ancients. This, then, was the picture that the early travelers and missionaries carried with them when they ventured forth in search of new sea routes to the fabled lands collectively called 'Asia'.

In addition to these sources of information, one other important element would have gone into constructing the horizon of expectations of these travelers–the Biblical framework. The framework would have been self-evident to both our monk and the university student. It was obviously true that the people of Asia were descendents of Noah. Though it was not known which of Noah's sons went to Asia and populated its empty lands, there was little doubt that it happened exactly the way the Good Book and its commentators described. In other words, the European travelers and missionaries 'knew' the origin of and the truth about the Asian people even before they set sail for the East. There was, however, a question regarding the extent to which the Asian people themselves knew of this truth. Then there was the question regarding the religion of these people. Had they preserved the true religion or had they succumbed to the devil?

Among their sources of information, there were the histories and conquests of Alexander, the writings of Strabo and Ptolemy, and the travel reports of Megasthanes and Pliny. These consist mostly of reports about the geography and the lay of the land, accounts of the heroic feats of Alexander, some descriptions of animals and so on. Regarding the customs of the people who inhabited the plains of the Indus, these ancient authors appear almost totally devoid of curiosity. There is a mention here and there of the existence of different social layers, of sophists or gymnosophists identified as 'philosophers', or of women who immolated themselves on the funeral pyres of their husbands, along with several reports of monstrous beings.

What is interesting about this situation is that these sources were nearly 1,600 years old when the Europeans took them as ethnographic descriptions of Asia of their own time. As one scholar notes:

> ...(I)n the take-over of anthropological tradition from Antiquity, the feeling for elapsed time was lost. Medieval scholarship seemed to have no realization that a people described by the ancients one thousand years before might no longer exist; that it might have moved out of its earlier homeland, or have been swamped by an invading culture, or, as the result of a cloud of circumstances, lost its old name and altered its old way of life. (Hodgen 1964: 34).

This was the horizon of expectations regarding Asia that the medieval travelers would have had when setting forth on their voyages in the fifteenth century: (i) it was an exotic land with strange creatures and strange customs; (ii) it was a wealthy land–a great deal of profit could be made; (iii) there were Christian communities they had to establish contact with and, if need be, win them over to the Catholic church; (iv) there would be also be pre-Christian groups, descendants of Noah, perhaps sunk in pagan practices–conversion would be necessary to save their souls.

Needless to say, the travel reports and the missionary tales that wound their way back to Europe were written within this horizon of expectations. The European populace that avidly consumed such writings shared the same framework. Let us look at some of these reports, and then meditate on the implications.

The Early Snapshots

One of the earliest travel reports by an anonymous Franciscan friar from the middle of the fourteenth century, titled the *Book of Knowledge of all the Kingdoms, Lands and Lordships that are in the World* is a good place to start a brief survey of the travel and missionary reports. This report is important because of its structure. The way this friar structures his description of other countries and peoples has remained the same across generations and centuries. In other words, between this friar's report and typical modern ethnography, a surprising similarity is to be found. Here is a passage from his report about India and Tibet:

> In the empire of Catayo there is a kingdom called Scim which borders on the kingdoms of Sarmagant, Bocarin and Trimic. The kingdom of Trimic is all surrounded by mountains which give rise to many fountains and rivers. This land has a very healthy climate...so that those who are born and live here have very long lives. They are men of clear understanding and good memories, learned in the sciences, and live according to law... That is because they are at the birthplace of the east, and the rest of the towns and great cities, and the root of this kingdom are all due to the temperate climate which tempered their bodies and the good extended to their spirits, and gave them better understandings and good memories... Beyond these are the people of India who are near the equinoctial line. Their land is very hot. Most of their towns are on the sea shore and there are many islands so that the air receives moisture from the sea, and tempers the dryness and heat. In this way are formed beautiful bodies and graceful forms, with fine hair; which are not produced by heat, except that it produces dark colour... (Markham, Ed., 1877: 49).

It is important to note that the author makes no distinction between *geo*graphy and *ethno*graphy. Both are at the same level of description and share the same status. There is no distinction between flora and fauna and the knowledge of peoples and cultures. He describes the weather, the rocks, the flags, the lay of the land and the human beings all in the same breath as if there were no distinction between them. Further, this anonymous Franciscan friar assumes that knowing about other people and cultures is equivalent to gathering information about them.

As time progressed and the number of travelers and missionaries multiplied, the ensuing reports retained the same structure. Today's anthropology and ethnography are heirs to our Franciscan brother, except that they are far more systematic. Today, we are treated to a neatly organized medley of information: the geography along with an accurate map, followed by the demography of the region, the sex distribution, the division of labor, the housing patterns, or the festivals of the particular village or tribe that the anthropologist intends to study. Then begins the ethnography. While this 'scientific' orientation distinguishes our modern-day anthropologist from his religious brother, what unites them is the idea that ethno-graphy is on a par with geo-graphy. To know a people and a culture is to have a descriptive acquaintance with them in the same way that knowing the flora and fauna of a region requires descriptive acquaintance. If you are a botanist or a zoologist, you need to go to the areas where the specimens are located so that you may meticulously observe and record. If you are an anthropologist, then the same practice is called 'doing fieldwork'.

The main difference between the sixteenth and seventeenth century travel reports when contrasted with the writings of the Ancients consists in two new domains they highlight: morality and religion. Running as a thread throughout these reports is a description of the sexual mores of the Indians. Generally they present a picture of these peoples as sexually loose and "much addicted to licentiousness." First, there are reports about the wives that the indigenous kings were supposed to have had. The numbers are exorbitant, varying from a mere thousand to an astronomical twelve thousand. Then there are stories about weird practices of deflowering virgins. Barbosa, for instance, speaks of one such practice in Vijayanagara in the following terms:

> And another sort of idolatry is practiced in this kingdom. Many women, through their superstition, dedicate the maidenhead of their daughters to one of their idols, and, as soon as they reach the age of twelve years they take them to the monastery or house of worship where that idol is, accompanied with exceeding respect, by all their kindred, holding a festival for the maid as though she were to be married. And outside the gate of the monastery or church is a square block of black stone of great hardness about the height

of a man, and around it are wooden gratings which shut it in. On these are placed many oil lamps which burn by night, and these gratings they decorate for the ceremony with many pieces of silk that they may be shut in and the folk outside may not be able to see them. On the said stone is another stone as high as a stooping man, in the middle of which is a hold in which is inserted a sharp stick. The maid's mother then goes inside the grating with her daughter and some other women of their kin, after great ceremonies have been performed "as to which I have scant knowledge by reason that they are concealed from view", the girl with the stick *takes her own virginity and sprinkles the blood on those stones,* and therewith their idolatry is accomplished. (Dames, Ed., 1812a: 222-223; emphasis added).

Second, reports abound regarding idolatrous priests given to deflowering virgins. Obviously, not all priests found the task of deflowering virgins pleasurable as this writer reports:

When the king takes a wife he selects the most worthy and most honoured of these Brahmins and makes him sleep the first night with his wife, *in order that he may deflower her. Do not imagine that the Brahmin goes willingly to perform this operation. The king is even obliged to pay him four hundred or five hundred ducats.* (Badger, Ed., n.d: 141; emphasis added).

The editor cites two other writers to confirm that this was indeed the practice of the king of Calicut. But the king of Tarnassari, a place about whose identity there is some controversy,

does not cause his wife's virginity to be taken by the Brahmins as the king of Calicut does, but he *causes her to be deflowered by white men,* whether Christians or Moors, provided they be not Pagans. (*ibid.* 202; emphasis added).

Third, they describe another interesting feature of the sexual practices of the Indians: wife swapping. Varthema, who tells us this story, must have been a living refutation of everything linguistic science tells us about language learning. He apparently picked up languages in a snap and understood conversations so well that he provides transcriptions of intriguing negotiations in these matters. The editor regrets that he could not reduce Varthema's narrative phrases into readable 'Malayalim'. Perhaps because it is not 'Malayalim' at all, as one of the experts he later consulted informed him. Varthema provides another report about the deflowering of virgins and wife swapping about which the editor in a footnote adds:

> I find nothing to confirm the flagrant profligacy described... Nevertheless, revolting as the custom appears to us, and difficult as it may be to account for so strange an illustration of human depravity, *I see no reason to doubt the veracity of Varthema's narrative.* (*ibid.*: 204; emphasis added).

Another scholar makes a more general point about Varthema's accounts.

> Varthema was an excellent observer, and there *is no reason to doubt the veracity of what he writes*; indeed the naiveté of his accounts of various events and activities give strong reason to believe that he is recording and not inventing. (Neill 1984: 396; emphasis added).

Apparently the rest of Europe thought the same way too, for Varthema's writing attained immense popularity. For scores of years, it remained one of the main sources of information about India in Europe. It was translated into several European languages and reprinted many times. If naiveté is to be the criterion to judge the veracity of ethnographic claims, it makes one wonder what to make of the equally naïve belief that people in many cultures have regarding European and American women–that they are all whores. The ethnography of the missionaries was precisely at this level of naïveté.

Let's move on from sex to God. The reports are unanimous in agreeing that Indians were heathens and idolaters. "The Kings of Malabar are heathens and worshippers of idols"; each 'caste' has "its own separate idolatry"; the entire province is "full of idolatry and witchcraft and every other heathen practice"; and the "heathens of Cambay are great idolaters and soft, weak people". The reports speak of "gods" that are worshipped throughout all of India and the feasts for the gods, performed "after the manner of ancient heathens"; and that the people of 'Guzerat' are "idolaters who worship the sun and the moon and cows." Many also identify Brahmins with the clergy, explicitly calling them "priests". Speaking of the Brahmins, Varthema says, "you must know that they are the chief persons of the faith, as priests are among us".

Barbosa identifies them as the "priests of the heathen" who manage and rule their house of prayer and idol worship and compares them explicitly with the "clergy among us".

Again, it is Varthema who spells things out very clearly:

> The king of Calicut is a Pagan, and worships the Devil... They acknowledge that there is a God who has created the heaven and the earth and all the world; and they say that if he wished to judge you and me, a third and a fourth, he would have no pleasure in being Lord; but that he has sent...his spirit, *that is the Devil*, into this world to do justice: and to him who does good he does good, and to him who does evil he does evil. Which Devil they call Deumo, and God they call Tamerani. And the king of Calicut keeps this deumo in his chapel...(which has) a wooden door covered with Devils carved in relief. In the midst of this chapel there is a Devil made of metal placed in a set also made of metal. The said Devil has a crown made like that of the papal kingdom, with three crowns; and it also has four horns and four teeth, with a very large mouth, nose, and most terrible eyes. The hands are made to look like those of a flesh-hook, and the feet like those of a cock; so that he is a fearful object to behold. All the pictures around the said chapel are those of Devils.... (Badger, Ed., n.d.: 37; emphasis added).

Naturally, such descriptions cannot stand alone without an appropriately diabolical mode of worship. The pagans, according to Varthema, pray in this manner:

> They lie with their body extended on the ground and very secret, and they perform certain *diabolical actions* (or motions) with their eyes, and with their mouths they perform certain *fearful actions* (or motions); and this lasts for a quarter of an hour... (*ibid.* 149; emphasis added).

To some, even the daily practices of the Jains appeared to be an expression of abomination and idolatry. The unwillingness of the Jains to hurt animals was, of course, idolatry:

> This people eats neither flesh nor fish, nor anything subject to death; they slay nothing, nor are they willing to see the slaughter of any animal; *and thus they maintain their idolatry and hold it so firmly that it is a terrible thing.* (Dames, Ed., 1812a: 111; emphasis added).

And so the reports go on and on, in much the same vein. The peoples of India were depraved heathens and idolaters. This relation between religion and morality is not a surprising connection. One of the beliefs that the Europeans of this period held was that morality required grounding in true religion. Where it was lacking–as among the heathens with their false religion–it was evident that morality would be absent. It should not come as a surprise that morality was described in terms of sexual mores. These travelers could easily find out when a commandment like "Thou shall not commit adultery" was violated; but how could they know when something like "Thou shall respect thy parents" was fulfilled or violated? Their problem was not an obsession with sex; the problem was that they simply did not know how to observe the fulfillment of a moral norm in other cultures.

The general picture that emerges from the foregoing account provides us with the image of India that was beginning to crystallize in the Europe of that period. What is more important for the purpose of this book is to emphasize that none of these travelers asked the question whether there was religion in India. In keeping with what they had learned from the Good Book, their assumption was that heathens and idolaters, that is, those who practice a false religion, populated the continent of Asia. This is precisely how they interpreted the facts. But this was only the first phase. In the coming period they began to ask more probing questions: What kind of beliefs guided these idolatrous practices? What were the varieties of false practices prevalent in the subcontinent? The following generations began to fill in the details. By then, however, the framework was set.

To continue further on our journey through history, we need to take a detour back into the heartland of Europe. It does not matter where the heartland of Europe is situated, because, as we know, "All roads lead to Rome..."

The Reformation

To understand the spirit and the times of sixteenth century Europe, we need to come to grips with the schism within Christianity created by the Protestant Reformation. This schism shook the very foundations of Papal authority and Catholic practices. The movement that brought about this split rested on four main pillars:

(i) the question of idolatry and the immense importance of battling against it; (ii) the degeneration and corruption of religion; (iii) the relationship between Man and God; and (iv) the issue of truth. These four points of reference can help us appreciate the way in which the age of Reformation defined the terms of the debate on religion, forcing all to respond likewise.

To begin with, the battle against idolatry assumed great importance. Within the Catholic Church, the role of icons and images had often been a contested issue and much blood had been spilt over this regularly over the centuries. What happened in the sixteenth century, however, went way beyond anything Catholicism had known before–in depth, in ferocity and in scope. From images to relics, from church altars to the saints, and ultimately the ritual celebration of the Catholic Mass itself–all of these came under vicious and pulverizing attack. The Protestants argued that there was little difference between Catholic rituals and those of the early pagans. Catholicism was corrupt, the Church belonged to the Anti-Christ and idolatry ruled over the faithful.

In order to make their claims plausible, the Protestants turned to early Christianity and its battle against the pagans to draw comparisons about the fall and corruption of Catholicism into the same pagan pattern. In the age of the Renaissance, the works of the pagan Greek and Roman thinkers had been re-discovered via Arabia, after having been banned, burned, and lost for over a thousand years. The dormant fires of the newly discovered theories from Antiquity were fanned to life. Pagan criticisms of 'religion' were pressed into service by friends and foes alike. Did Catholic rituals not show a surprising similarity to pagan rituals? The Catholics claimed that it merely confirmed the fact that all peoples had a common religion 'once upon a time', and the memory of this common religion was preserved in the Catholic rituals. This accounted for the similarities that the Protestants were up in arms against. The Protestants would have none of it. To them, the similarity testified to the fact that Catholicism had taken to idolatry. In brief, Catholic Christianity was merely 'Christian paganism'.

To make matters worse, the Reformation thinkers postulated a more intimate relation between Man and God. They spoke of man bearing witness to God directly, without the intervention of priests.

According to them, both Nature and the Book made it impossible that an individual could not see the revelation of God. Cicero was once again pressed into service. Had he not said that all men had an innate sense of divinity? Consequently, God ought to be worshipped properly, that is, one had to study the Book afresh to find the scriptural grounds for worship. In fact, what distinguished human beings from beasts was the relation between Man and God. Now, within the context of Roman *religio* and its relation to culture, it is obvious why man is but a beast if he does not revere the gods. But when Calvin appropriated this idea he turned it into a theological truth. In brief, the Reformation suggested that a religious sense was deeply ingrained in human consciousness.

Of course, this alone is not sufficient for human salvation, which brings us to the question of truth. Between the so-called natural religiosity and human salvation there exists both a chasm and a bridge. The chasm was the degeneration into idolatry; the bridge was provided by the 'true' religion. But how was one to know which was the bridge and which merely an illusion? One had to choose, at the risk of eternal damnation, between competing Christian groups. Christians now began to define their loyalty along different lines of affiliation than the ones before. Two fundamental consequences of this are important to note. First, this period defined the way in which European intellectuals would approach the question of religion from now on. Second, in so doing, it posed the question about the truth of religion in an excruciatingly sharp form.

Thus, paganism once again became an issue in the sixteenth century. The resurfacing of this theme nearly sixteen hundred years later is, however, deceptive. It was not the same paganism despite the fact that the same figures (Cicero, Plutarch) spoke the same words. Now it was paganism with a Christian soul. The arguments of the early church fathers against Roman *religio* were now used as a weapon against Catholic Christianity. For example, Plutarch's *On Superstition* was wielded as a weapon against the Catholics. This indicates not only the distance separating the European intellectuals of this period from their own cradle, but also the extent to which the 'other' had now become a domesticated variant of one's own 'self': paganism became a recognizable deviation in Christianity.

On the Eve of the Age of Reason

The religious schism within Europe had many consequences for the study of newly discovered cultures. The earliest consequence had to do with human resources. The battle with the Protestants reduced the number of available missionaries able to stay for a long period among the heathens. Those available were reluctant to learn the local languages. The result was that during the early centuries of contact between the Europeans and Asians, the knowledge that the Europeans had of 'religions' in India was based on what the Indian natives proficient in European languages could or would tell the missionaries. Their answers depended on how well they understood the questions raised by the Christian missionaries. The missionaries' questions, of course, would have been constrained by their horizon of expectations. Consequently, we can compress the 'knowledge' the European missionaries had of India thus: heathens and idolaters populated most parts of the Indian subcontinent. The situation would not have been so bad had this perception not been colored by the Protestant conflict with Catholicism raging at the time. By raising paganism from the dead, by characterizing Catholicism as Christian paganism, the Protestant Reformation posed the question of religion as a relation between false and true: the false worship of the pagans as contrasted with the true worship of the Christians.

Knowledge of the Natives and the Problems of Proselytisation

The previous chapter spoke about the way in which Christianity appropriated the history of humankind in terms of the past of one people. The missionaries and travelers who began to rediscover the countries and cultures of Asia gave flesh and blood to this picture. The heathens and pagans were the descendants of Noah who had somehow managed to retain vague memories of their past. Among other things, this belief meant that the Europeans had knowledge about the people of Asia that the Asians themselves did not have. One of the implications of this belief was the tacit acceptance of the idea that there was little for European Christians to learn from heathen societies. Consequently, the only kind of knowledge they acquired about the natives was no different in kind from that which they acquired of the flora and fauna of these countries. Quite obviously, as time progressed, the demand grew for more accurate knowledge about the natives. It was not sufficient simply to describe the people as heathens and idolaters, which they surely were, but one also needed to make sense of their abominable practices.

As previously noted, Christianity had established a specific relationship between beliefs and practices. According to this notion, actions expressed or embodied the beliefs that an individual held. Protestantism revitalized this idea by emphasizing that the outer trappings of worship must be congruent with inner reverence towards God. Even though the service of God, argues Calvin, is located primarily in one's heart, external actions are the public confessions of faith. In other words, acquiring knowledge about the natives meant finding out what the natives believed in. To describe the belief system of the heathens was to understand and make sense of their actions. More importantly, perhaps, it would enable the Christian missionaries to spread the Gospel by suitably reinterpreting it, using the languages and belief system of the natives.

The problems that the Christian missionaries faced in India were the eternal problems faced by any proselytizing religion: how best to root out erroneous beliefs and replace them with correct ones? Christian missionaries tried the only two routes that they knew: persecution and criticism of beliefs. The Portuguese, for example, declared an all-out war on the Brahmins, who apparently offered the greatest resistance to conversion. In 1545 King John III of Portugal produced a series of detailed instructions for the Governor of Goa:

> In this brief the king orders that neither public nor private idols be tolerated on the island of Goa and that severe punishment must be meted out to those who persist in keeping them. The houses of people suspected of keeping hidden idols are to be searched. Heathen festivals are not to be tolerated and every Brahman is to be banished from Goa, Bassein, and Diu. Public offices are to be entrusted to neophytes and not to heathens; Christians are to be freed from heavy labour at the port of Goa, such tasks in the future being reserved exclusively for heathens. Portuguese, under pain of severe punishment, are forbidden to sell heathen slaves to Muslims, since heathens are converted more easily to Christianity under the Portuguese and to Islam under Muslim ownership. Revenues previously used for the support of mosques and temples should be diverted to

aid in spreading the gospel. The governor should help the vicar by building churches and schools, by limiting the anti-Christian activities of the King of Cochin. (Lach 1965: 239-240).

The persecution of the heathens, however, was apparently neither consistent nor thoroughgoing enough to satisfy the bloodlust of the missionaries in Goa. They also tried to reward the heathen converts by providing jobs. Notwithstanding the persecution, paganism appeared difficult to eradicate. They could, and did, ban festivals and burial of the dead according to heathen practices:

> In Goa...the destruction of temples and attempts by ecclesiastical councils to eradicate the rites and ceremonies of the Hindu and other religious communities, as well as efforts to convert the local population to Christianity met with no...(great) success. (Massarella 1990: 44).

Another report goes thus:

> Although temples were destroyed, baptisms forced, and religious leaders exiled, the church found that conversion to the ideas, values, and practices of Christianity was impossible to effect quickly. Clearly it took more than baptism, a European suit of clothes, and a new job to make a Hindu desert the customs of his fathers and take up foreign practices of the Christians. (*ibid.*: 243).

Goa was not the Roman Empire and paganism in India was not the same as that of Rome. Thus, an important weapon in the Christianizing of the Roman Empire did not deliver the goods this time around. That is, the backing of political power with the economic and coercive power that goes along with it did not have much effect in the Indian context. It was not simply a matter of converting the king and expecting the rest of the populace to follow.

Thus, the missionaries were forced to take the second route, that is, the criticism of beliefs. This is how they began creating the Gestalts or forms that we recognize today: Hinduism, Buddhism, Shintoism, Taoism, Confucianism, etc. These Gestalts were built initially by reporting the beliefs that Indians held about their gods. The Europeans were convinced that these beliefs were scripturally sanctioned and a furious hunt was on to locate the 'Holy Book' (to begin with, in singular) of the Hindus. Criticisms about the immorality of their gods, and the inconsistencies in the texts began to be launched on an ever larger scale. It did not occur to these missionaries that they might just be fabricating religions around the texts that they were so feverishly searching for. They were convinced that to make sense of the pagans, they needed only to find their 'theology'. Thus, the Hinduism, Buddhism, etc. that we know of today, began to take shape. And waiting in the wings, to confound matters further, were the ideologues of the Enlightenment.

The Enlightenment

In a way, the French Enlightenment sealed the way in which questions about religion have been raised ever since. The generally held opinion is that the French philosophers were pioneers in the criticism of religion and that the Enlightenment period neatly breaks with the religious doctrines and dogmas that had held men in bondage for centuries. Let's see whether this opinion holds up under scrutiny; or is it the case that the Enlightenment thinkers merely continued the Christian discourse under a different guise?

To begin with was the question that Protestantism raised–of the relation between paganism and Christianity. Since modern-day paganism (i.e., Catholicism) had masqueraded as the Christian religion for centuries, the question was really about the truth claims of Christianity. Which of the Christian religions is the true religion? To answer this question, some understanding about paganism was required since the evidence it would provide was vital to settling the question about religious truth. To the Enlightenment thinkers, this issue was also the starting point.

Although the Enlightenment thinkers accepted the evidence that paganism presented, it nevertheless presented a double problem. How to understand the ancient pagan texts and how to make sense of the living pagan cultures? They solved the problem in the most evident way–by making use of one to illuminate the other. The texts from Antiquity rendered the religious practices and beliefs, ceremonials, and rites of both the savage and the civilized parts of the world meaningful. In the same way, contemporary pagans helped Europeans understand the Ancients better. That is to say, over the generations, Europeans began to see a common human experience in these 'congruencies'.

Christianity's claim about the universality of religion, that each human being carries a sense of divinity in him, was, to be sure, challenged by the *Philosophes*. Yet they accepted as a matter of fact that all cultures had religion in some form or another. They accepted the existence of the domain of religious experience that was universal across cultures. How else could they use Greek and Roman texts to understand the meaning of Egyptian, Indian and Native American ceremonies or rites, and the latter to understand the texts of the Ancients? Only by *presupposing that they had to do with the same kind of experience*. Instead of all individuals having an innate sense of divinity inscribed in their hearts, it would now appear that all cultures have an identical experiential domain– the religious.

It is ironic that in this case there is a fundamental superiority of the religious claims over the theories of the Enlightenment thinkers. Christianity insisted that there was a difference between being 'religious' (which meant being Christian, to be sure) and being a 'heathen'. Irrespective of the grounds on which such claims were made, Christians did not generalize their experience across time, space and culture. Our Enlightenment thinkers had no such qualms. Why restrict the religious domain as the exclusive property of the Jews and the Christians? Their own alternative was a singular statement: All cultures know of one common domain– the religious.

Consequently, both kinds of pagans could be assimilated into each other as expressions of heathendom. The multiple gods of the Indian subcontinent were just like the pantheon of the Greeks and the Romans. Both were witnesses to idolatry and polytheism. In charitable moments, they were even willing to reconcile the worship of animals as a way of allegorizing virtues. Even though it took a while, this assimilation of Ancient Greek and Roman 'religions' into Asian paganism was an accomplished fact by the time the Enlightenment was in full swing. A neat division of the world into heathens, Christians, Jews and, in some cases Muslims (often called Mahometans) came into being by virtue of this assimilation. This was not the only legacy of the Enlightenment. The world was neatly divided in other ways too.

In this Age of Reason, the sentiment was that the 'moderns' were far ahead of the ancient civilizations of Greece and Rome. The various traveler and missionary reports had laid bare the superstitious, licentious and barbaric practices of contemporary pagans. The idolatry and zoolatry of the Indians that demeaned the dignity of man; the 'Sutti' tradition of burning widows on the funeral pyre of their deceased husbands, the adultery and wife-swapping that ran through the daily life of the Indian people were part of this picture. These images were rendered more vivid with the discovery of half-naked savages running around in Africa and the Americas, cannibalizing each other, lacking script or culture, leading a life fit only for the beasts. The time, in other words, was ripe for a developmental ordering of human history with paganism representing the 'childhood' of Man.

The *Philosophes* met this intellectual challenge by spinning out splendid tales of the growth of Man from childhood to maturity. Pagans, whether living or dead, were at a lower rung of the ladder, separated by the brutish savages of the Americas and Africa by one rung. Not all Indians shared this singular honor of being placed alongside the Greco-Roman world. There were whole groups of people in what is now Sri Lanka who did not even have a language. The poor souls went round grunting to each other like the animals that they were:

> Max Müller quotes Sir Emerson Tennent to the effect that the Veddahs of Ceylon have no language: "they mutually make themselves understood by signs, grimaces, and guttural sounds, which have little resemblance to definite words or language in general." In fact they speak Sinhalese (an Indo-European tongue). (Evans-Pritchard 1965: 106).

Hence came into being the tale of the 'primitive': a man, a psychology and a society. Human history also achieved a developmental ordering, stretching from the primitive to the modern. The order in nature cannot be apprehended by the primitive man, claimed this thesis, as this order could only be experienced by those who knew that the universe embodied a divine plan. Primitive man did not experience the world this way because he could not think abstractly. Instead, what characterized the primitive man was his 'concrete' thinking. Now, of course, the primitive man did not look at the world the way the Christians did because he did not know of this religion. But this is not how it appeared to the 'enlightened' thinkers of the time. To them, the perception of harmony as a divine plan was a measure of the extent to which humankind had progressed from its primitive days. By definition, primitive man was not capable of reflection and abstract thought and therefore incapable of perceiving this harmony that was evidence of the divine plan.

Hume, in *The Natural History of Religion* accepts this argument. He believes that the personification of natural forces accounts for the origin of religion. It is idolatrous in nature and those who are idolatrous are barbarous because of their defective cognitive development:

> In the very barbarous and ignorant nations, such as the Africans and Indians, nay even the Japonese, who *can form no extensive ideas of power and knowledge,* worship may be paid to a being, whom they confess to be wicked and detestable; though they may be cautious, perhaps, of pronouncing this judgement of him in public, or in his temple, where he may be supposed to hear their reproaches.

> Such rude, imperfect ideas of Divinity adhere long to all idolaters; and it may be safely affirmed, that the Greeks *themselves never got entirely rid of them.* (Hume 1757: 353; emphasis added).

Contrasted with this was the notion of a 'higher' and 'more advanced' deity. The God of the Semites is an advance because it shows that man has begun to form abstract conceptions. Here is Hume again:

> But (to) a barbarous, necessitous animal (*such as man is on the first origin of society*), pressed by such numerous wants and passions...an ordinary spectacle... Ask him, whence that animal arose; he will tell you, from the copulation of its parents. And these, whence? From the copulation of theirs. A few removes satisfies his curiosity, and set the objects at such a distance, that he entirely loses sight of them. Imagine not, that he will so much start the questioning, whence the first animal; much less, whence the whole system or united fabric of the universe arose. (*ibid.* 312; emphasis added).

There is a delicious irony to this passage. The primitive man is satisfied with the answer that some few members have an ancestor and does not persist in following it through until he reaches the absolute beginning. In both Christian theology and the philosophy of religion, there is an argument that does precisely this. Called the 'cosmological argument' for proving the existence of God, it argues that since each member in such a series has an ancestor, there must be a single beginning for the entire series. This argument is, however, fallacious, if applied to infinite sets. Here, a given member could have an ancestor without it being true that there is one absolute beginning for an entire series such as animals, human beings, inanimate objects. Moreover, since we are talking about events, processes and objects within the universe, it is not evident what kind of sets we are dealing with. As Bertrand Russell pointed out:

> I can illustrate what seems to me your fallacy. Every man who exists has a mother, and it seems to me your argument is that therefore the human race must have a mother, but obviously the human race hasn't a mother–that's a different logical sphere. (Russell and Copelston 1948: 479).

The primitive man who supposedly cannot reason abstractly is nevertheless being logical when he does not pursue the question of the beginning. The 'civilized' man, allegedly more advanced in abstract thought commits a logical fallacy. What makes this even more insidious is that such ideas survive to this day in domains such as psychology and anthropology. In psychology it is axiomatic that children and the 'primitive' think concretely whereas the hallmark of adult and scientific thinking is that it is abstract. In anthropology, the fieldwork of the last two centuries was in and about 'primitive' societies. A reputed anthropologist, Adam Kuper, debunked the 'myth of the primitive' and even if most anthropologists are rid of this myth today, it is canonized in the writings of Piaget, Vygotsky and their followers. It is fascinating to note how a religious and theological idea–the distinction between 'concrete' and 'abstract' thinking acquired universal currency in a secular mantle.

The Enlightenment of World History

One of the most important characteristics of this movement was its indulgence and obsession with the question of the origin of religion. Speculations regarding this matter focused upon paganism and the primitive man. This contributed to the assimilation of Asian culture with that of the Ancients. The distance between the two was bridged by the 'evolution' of mankind–from the primitive to the modern through the pagan. European history became *de facto* the history of humankind.

The identification of human history with world history is hardly novel, of course. Biblical chronology had already performed this feat long ago. After all, human beings were the descendants of Noah directly and of Adam indirectly. When this was the history of the Cosmos, how could it not apply to the rest of humankind? This Biblical chronology exercised an intellectual dominance for centuries. What happened during the Enlightenment is simply a secularization of the ideas presented in the religious identification of human history with Christian history. A new twist was added to the old story where multiple histories of multiple peoples were mapped on to two constant factors: a shared beginning and an underlying pattern.

Where did religion fit in this picture? Again, the Enlightenment thinkers presented secularized versions of the Protestant polemic against Catholicism. Instead of 'degenerate', the idolatrous religious developments were characterized as 'errors'. Their history of humankind was, of course, able to shed light on this phenomenon–it was because of the inability of some folk to think abstractly.

Within the cultural matrix of the Protestant Reformation, scholars and intellectuals began to create a picture of the 'other' based on at least one common assumption: to know their 'religion' was to know the other. The travel reports from this period built a series of images of other cultures in two distinct ways. On one hand, there was a description of cults, religious practices and beliefs; on the other, an interpretation and explication of these by reference to 'similar' phenomena involving the Ancients.

What were some of the consequences of this scholarship on religion? The concept of the universality of religion took on a more insidious form—a universal domain of religious experience. Such a domain was but a mere restriction in scope of the earlier Christian belief in the universality of religion. This enabled a division between modes of thinking. One could distinguish between a superstitious and a rationalist mode of thinking. With this division, the problem of progress could be formulated differently, the answers to which were to color the intellectual outlook in Europe for a long time. How did this superstitious mode come into being and what sustains it? How could one make a transition to a rational way of cognition? The notion of the primitive man and his society began to crystallize. The invention of the primitive was the counterfoil against which the progress of Europe could be recorded and measured.

Thus, the Enlightenment philosophers simply traveled further along the road to Jerusalem. A whole series of beliefs that are typically Christian were secularized by the sons of the Age of Reason. While it is true that they fought battles against religion, their own contribution was simply to strengthen the grip of religious ideas by reproducing them in a secular mantle. Remarkably enough, at a time when even the Pope was willing to acknowledge that a nation could exist without religion, the Enlightenment philosophers began to construct theories of religion to explain why it had to be a universal phenomenon. Instead of calling religion God's gift to humanity (as the Christians saw their own religion) they made it nature's gift to humanity. Empirical questions about the origin of Christianity were turned into theoretical questions about the origin of religion. 'Why did Christ emerge among the Jews?' became 'Why did the gods emerge in human communities?' Thus they universalized religious themes by secularizing them.

CHAPTER IV

MADE IN PARIS, LONDON, AND HEIDELBERG

The framework and the questions for understanding religions in India were decided in Europe. The answers, of course, had to be provided in India. The way Europeans would approach these questions was once again determined by the religious developments on their own continent. Let's pick up our story around the end of the eighteenth century–the tail end of the French Enlightenment–with an examination of two fundamental problems that Christian missionaries confronted in bringing God's word to the heathens in India.

As emphasized earlier, Christianity postulated a specific relation between beliefs and actions. The Christian understanding of Man suggested that actions mostly express beliefs held by individuals. This orientation presented a slew of theological dilemmas and debates within Christianity on what it means to 'act' like a Christian. Questions such as: what is the relationship between willing ('intending' in today's idiom) and acting? What can one say about intentions by looking at the actions of individuals? What kind of gap exists between intending and acting? Such were the questions that arose within the religious and moral context of Christianity.

A Conceptual Quandary

When missionaries or intellectuals from one culture approach another within this framework, some problems are bound to arise. For starters, the stock of concepts that the Europeans used in understanding the other was rather poor: 'heathen', 'pagan', 'idolaters', 'devil worshippers', 'zoolaters'. These few concepts pretty much exhausted the intellectual richness of the European cultural framework. For more than two centuries these concepts had proved sufficient as far as the Europeans were concerned to understand the cultures and peoples of Asia, Africa and the Americas (not to mention Greece and Rome). The attitude of the Evangelical Protestants of the nineteenth century is summed up nicely here:

> Non-Christian religions (in this case Hinduism) were a piece with the corrupt world, and were summed up as "heathenism" or "idolatry". Early evangelical missionaries were normally convinced as a matter of theological fact that the individual "heathen" in his darkness was doomed, unless he turned in faith to the sole remedy for his sin, the atoning death of Jesus Christ... Hinduism was a "false religion" *a priori*, the work of the prince of this world, not of God. Thus it was typical that Alexander Duff should call Hinduism "an old, pestilent religion" and that his fellow-Scotsman John Wilson should characterize Hinduism as "the grandest embodiment of Gentile error". Such terms of opprobrium might be multiplied almost indefinitely from the missionary literature of that period. (Sharpe 1965: 25-26).

The dominant writings in Europe of this period show no sign of protest that such concepts were of no use in understanding other cultures. As though this were not enough, the theoretical 'sophistication' of the Enlightenment criticisms of religion was based on the data provided by the missionary and travel reports.

But, there are idolaters and there are idolaters. How to distinguish between them? Barbosa had already confronted this problem with respect to the several Indian 'castes' he had met. His conceptual framework allowed him only to note that each of these groups "practices its own idolatry". Consequently, the only way of distinguishing idolaters from each other would have to consist in identifying the differences in their beliefs.

Sources of Belief and Belief in Sources

Thus, a search for these beliefs began in earnest. To Christians, it could not be anything other than texts. But Indian culture, being a literate one, had many, many texts. Clearly, they had to search for the 'religious' texts, but the problem was how to recognize them.

The only possible way open to them was to ask the natives. This was easier said than done. How to make themselves understood by the natives? Through their ethnological efforts they learned that Indians often spoke of the incarnations of Vishnu. Clearly this story had to have come from a holy book. Besides, references were often made to Shastra and thus, they concluded, Indians had a holy book called 'Shasta'. Slowly it became clear that there was yet another holy book, or was it a series of them? Now it became clear that the holy book of the Indians was called 'vedam'.

Though many Indians had heard of the 'vedam' and spoke of its authority, not many knew what was in them. This state of affairs confirmed to the missionaries that not only was the 'vedam' a holy book, but also, precisely because of its holiness, a secret book. This was to be expected. The books of magic, which the worshippers of the Devil relied upon, were secret and only in the possession of a few. It is thus that the first translations of the Indian 'holy texts' began. Heathens were to be distinguished according to the beliefs sanctioned by their scriptures. That is to say, the Europeans believed that communities were united and differentiated from each other according to the beliefs that they entertained. To be sure, this was the experience of the Europeans. But whether this stance can be applied to other cultures and contexts depends upon the truth of other premises in their reasoning. In other words, this is a matter for empirical investigation. Faced with the empirical problem of transmitting God's word to the heathens, the Christian missionaries came up with theological solutions. Some kinds of texts were 'holy', practices were guided and sanctioned by these 'scriptures', and communities were divided according to the scriptures they apparently accepted.

A Social Quandary

But the task of converting heathens to Christianity proved to be a difficult job—so tells us the Public Relations Department of the Church of God. It identified three fundamental obstacles in the conversion of natives into Christianity: (i) the nature of Hinduism; (ii) the structure of social life; (iii) the role of the 'priests' of Hinduism, i.e., the Brahmins. Let us briefly take a look at these difficulties.

Hinduism, the 'religion' of the Hindus, was nebulous. It was very difficult for the missionaries to target their attack:

> Hinduism has never prepared a body of canonical Scriptures or a Common Prayer Book; it has never held a General Council or Convocation; never defined the relations of the laity and clergy; never regulated the canonization of saints or their worship; never established a single centre of religious life, like Rome or Canterbury; never prescribed a course of training for its priests. This is not due to the fact that war, or civic tumult, or foreign domination prevented the growth of institutions of this kind; but simply to the fact that all such action is essentially opposed to its spirit and traditions. (Crooke 1913: 712).

Such a Hinduism appeared to resist the onslaught of foreign religions, or "anarchy and persecution", and held its ground for ages. It seemed to possess "wonderful powers of adaptation to novel conditions"; because it "has a fully organized and articulate social system". Long before this, Hume had pointed to an analogous difficulty in describing the nature of pagan traditions:

> The pagan religion...seemed to vanish like a cloud, whenever one approached it, and examined it piecemeal. (1757: 349).

James Mill, in *The British History of India*, a book that was extremely influential in defining colonial policy, notes:

> Whenever indeed we seek to ascertain the definite and precise ideas of the Hindus in religion, the subject eludes our grasp. All is loose, vague, wavering, obscure, and inconsistent. Their expressions point at one time to one meaning, and another time to another meaning; and their wild fictions, to use the language of Mr. Hume, seem rather the playsome whimsies of monkeys in human shape than the serious assertions of a being who dignifies himself with the name of the rational. (In Schweinitz, Jr. 1984: 9).

It did not occur to people then, as it does not seem to occur to people now, that the amorphous nature of Hinduism had to do with the fact that Hinduism *did not exist*. It was an imaginary entity, conjured up in the minds of Europeans due to their absolute conviction that there had to be a religion among the natives. It was literally inconceivable to the Christian missionaries that the case could be anything else. To attack Hinduism as a false religion they were compelled to criticize its doctrines, and since these doctrines could only be found in texts, by default all the texts they came across–from the *Vedas* through the *Upanishads* to the *Puranas*– became religious texts.

Unless it could be explicitly shown that a text was not religious, say because it talked about the rules of grammar, it became part of the 'holy books'. This may have been a convenient strategy, although not a particularly useful one. To appreciate this point better, consider the texts and their variety. They discuss rituals or provide instructions on how to carry them out; they speculate about the structure of the cosmos or instruct people how to live on earth; they tell stories or just melodiously string names together. Now if all of these are religious texts, then this 'religion' would dominate the totality of social life and human existence. If everything is part of religion, the very word loses its meaning and becomes trivial. Yet our scholars deny this implication by suggesting that it is typical of the Hindu religion to pervade every aspect of social, intellectual and emotional life! This convenient strategy is actually a confession of ignorance. The tragedy lies in the fact that this confession of ignorance has become the truth about 'Hinduism'.

But there was another hitch to all of this. Even though the missionaries managed to locate the 'holy books', they soon discovered that most Indians were either ignorant of or completely oblivious about the 'doctrines' that the European intellectuals identified in them:

> In confirmation of this opinion of the general ignorance of the Brahmins, it is recorded, *that they cannot even read the books which contain their sacred records*, but are altogether immersed in such deep sloth and depravity, that immoral practices, which the most barbarous nations would have feared to adopt, are at this hour, openly allowed and sanctioned, in the most public places and polished cities of Hindoostan. Of the people, the description is generally degrading; uninformed, and only careful of their ablutions and the particular customs of their caste, they are said to *have as little acquaintance with the moral precepts of their Sastras*, as the Samoeides, and Hottentots, with the elegant arts of sculpture and painting. (Chatfield 1808: 212-13; emphasis added).

Moreover, the Indians appeared to be indifferent to the inconsistencies between their different texts which the "logical and rational mind of the West" found incomprehensible.

In their frustration, the missionaries turned to denouncing the practices of Hinduism, which would disgust and raise the hackles of any civilized person. Their unfavorable impression was strengthened by what they regarded as a "fatal cleavage" in Hinduism between religion and moral behavior. Part of the missionary heritage was, of course, based on the Protestant Reformation's emphasis on morals. The post-Reformation period laid great stress on the relation between beliefs and actions. To save one's soul from eternal damnation, it was not only necessary to have appropriate beliefs but these beliefs must find an adequate expression outwardly. Hinduism fell short of the missionary ideal. What they saw disgusted them. A religion which countenanced and even recommended practices such as adherence to caste, sati, or infant marriage, degraded its followers, they felt. They began to draw a distinction between a doctrinal core and common practice. That is to say, they created a difference between a philosophical Hinduism and the popular Hinduism that was found in its current practice.

> Comparatively soon Europeans had begun to make the distinction, which was to have so long a life, between what they regarded as 'popular' Hinduism and 'philosophical' Hinduism. Popular cults were described to be condemned or ridiculed, but most writers were also prepared to admit the existence of metaphysical assumptions and ethical doctrines in Hinduism of which they could approve because they seemed to be similar to western concepts, *although the similarities which they found now seem to depend largely on the inability of the European to describe a religious system except in Christian terms.* (Marshall 1970:20; emphasis added).

While it may have been very convenient to draw this distinction, it was, of course, not very conducive to understanding 'Hinduism'.

> They invariably made a distinction between 'popular' Hinduism, which they did not deem worthy of study, and 'philosophical' Hinduism, which they tried to define as a set of hard and fast doctrinal propositions and to place in current theories about the nature and history of religion. All of them

> wrote with contemporary European controversies and their
> own religious preoccupations very much in mind. *As
> Europeans have always tended to do, they created Hinduism in
> their own image. (ibid.*: 43; emphasis added)

In any case, the conclusion during this period, just as in the ones
past, was that Hinduism is immoral. It was "idolatry of the basest
kind, represented by numberless idols and symbols of the most
revolting character". As the late lamented Reverent Sherring put it
after having lived among Hindus in the 'headquarters' of
Hinduism, i.e., Benaras:

> (Here) idolatry is a charm, a fascination, to the Hindu. It is, so
> to speak, the air he breathes. It is the food of his soul. He is
> subdued, enslaved, befooled by it. The nature of the Hindu
> partakes of the supposed nature of the gods whom he
> worships. And what is that nature? According to the traditions
> handed about amongst the natives, and constantly dwelt upon
> in their conversation, and referred to in their popular
> songs...yet more especially according to the numberless
> statements and narratives found in their sacred writings, on
> which these traditions are based, it is, in many instances, vile
> and abominable to the last degree. Idolatry is a word denoting
> all that is wicked in imagination and impure in practice.
> Idolatry is a demon...an incarnation of all evil...but
> nevertheless bewitching and seductive as a siren. It ensnares
> the depraved heart, coils around it like a serpent, transfixes it
> with its deadly fangs, and finally stings it to death. (In Urwick
> 1885: 133).

The System of Caste

If Hinduism melted away into thin air when one stared at it long
enough, its social organization promised greater solidity as long as
one did not look at it too closely. It appeared to the missionaries
that Indian society was controlled and governed by a system of
caste hierarchy with the Brahmins at the top. The problem the
Christian missionaries faced with this social set up had little to do
with the socio-economic inequalities which they found in Indian
society. After all, the cultural and social gulf between the nobility
and the common folk in their own society was a matter of daily
experience to the Europeans. Rather, the problem was that the
caste system got in the way of the acceptance of Christianity.
Unable to convert the higher echelons of Indians, the missionaries

had to rest content with the induction of lower caste groups. In effect, this meant that Christianity was identified with the lower echelons and began to be socially marginalized. Even those few Brahmins who became converts found themselves getting isolated. Moreover, even the converts into Christianity continued with their former practices of caste discrimination.

Much like the social theorists of today, the Christian missionaries of yesterday had no clue about what they were confronting in the caste system. People appeared to follow some rules, without being clear what the rules were. Caste appeared to rest on authority, but it was not clear whose authority or which authority. Again the missionaries had but two guesses: the holy books of the heathens must have sanctioned this social organization; and the 'priests' of the heathens must be responsible for the continued sway of the caste system. Their rage and fury now turned against both of these things.

The Duplicity of the Devil's Messengers

The missionaries identified the Brahmins as the 'clergy' or the 'priests' of Hinduism. Now, the Reformation period had launched a furious attack against priests, albeit of the Catholic variety. The Protestants had left no stone unturned in attacking the Catholic clergy, including, of course, emphasizing the similarities between the heathen priesthood and the Catholic priesthood. The Catholics had to defend their position by showing that they were not at all like the heathens. Thus, during this period, both the Protestants and the Catholics ended up launching a sharp attack on heathen priests–their immoral character, their devilish practices, etc.

This explicit hostility towards heathen priesthood was not helped by the inability of the messengers of God to convert the Brahmins to Christianity. In Brahmins, they found a literate group that was also the only source of information about India as far as the missionaries were concerned. They were schooled to perform many administrative tasks, were mostly the only ones able to communicate in European languages and appeared to be the most intellectual and influential layer in the Indian social organization. Conversion of the heathens in India appeared to depend on converting the Brahmins. But, as Xavier saw the Brahmins:

These are the most perverse people in the world...they never tell the truth, but think of nothing but how to tell subtle lies and to deceive the simple and ignorant people, telling them that the idols demand certain offerings, and these are simply the things that the Brahmans themselves invent, and of which they stand in need to order to maintain their wives and children and houses... They threaten people that, if they do not bring the offerings, the gods will kill them, or cause them to fall sick, or send demons to their houses, and, through fear that the idols will do them harm, the poor simple people do exactly as the Brahmans tell them... *If there were no Brahmans in the area, all the Hindus would accept conversion to our faith.* (Neill 1984: 146; emphasis added).

Here, the Christian missionaries failed abysmally. They could not persuade the Brahmins to give up their 'religion'. Why is that? As emphasized several times, Christianity believed that practices were guided by beliefs and that criticism of the former was identical to criticizing the latter. The Brahmins were mostly unimpressed by the Christian criticism of their beliefs. In fact, they even agreed with them on several issues. As Abbé Dubois, the nineteenth century missionary, chronicled: The Brahmins clucked at the foolishness of the masses who worshipped in the temples, shaking their heads sadly at the credulity of the gullible folk for 'idol worship'; they agreed enthusiastically that there was only one God, the Supreme One, and that was that; they exhibited no fear and little respect towards those very same idols in whose temples they officiated as 'priests'; and had little problem in saying that the gods–whose stories they themselves were telling–were indeed immoral and definitely not worthy of supplication. In other words, the criticism of the missionaries did not seem to perturb the Brahmins. With respect to the charge that Hinduism is 'polytheistic' this is what they had to say:

We teach the People to worship One only, and not many Gods... God is variously represented under different Attributes and forms; yet he is still but one God, as Gold is but one, as to its kind, tho' wrought into a Thousand different Figures. (Excerpted in Young 1981: 24).

Why would they not convert to Christianity? Bernier, in his famous *Voyages*, recounts a conversation that he had with some Brahmins regarding the frequency of their ablutions:

> When I told them that in cold countries it would be impossible
> to observe their law during the winter, which showed that it
> was nothing but a pure invention of men, they gave me this
> rather amusing reply: that they were not claiming that their law
> was universal, but that God had made it for them alone, which
> was why they could not receive a foreigner into their
> religion;...they were not in the least claiming that our religion
> was false, but that it might be good for us and that God might
> have made several different paths to heaven; but that they
> would not agree that as ours was general for the whole world,
> theirs could be but fable and pure invention. (Chatfield 1808:
> 324).

In other words, the Brahmins remained Brahmins in spite of, or
precisely because of the very same arguments. How could
Europeans with their belief-fixations even begin to understand
this? In the same way that the Enlightenment thinkers suggested
that the pagan writers of Greece and Rome were inauthentic, the
Brahmins were suspected of being inauthentic, with the only
difference being that the attack against them was much more
unrestrained. After all, there was little to learn from these
idolatrous priests. The hatred against the heathen priesthood,
recently highlighted by both Protestants and Catholics during the
Reformation, the impotence in converting the Brahmins, the
identification of Brahmins as 'priests', the inability to understand
the culture they were functioning in, and a supercilious arrogance
were the ingredients that went into concocting the charges of
duplicity, unauthenticity and immorality against the heathen
priestly caste.

As time progressed, this attack would also target the 'caste
system'.

> Missionaries united in condemning the caste laws–"a lie
> against nature, against humanity, against history"–as being
> contrary to the spirit of Christian brotherhood; they declared
> caste to be the "bane of India", and demanded that caste should
> be utterly rejected by all converts to Christianity. (Sharpe
> 1965: 31).

The caste system, together with the priestly caste of the Brahmins,
epitomized all that was wrong with this nation of idolaters–and
there were plenty of wrongs to talk about. And talk they did, all the

way into the 20th century. William Hastie had this to observe in *Hindu Idolatry and English Enlightenment*:

> Senseless   mummeries,   loathsome   impurities...every conceivable form of licentiousness, falsehood, injustice, cruelty, robbery, murder... Its sublimest spiritual states have been but the reflex of physiological conditions in disease. (Cited in Maw 1990: 8).

And so the attacks continued. The only thing that changed over the centuries were the types of wrongs identified in Indian culture, in keeping with the changes in the times and tastes. Yesterday, the heathens were impervious to the message of the Gospels; today they are impervious to the message of social and economic progress. Christian missionaries made a moral issue about the Brahmins and the caste system; their heirs, the social scientists of the twenty-first century, faithfully continue to do so, oblivious to anything but their own sanctimony. What further unites them is their ignorance of what they were or are talking about.

Similar difficulties were encountered by the march of Christianity elsewhere across the Asian continent. In Japan and China too they met with an immovable object. It is easy to guess what was to blame: the heathens and their duplicity, of course. As the Mission Superior of Japan, Padre Francisco Cabral voiced his thoughts about the induction of Japanese into the Jesuit Order:

> If one does not cease and desist admitting Japanese into the Society...that will be the collapse of the Society, nay! of Christianity, in Japan, and it will later hardly prove possible to find a remedy... I have seen no other nation as conceited, covetous, inconstant, and insincere as the Japanese...they are educated to be inscrutable and false. (In Elison 1973: 16).

The 'red race' was primitive, it could be decimated; the 'blacks' were backward, they could be enslaved; the 'yellow' and 'brown' were inferior, they could be colonized. But how to convert them? How to respond to their indifference? For if there is one word that can capture the attitude of the heathens towards Christianity, it is this: indifference. The shrill and strident tone of the Gospel and its messengers is itself suspect. If their beliefs are all that superior, why the need to shout?

This was the context within which the first translations, the first texts, and the first discoveries were to filter down to the European continent. The broader context, as it remained for a long period, was the preoccupation of the European intellectuals with their own religious schisms and controversies. The Portuguese referred to the Indians as 'gentues' which the British made into Gentoos. The eighteenth century world allowed one to speak of the 'religion of the gentoos', the 'law book of the Gentoo people'. The same gentoos were also known as 'Hindus' to the Persians because they lived on the other side of the Sindhu river. This name was adopted in the nineteenth century, and the 'religion of the gentoos' became the 'religion of the Hindoos', later to achieve full recognition as 'Hinduism'. In the initial stages, this 'Hinduism' merely signified the idolatrous religion of the Hindoos, so named by the Moguls to designate the people who lived on the banks of the river Sindhu. How this 'Hinduism' metamorphosed into a full-blown religion has to do with some conceptual requirements and historical accidents, a brief sketch of which may not be out of place now.

Romanticism

The year is 1783. The man is William Jones. Son of a mathematician, this man is a gifted linguist. He wrote and published poems in Greek by the time he was fifteen; produced a remarkable Persian grammar and translated it into French when he was twenty-five and before his death at the age of forty-eight, he would thoroughly know thirteen of the twenty-eight languages that he would study. This brilliant jurist is on his way to Calcutta to serve in the East India Company under the guidance of Warren Hastings. Jones, Hastings, and another gifted mind by the name of H.T. Colebrooke, together set up the Asiatic Society and brought out the celebrated *Asiatick Researches.* Intellectuals from London to Rome would be indebted to them. The arrival of William Jones in Calcutta would mark the end of one era and the beginning of another.

This period was to be known as the "Second Renaissance", and it was anticipated that it would be as productive as the first one. It was also dubbed the "Oriental Renaissance" to distinguish it from the "Italian" one. Today, not much is known about the second renaissance, perhaps because, as Eliade remarks, it did not deliver the goods that were anticipated of it.

> The "discovery" of the *Upanishads* and Buddhism at the
> beginning of the nineteenth century had been acclaimed as a
> cultural event that presaged considerable consequence.
> Schopenhauer compared the discovery of Sanskrit and the
> *Upanishads* to the rediscovery of the "true" Greco-Latin
> culture during the Latin Renaissance. *One expected a radical
> renewal of Western thought as a consequence of the
> confrontation with Indian philosophy.* As is known, however,
> not only did this miracle of the "second Renaissance" not take
> place...but the discovery of the Indian spirituality did not give
> rise to any significant cultural creation. (1969: 55; emphasis
> added).

These words summarize the context and the result of the second
European encounter with India. Not only was there an anticipation
of a renewal in European culture that the second contact with India
would bring, but also a yearning and desire that it would
effectively take place. This longing was genuinely a part of the
spirit of the times and not a description projected by later scholars.

Let a Hundred Flowers Bloom?

A brief detour into the goings-on back on the European continent
will better illustrate the scene. The Protestant Reformation that had
split Christianity into two began to undergo divisions in its ranks.
We could try and look at this as a sort of a let-a-hundred-flowers-
bloom scenario, but this would be a hard case to argue considering
that ninety-nine of those flowers were considered to be deadly and
poisonous and only one invigorating and healthy. In any case, none
of the variations on the Christian theme escaped the iron grip of
the questions as they were formulated by the Protestant
framework. Caught in this atmosphere of persecution and
polemics, many intellectuals began to seek commonalities among
the competing Christian groups in the hope of finding a foundation
for their religious quest.

The earliest attempt was that of Lord Herbert Cherbury who
sought to discover a shared way of getting out of problems that
confronted the seventeenth century believers. Standing at the head
of a trend which was later to bloom into various shades of deism
and natural theology, Cherbury argued that there were certain
"Common Notions" concerning religion which were not only self-
evidently true but also innate in all men. These common notions

included the existence and nature of God, the duty of worshipping Him, the connection between virtue and piety, reconciliation through repentance, and the threat of punishment and reward in an afterlife. While in the initial stages this attempt was oriented towards Christian communities, very soon it spilled out to incorporate Judaism and Islam. As information about the heathen religions began to filter through and accumulate, it was inevitable that the attempt to catch all religions in one net should be extended to them as well.

A term that kept resurfacing in the discussions and disputations during this period was that of 'natural religion' although it was far from clear what exactly it was supposed to refer to:

> For some 'natural religion' referred to the religious beliefs which all men could in theory determine from nature and mankind by the use of their reason; for others it meant the beliefs which were innate in all men; for others 'natural religion' was religion which God revealed to Adam and, from Adam, was transmitted in theory and practice to all mankind; for others it denoted the beliefs and practices of those who were 'natural' men–unaffected that is, by civilization; for others it meant the religion of those who were unaffected by divine revelation–that is those outside the influence of Judaism, Christianity and Islam (since Mahomet was held to have adopted many of his ideas from Jewish and Christian teaching). For some, talk about natural religion has a theoretical context, while for others it has primarily an empirical use. For some, natural religion was the pure and sufficient religion for all men; for others it was a human product which showed that valid religion can be derived only from a divine revelation accepted by faith. (Pailin 1971: 86-87).

This was the background in Europe by the time William Jones set sail for Calcutta. As for knowledge about India, the Dutch, French, Danish, Italian, and English missionaries discovered and announced the existence of a language in India which was,

> a dead language, sacred, liturgical, and erudite, restricted to a high priestly caste, renowned for an immense and mysterious body of literature, and written in a script to which the key was missing. Formidable barriers defended this treasure from the impurity of the Europeans, who called it by various names,

according to the dialect in which they first encountered it. For Abraham Roger it was Samscortum. Bernier employed the curious form Hanscrit which, with two exceptions, Voltaire also used. Sahanscrit, and worse, can be found in the *Lettres édifiantes*. Anquetil called it Samscroutam or Samcretam at first. Sonnerat called it Sanscroutam, Samskret, Hanscrit and Grandon (after Grantham). In 1806, Adelung termed it Samscrada. (Schwab 1950: 31).

Meanwhile the missionaries had also amassed evidence about the existence of a holy book called 'Shaster', 'Shastah', 'Beed', 'Bede', 'Bedam' or 'Vedam'.

Into this parched ground fell the fresh drops of rain by way of the first authentic translations brought about by Jones, Colebrook, Wilkins, and others. This, in turn, paved the way for the Romantics. With respect to the theme of this book, there are two aspects of relevance. The first relates to the continuity in the line of thinking between the Enlightenment and Romanticism, and the other relates to the legacy of Romanticism.

The Romantic Heirs of the Enlightenment

The previous chapter talks about the emergence of the domain of a universal history brought about by the absorption of living heathen culture into the paganism of Antiquity. Generally, the eighteenth century thinkers argued that the origin of religion, specially the primitive heathen ones, had to do with the fact that they gave material substance to natural forces, attributing semi-divine qualities to these forces. Thus the primitive man invented his pantheon of gods. Not yet capable of rational thinking, Early Man used the fanciful imagination that he was endowed with. This was at the root of those fantastical creations and absurd stories that constituted his religious world. These stories were the product of 'mythical' thought as opposed to 'rational' or 'scientific' thought.

The Romantics, from Herder to Schlegel and beyond accepted this Enlightenment legacy. Consequently, the rediscovery of India and its culture meant the discovery of an ancient culture that was contemporaneous with the modern one. The ancients represented the childhood of Man. Thus, the Romantics projected an image of India as the cradle of world civilization. The plains of the Ganges were supposedly populated with gentle people with noble souls; its poetry, according to Goethe, was the last word on the subject; and so on.

A bit of unpacking of the notions of 'childhood' and 'cradle' is necessary to understand what the German Romantics were really saying. Irrespective of what any single thinker said, each of them had accepted the framework of a universal history of humankind. There was a consensus that European culture had matured. They may mourn the absence of innocence and the spontaneity of childhood but it remains incontrovertible that this is how an adult looks back. By calling Indian culture the childhood of Man, the Romantic thinkers did not go beyond or against the Enlightenment tradition. They merely extended it, albeit with a fanciful twist. The same reflections are applicable to the term 'cradle of civilization'. To use this term with reference to a culture that is long dead and gone, like that of the Greeks and Romans, might be construed as a way of paying homage to the contributions of the past. What does it mean when it is used to characterize a living culture? It can only mean that those who live in this culture are still in their cradles, and have been there for the past thousand years, unlike their European counterparts.

That German Romanticism accepted the legacy of the Enlightenment, despite the alleged antagonism between them, is evidenced in the way they treated the subject of religion. Herder, the recognized leader of German Romanticism, places the cradle of humankind in the Orient. It is the land of gold and precious stones mentioned by Moses, the cradle of human desires and of all religion:

> There, Land of the east! The *cradle* of the human race, human drives, and all religion. (In Willson 1964: 51; emphasis added)

As Willson further remarks:

> Herder believes that the first faint stirrings of religion were to be found in the worship of natural phenomena, *in reverence and awe before its revelations*... Herder points out that he considers the mythology of India older than that of any other land... He looks upon the mythology of the Hindus as *first, childlike attempts* to arrange objects systematically in ideas or images... (*ibid.* 60-61; emphasis added)

Georg Forster, in his German translation of *Sakontala* from the English version rendered by Jones in 1789, recommends in the introduction:

> ...(the) Indic literature as represented by *Sakontala* for the simple relationship the Hindu, *in a childlike and unspoiled state*, has with nature. The Modern European, *living in a highly civilized culture*, he says, has lost this intimate identification of himself with nature. He reminds his reader that, disposed by scientific refinement in skills and customs to an artificially gauged and rationalized way of life, the European could easily lose sight of an ingenious feeling for nature, *if he did not still encounter it in less sophisticated peoples*. (*ibid.* 73; emphasis added).

Eulogizing further about this piece of poetry:

> Forster emphasizes that the *childlike imagination* of the Hindu personified all of nature, even the plants; the animating powers of the trees were divine creatures... Very closely connected with this belief is the sanctity and inviolability of the woods and groves in which those men favored by God reside. (*ibid.* 75-76; emphasis added).

How far is this from the explanation about the origin of religion that the Enlightenment thinkers gave? Friedrich Ast, a German philosopher, suggests that there are three periods in the history of human civilization:

> That of the Hindu, in which the root of religion falls, where nature and love were intimately reciprocal, the period of golden innocence, of undivided religion, philosophy, and art;... India...is an idyllic paradise where nature is entwined with love; the emotion and the object are inseparable, each includes the other. *In India there was a pure, golden innocence, the innocence of childhood.* (*ibid.*: 89; emphasis added).

Indian culture of the eighteenth and nineteenth century not only represented the childhood of Man but was itself the childhood of Man. Its people were naïve, innocent and good. They had retained the primal religion, which permeated all aspects of their existence—religion, philosophy, poetry, knowledge was all one. As Hegel put it in less flattering terms, "fantasy makes everything into a God here".

Based purely on the texts they read in translations, people built these images of India. The first obvious conclusion we can draw is that German Romanticism did not go any further than its predecessors in empirically investigating the existence or non-existence of religion in India. It merely strengthened the grip of the Biblical story of an original religion by depicting India as the seat of this primal culture. The legacy of the Enlightenment-Romanticism period has allowed the generations that followed it to accept these images as facts about Indian culture and to continue spinning the same image. Consider the image of the people of India constituting the childhood of Man. If a few thousand years ago they were in their childhood and remain in that phase, how would one describe their development over these years? It can only be a static and stagnant civilization. As Stevenson, a missionary in Madras, was to put it in his *Hinduism and Christian Religion*:

> The implements of trade and agriculture have been unchanged for ages; there are no changing fashions even in women's dress; little original has been produced in literature or philosophy worth speaking of; and religion has become...a tremendous fossilized organism, dead at the core, yet standing strong by its vast mechanical solidity and hoary antiquity. (Cited in Maw 1990: 1-2).

From Hegel through Marx and beyond, this has been the description of India. What caused the stagnation of India? If you are a twentieth century liberal your choices are limited. You can only identify the social structure as the cause for this stagnation. This means the caste system of course. Thus, from Marx through Weber and beyond, we hear incessant chatter about the obsolete caste system which has caused this stagnation.

There is yet another element to the legacy of the Romantics. One consequence of an extended childhood is the dominance of religion in all aspects of human life. This longing of German Romanticism has ended up becoming the truth about Indian (Asian) society and culture today. From the scholar to the street sweeper, from the tourist to the television reporter, everyone insists that religion pervades everything in India. Here, at random, is one such example:

> There can never be a clear-cut understanding of the East on the part of the West until Westerners realize that all Asian thought

is religiously conditioned... I can think of no single department of human activity in Asian lands that is not encompassed by religious concepts. (Abbot Sumangalo 1972: 19-20).

If religion is everywhere in India, what is the problem in saying what it is? Yet apparently these religions defy description.

Such mythical, romantic images can never survive the onslaught of facts for long. Herder may have sighed about the childlike Hindus, all noble and good, dripping sugar and honey. Not so our intrepid Abbé Dubois who lived in India for thirty years.

> Certain it is that there is no nation in the world who think so lightly of an oath or of perjury. The Hindu will fearlessly call upon all of his gods–celestial, terrestrial, infernal–to witness his good faith in the least of his undertakings; but should fresh circumstances demand it, he would not have the smallest scruple in breaking the word that he had so solemnly pledged...
>
> The unscrupulous manner in which Hindus will perjure themselves is so notorious that they are never called upon to make a statement on oath in their own courts of justice... (1816: 662).

In case you are of the opinion that the words of a Catholic missionary hardly count as facts, here is another random citation from a non-Catholic. Speaking of Hindus, he claims:

> In nothing is the general want of principle more evident, than in the total disregard to truth which they show; no rank or order among them can be exempted from the implication. The religious teachers set the example, and they are scrupulously followed by all classes. Perjury and fraud are as common as is a suit of law; with protestations of equal sincerity will a witness stand forth who knows the falsehood of his testimony, and he who is ignorant of what he professes to testify. No oath can secure the truth; ...Venality and corruption are universal; they are remarkable, too, for their ingratitude. (Massie, Vol. 1, 1840: 466-467).

Thus, under the harsh sunlight of truth, the misty image of German Romanticism just faded away. There were other historical realities that contributed to this: the tighter control of the British over colonial rule in India; the dissipation and dissolution of the Asiatic

Society; and the determined effort to spread English education, among other things.

Buddha, the Savior

It's now time to move on to the nineteenth century to meet The Buddha, the Savior of the people. You might have wondered why it has taken so long to meet this legendary figure. The reason is simple. The creation of Hinduism antedates that of Buddhism. This does not mean to imply that Hinduism existed in India before Buddhism came into being. This is the standard textbook claim, of course. It just means that the Europeans created Buddhism after they had created Hinduism. The thesis about the creation of Buddhism has been argued superbly by Almond (1988), therefore, let's allow him to speak in his own words:

> ...in the period from the later part of the eighteenth century to the beginning of the Victorian period in the latter half of the 1830s is the *creation* of Buddhism. It *becomes* an object, is constituted as such; it takes form as an entity that 'exists' over against the various cultures which can now be perceived as instancing it, manifesting it, in an enormous variety of ways. During the first four decades of the nineteenth century, we see the halting yet progressive emergence of a taxonomic object, the creation of which allows in turn the systematic definition, description, and classification of that congeries of cultural 'facts' which instance it, manifest it, in a number of Eastern countries.

> The creation of Buddhism took place in two more or less distinct phases. The first of these coincided with the first four decades of the nineteenth century. During this period, Buddhism was an object which was instanced and manifested 'out there' in the Orient...

> This would subtly change in the first twenty-five years of the Victorian period. Originally, existing 'out there' in the Oriental *present*, Buddhism came to be determined as an object the primary location of which was the West, through the progressive collection, translation, and the publication of its textual *past*. Buddhism, by 1860, had come to exist, not in the Orient, but in the Oriental libraries and institutes of the West, in its texts and manuscripts, at the desks of the Western savants who interpreted it. It had become a textual object, defined, classified, and interpreted through its own textuality.

> By the middle of the century, the Buddhism that existed 'out
> there' was beginning to be judged by a West that *alone* knew
> what Buddhism was, is, and ought to be. The essence of
> Buddhism came to be seen expressed not 'out there' in the
> Orient, but in the West through the West's control of
> Buddhism's own textual past. (*ibid.*: 12-13).

None of these developments should come as a surprise to the
reader who has followed the arguments presented in this book so
far. Rather than reproduce the arguments presented in Almond's
book, it is worth highlighting the contexts–both the European and
the Indian ones–in which the creation of Buddhism took place.

The Contexts of Creation

The European context, first. Even though the mythical image that
the German Romantics projected on India disintegrated pretty fast,
one of the dissatisfactions that had brought it about did not.
Though caused initially by the schismatic movement within
Christianity, the 'spiritual solace', as people formulated it, could
not be found within the existing Christian traditions. The Christian
worldview was increasingly incapable of providing satisfactory
answers to the questions it itself had spawned regarding the
meaning of life, the goal and origin of human beings, etc. It was
unable to answer existential questions like what it means to lead
the life of a Christian industrialist, Christian plumber, or a
Christian intellectual. It is one thing to shout from the rooftops that
you must continue to live your life like a Christian in a secular
world, but quite another to say what such a life consists of. The
growth of secular ethics appeared to sever the relationship between
religion and morality. To reduce Christianity to a variety of ethics
appeared not only blasphemous but a downright degradation of the
idea of religion itself. This unsettling, if vague, disturbance within
Christianity was one of the strands that lived on even after the
Romantic mythical image and longing had died out.

This disquiet was further sustained by the evangelizing work of
Christianity itself. The realization that the conversion of heathens
required an understanding of their experiential world implied
digging into the culture of India–albeit with European instruments
and expertise. The work of the British Orientalists, the translation

of the Gita, and other texts, began to create an audience faintly receptive to 'Oriental wisdom'.

As for the Indian context, it had more to do with the Christians and Europeans in India during this period, than Indian culture itself. The missionaries had reached an impasse in their efforts to convert the heathens. As they saw it, the Brahmins and the ubiquitous 'caste system' appeared to impede the progress of Christianity in India, or even worse, threatened to marginalize it. As information accumulated about the different parts of Asia, it became evident that there was yet another idolatrous practice which appeared to be dominant in Ceylon (Sri Lanka), Siam (Thailand), Cathay (China) and Japan. The definitive breakthrough in the 'scientific' study of Buddhism, according to the consensus of scholars, was the appearance in 1844 of the *Introduction á l'Histoire du Buddhisme Indien* by the French scholar Eugène Burnouf. This volume apparently set the standard and provided the guidelines for the further study of Buddhism. To this day it is reckoned as an exemplar to follow.

While this signaled the beginning of the deluge of translations of Buddhist texts from Sanskrit, Pali, Tibetan, and Chinese, it is to the credit of Edwin Arnold to have made Buddhism popular in the West. In 1879, his poem *The Light of Asia* fell amid an audience which swallowed up more than a hundred editions in England and America, and had it translated into several foreign languages. From then on, the deluge became a veritable flood.

It is important to note that the religion called Buddhism was built around those many texts that found their way to the various institutions of learning in Europe. The different kinds of Buddhism that flourished in Asia were discovered and reconstructed through translations and commentaries; the outline, feature, Gestalt, the very identity of Buddhism was captured and delineated by the translations of these texts; the 'doctrinal core', the history, the evolution, and the transformation of the religion were decided by means of deciphering the texts. Most of these texts were old, sometimes a thousand years old, at other times even older than that.

The only difference between the creation of Hinduism and that of Buddhism was that in the case of Buddhism this creation is easily discernable because the speed with which it came about was so spectacular, occurring in less than seventy years. In the case of Hinduism, it was more long drawn but no less insidious for it. As Almond convincingly argues:

> Buddhism had become by the middle of the nineteenth century a textual object based on Western institutions. Buddhism as it came to be ideally spoken of through the editing, translating, and studying of its ancient texts could then be compared with its contemporary appearance in the Orient. And Buddhism, as it could be seen in the East, compared unfavourably with its ideal textual exemplifications contained in the libraries, universities, colonial offices, and missionary societies of the West. It was possible then, as a result of this, to combine a positive evaluation of a Buddhism textually located in the West with a negative evaluation of its Eastern instances. (1988: 37)

This creation of Buddhism went hand in hand with the interpretation and appreciation the West showed for it.

On How the Buddha Saved Souls

As mentioned multiple times already, the Brahmins, who were conceived of as a priestly caste, together with the caste system, had frustrated the messengers of God in saving the lost souls of the Indians. This resulted in a moralizing discourse about both of these phenomena that the Europeans had no understanding of. It was done in the name of such principles as equality and the dignity of man. The British missionaries, of course, had little love for Roman Catholicism, 'Romish' priests or Catholic rituals. After all, these had been the primary targets of the Protestant Reformation. Buddhism, as the European savants viewed it, was precisely a reaction against Brahmanism, the priestly caste of India. In no time at all, the Buddha became the Martin Luther of India rebelling against the 'Roman Catholic' Brahmanic priests.

> 'Original' Buddhism...was often called the Protestantism of Asia. (The Lamaism of Tibet, on the other hand, was frequently compared by English writers to Roman Catholicism and regarded as a priestly, ritualistic corruption of original Buddhism.)... Max Müller gave broad currency to the view that Buddha was another Luther who, sweeping away the superstitions and rituals with which the Brahman priesthood

had enshrouded India, took religion back to its simple and pure origins. (Clausen 1975: 7).

In 1850, *The Prospective Review* declared that "Gotama was a Protestant against the Religion of his Country"; *The Christian Remembrancer* argued in 1858 that the comparison of Protestantism to Catholicism and Buddhism to Brahmanism held up, even down to minute points of resemblance. *The Journal of Sacred Literature* exclaimed in the 1860s:

> Gautama did for India what Luther and the reformers did for Christendom; like Luther, he found religion in the hands of a Class of men who claimed a monopoly of it, and doled it out in what manner and what measure he chose; like Luther, he protested that religion is not the affair of the priest alone, but is the care and concern of every man who has a reasonable soul; both labored to communicate to all the knowledge which had been exclusively reserved for the privileged class... And as Europe bestirred itself at the voice of Luther, so India awakened heartily to the call of Gautama. (Almond 1988: 73).

It is no wonder that such a Martin Luther would receive applause from an appreciative audience, considering what they thought about Hinduism. Though this has already been elaborated upon, it is worth presenting one or two citations that provide an overview of the context for the Indian Luther. "There is universal agreement," claimed James Mill in *The History of British India*,

> Respecting the meanness, the absurdity, the folly, of the endless, childish, degrading, and pernicious ceremonies, in which the practical part of the Hindu religion consists... Volumes would hardly suffice to depict at large the ritual of the Hindus, which is more tedious, minute, and burthensome; and engrosses a greater portion of human life than any ritual which has been found to fetter and oppress any other portion of human race. (Almond 1988: 71).

Buddha came to the rescue of the European intellectuals in finding an answer to the riddle of the Brahmins in yet another way. One of the issues that the Protestants had pounced upon during the Reformation was the corruption and degeneration of religion. Textual Buddhism now allowed the same question to be put to Buddhism. The answers they came up with only confirmed the providential role that the Europeans played in civilizing the peoples of Asia. The practice of Buddhism in all countries of Asia had degenerated into gross idolatry and superstitious idol worship. This corruption, dubbed the 'popular Buddhism', was very different from the pure, simple, and original 'philosophical' Buddhism of the founder himself. This 'philosophical' Buddhism was, of course, delineated in the texts of the Buddhist tradition known to the European intellectuals. Consequently, they could measure and pronounce upon the practices in the Asian continent. In this sense there was no difference between the missionaries and these intellectuals: popular Buddhism was corrupt and degenerate. One could wonder at and admire the good things that Indian civilization had to offer, without having to admire its current state, living inhabitants and the actual culture.

Of course, not all European intellectuals were equally drawn to Buddhism. As Robert Childers notes in the *Contemporary Review* in 1876:

> Much diversity of opinion appears to exist respecting the teaching of Buddhism. According to one it is a system of barren metaphysics, according to another it is sheer mysticism; a third will tell you that it is a code of pure and beautiful morality; while a fourth looks upon it as a very selfish abstraction from the world, a systematic repression of every impulse and emotion of the heart. (In Clausen 1975: 7).

More importantly, even those sympathetic to Buddhism, like Max Müller or Rhys-Davids felt compelled to contrast it with Christianity only to find the former inferior. Buddhism might have been one of the best pagan religions they encountered, but in the end it was "almost but not quite" as good as Christianity.

Such, then, was the Buddhism as the West created it by the time we reach the turn of the century: moral, repellent and fascinating, pure and corrupt, it was a religion which came into being in Paris and London.

> It was the Victorians who developed the discourse within which Buddhism was circumscribed, who deemed it a worthy focus of Western attention; it was they who brought forth the network of texts within which Buddhism was located. And it was they who determined the framework in which Buddhism was imaginatively constructed, not only for themselves, but

also *in the final analysis for the East itself.* (Almond 1988: 140; emphasis added).

A Conceptual Gap

Through the centuries, the portrayal of Indian culture by the Europeans–whether it was the missionaries, the travelers, or the scholars–did not alter the framework of the image it depicted. The later reports merely modified the details that the former reports had provided. Common to all of them is this single belief: to know and understand a culture is to study the relevant texts. Or, to know and understand a culture is to find out what people believe in. Consider how ridiculous this really is by reflecting on the following. What could one say about European culture and its people of the eighteenth century by studying The Bible? Just imagine a group of scholars in India, none of whom knows either the classical or modern languages of Europe, studying some gibberish translation in their vernacular of a fragment of the Bible to make pronouncements about a culture and society thousands of years later. Even the French Enlightenment thinkers would find it absurd. Yet this happened in Europe with respect to India for over two hundred years. What makes this absurdity an absolute farce is its continuation today. How many treatises do not refer to the *Laws of Manu* in order to talk about Indian ethics? How many ethnographic works talk about the caste system without solemnly mentioning the four 'varnas'? But how many Brahmins have ever read the *Laws of Manu*? How many know what the *Dharma Shastras* contain?

This farce has assumed tragic proportions because the Indian (Asian) intellectuals have made this attitude, this posture, this stupidity their very own. What started off as a Protestant criticism of Catholic priesthood, and was then conveniently used to describe the Brahmins by the ignorant West, has now become the regular stock-in-trade of any 'progressive' intellectual you would meet in India. A self-evident set of notions becomes 'obvious' due to its long currency; the ideas become truisms and trivia to most anthropologists, philosophers, and students of religion. The circle is complete when intellectuals from other cultures accept these ravings as scientific truths.

The reason for believing that India knows of indigenous religions is religious in nature. This belief is generated by and thrives because of standard Christian beliefs. This has never been a scientific, empirical question. Ever. Both the question and the answer are theological. It is an article of faith. Why do people in the twenty-first century accept this idea as well? It is because this theme has become an unexamined triviality due to its long currency. Besides, to deny religion to a people is to deny them culture and civilization. This is partly the old association between *religio* and *traditio,* and partly the not-so-old legacy of the relation between being 'not-primitive', thus having the ability to think abstractly, and having a home-grown religion. The intellectuals of India (Asia) accept this because of their peculiar relation to their old colonial masters. This is part of the answer. The other parts of the answer will be tackled in the following chapters.

PART II

A Christian theoretical framework guides the study of religion, including the study of naturalistic religion. All studies of religion presuppose the truth about Biblical themes, even as they couch them in secular terms. Our so-called secular world is, in effect, a secularized religious world.

CHAPTER V

REQUIEM FOR A THEME

Sometime in the eighteenth century, there emerged a new paradigm for developing theories in the field of religious studies– the naturalistic paradigm. Instead of appealing to the 'supernatural' to account for the origin of religion, this paradigm turned to 'natural' causes to look for an explanation. Instead of providing theological explanations such as the classic Biblical account that God gave religion to mankind, it sought to provide a secular account.

> If there is one person...whose achievement might be marked as the completion of a paradigm shift, it is Hume...(who) produced a thoroughgoing naturalistic critique of all available theological explanations of religion... (He) not only undercut all appeals to supernatural or transcendent causes of religion, but went on to propose alternative paths of explanation of the available data–paths that are travelled still by scholars. (Preus 1987: xiv-xv).

If we are to believe the above, it would appear that from Hume onwards we should not stumble upon any theological residue in the naturalistic explanations of religion. To assess this claim, we need to be clear about the problems these theories tried to solve and the answers they provided. The problem they tried to address was: if we cannot take the existence of God as a given, how can we explain the universality, variety, and persistence of religions? The answers they tried to provide would revolve around natural causes.

A word about theories and theory formation will be helpful at this point. Suppose we want to ask why the grass is green? If we already have some knowledge and theories about color, vision, chlorophyll, and sunlight, it is possible to provide a satisfactory answer. If we have no theories at our disposal, the same question admits several kinds of answers: "Because God made it so"; "Because elves come and paint it every night"; "Because it's in the nature of grass to be green". That is to say, the question does not impose any constraints or limits on the process of seeking answers. It is not even clear where we need to look for an answer. This is an example of an ill-defined cognitive problem. The more we know about a phenomenon, the more focused our questions and answers can be.

It is important to note that the several theories that emerged from the naturalistic paradigm did not undertake to study the historical causes for the origin of specific religions. What they did was to account for the emergence of the phenomenon of religion as such. In other words, the naturalistic paradigm undertook to explain why religion is a culturally universal phenomenon or why human beings had to invent religion.

Now, if we are to take these theories seriously, then one of the fundamental requirements would be that they do not presuppose the truth about what they are trying to explain. But this is precisely what the naturalistic theories do. They purport to explain why religion is necessarily a cultural universal, but they assume this 'fact' as a given. If this is the case, such a theory will come up with *ad hoc* explanations. An *ad hoc* explanation is an explanation specifically invented to explain a fact or a set of facts. To be more than just an *ad hoc* explanation, a theory must be able to account for and link together several other independent facts than the facts it originally faced (say, in the way the original fact that grass is green ties in or fits into other independent facts about sunlight, chlorophyll, and our theories about vision, color, etc.)   The problem in the naturalistic explanations of religion is that they first presuppose the truth of the claim that religion is a cultural universal and then come up with *ad hoc* explanations designed to fit this fact. For all its intellectual pretensions, an *ad hoc* naturalistic explanation is no better than an *ad hoc* supernatural explanation.

It is equally essential to note that during this period the ethnographic data about other cultures was not exhaustive. It was not even free of ambiguity or inconsistencies. During the period of

Hume, or even Freud, anthropological investigation had not come up with indisputable evidence showing that religion was a cultural universal. Therefore, we would be justified in saying that these theorists tried to provide an explanation for something that was not an established fact.

Let's suppose we come across a culture that has no religion. What precisely would the importance of such a discovery be and what would be the consequences for the theories of religion? Here are three possibilities: Consider the naturalistic theories that say that religion is an experience of the holy; or that it is a human response to the transcendent; or that it is an expression of human alienation; or that it is a cementing bond for the community. Armed with these theories, let us assume that we examine all cultures only to find that some cultures do not have religion. What do we learn? We conclude that either this theory is false; or the members of such a culture do not have an experience of the holy; they have no response to the transcendent; they are not alienated; they lack a cementing bond for the community, etc. So what? There are no consequences other than the realization that we had entertained false beliefs and that we had better find another theory.

Or it might be that our theories are not false but rather they are simply inadequate. With respect to theories that define religion as a "mechanism for social integration" (e.g., the functionalists), or as an "experience of the sacred" (e.g., the phenomenologists), if we come across cultures with no religion we can conclude, for instance, that these societies use other mechanisms of social integration or that they have something else that replaces the experience of the sacred. At this point we could say that our definitions, as embedded in these theories, are inadequate because we had wrongly assumed that these specific mechanisms and these typical experiences were somehow necessary. Again, so what? We learn a methodological lesson that we should provide adequate definitions but this tells us very little about the real issues at stake in the particular case.

There is a third possibility. Suppose some culture just does not have a "mechanism for social integration" or lacks the "experience of the sacred" as stipulated by the theories of religion. This scenario is not cognitively interesting since it hinges entirely on the stipulative definition of religion, i.e., a definition that is based on how some author decides to define the word. It does not require the rethinking of any major issue, except that of revising the stipulative definition.

This situation is rather odd, to put it mildly. It is self-evident to most that all cultures have religion and yet it is not possible to say what the consequences of its absence are. It is clear that there is something suspicious about the claim regarding the universality of religion. These theories simply assume that there is religion everywhere; they assume its diversity too, insofar as all cultures supposedly have some religion. Having assumed the truth of that which they need to explain, they then fish around to find a set of plausible-looking claims which might explain the phenomenon in question. Laudan describes such a procedure and the problems involved with it rather succinctly:

> Suppose that I find some puzzling fact that piques my curiosity, maybe I find a massive fossilized bone while digging in my backyard. I may develop a low-grade "theory" to explain this fact: perhaps I conjecture that God put it there to test my faith in the literal reading of the Scripture. Now although my hypothesis arguably explains the fact of a fossil bone in my backyard, that hypothesis is not tested by the fossil bone. On the contrary, my hypothesis was specifically constructed to explain the bone. My hypothesis might be testable but I would have to look further afield to find something which counted as a genuine test of it...
>
> (A)n observation or set of observations is a "test" of a theory only if the theory or hypothesis might conceivably fail to pass muster in the light of the observations. If, as in my hypothetical case, the theory was invented specifically to explain the phenomenon in question, and was groomed specifically so as to yield the result in question, then there is no way in which it could fail to account for it. *Where there is no risk of failure, there is no test* involved. (1990: 20; emphasis in original).

In other words, there must be some way to test a theory. If the naturalistic theories of religion simply provide *ad hoc* explanations designed to fit their hypothesis, their lack of explanatory power becomes understandable. The claim about the nature and universality of religion is not part of any one theory of religion. If it were, we would immediately see the consequences of these theories if we found a culture without religion. Rather, it appears to undergird all theories of religion.

The only way we can test these theories is by assuming the negation of the claims that they are trying to explain, i.e., by assuming that not all cultures have religion. Let's see what the consequences of this assumption would be.

First, it would mean that judgments about religion are pre-theoretical in nature. That is to say, they would undergo all the ups and downs that pre-theoretical intuitions are subject to. There would be variations in inter-generational and even inter-individual judgments regarding the same phenomenon. This consequence appears to be true–at times the Native Americans are said to have religion, and at other times not; at times Buddhism is a religion, at others times it is not, and at yet other times it is devil worship. Second, since 'religion' is not a concept in any axiomatized theory, since it is a pre-theoretical concept, any definition of religion will show all the arbitrariness of a stipulative definition. The words of Lott support this consequence:

> Any attempt at an anatomy of religious life immediately faces the vexed question of a definition of religion. The field of religious studies is bestrewn with corpses of rejected definitions, found to be either too vague to be of any foundational value, or too specific to include types of religion that are found at the other end of the spectrum; or perhaps too cumbersome to be anything other than a summary description of typical features found in traditions which by general consent are part of comparative field of religious studies. (1988:15).

Third, it would be possible to demonstrate that the ideas about the universality of religion are based on grounds other than serious factual investigation of cultures and peoples. This has been amply demonstrated in the previous chapters. Fourth, it would be possible to account for the persistence of the stubborn superstition among scholars that cultures without religion cannot possibly exist. The following chapters will attempt to establish this. Meanwhile, let's examine these naturalistic theories of religion a bit more closely.

The Metaphysical Speculations

It is often said, in a half-joking and half-serious vein, that cultures are driven to create religions if they do not have one. This statement is based on claims about the nature and needs of human beings and refers to the various attempts at a speculative reconstruction of the origin of religion. The early discussions about the universality of religion took this form. The examination of these discussions is aimed not so much to show that such speculations are false, but that they are nothing more than theories specifically designed to explain a particular phenomenon. In the process of exhibiting their *ad hoc* nature, it will hopefully become clear why these assorted theories appear plausible even though they are not.

To the question "why does religion come into being?" there's pretty much one basic answer with many variants: confronted with a chaotic world, primitive man had to impose some order on his experience. Experiencing phenomena that were both random and inexplicable, primitive man devised mythical, magical or naturalistic religious explanations. This enabled him to survive in a hostile world. From the beginning man was confronted with two great mysteries: birth and death. To make sense of these, he devised elaborate religious explanations. These are the basic accounts that come with assorted embellishments and variations on the theme. Here is one, as an example:

> Primitive man's life is a life of great uncertainty combined with little knowledge. His universe confronts him with an unpredictable alteration of abundance and dearth, prosperity and famine, life and death. He *necessarily* experiences it as whimsical and unreliable, *threatening* him on vital points of subsistence and survival with far greater frequency than it does modern man. More often than the latter, primitive man has *reason* to experience events as intentional, as carrying hidden messages of some sort. (Van Baal 1981: 155-56; emphasis added).

Another scholar states it thus:

> So far as Early Man is concerned, the three most arresting situations with which he was confronted were those of birth, propagation, subsistence and death. These, in fact, have been

the fundamental events and experiences in the structure of preliterate society at all times, creating a tension for the relief of which ways and means had to be found. In the palaeolithic period, when life depended largely on the hazards of chase and of the supply of roots, berries and fish, the vagaries of seasons, and so many unpredictable and uncontrollable circumstances by the available human means, the emotionable *strain and stress* was endemic. To sublimate this a ritual technique was devised and developed to meet these requirements and to maintain equilibrium in an expanding social and religious organization. (James 1969: 23-24; emphasis added).

How sensible are these explanations? Not very. If anything, primitive man should have been very impressed by the orderliness of the seasons, astronomical regularities, or just the plain stability of the world around him. Water did not change into wine, streams did not flow uphill, objects always fell down when let go, and so on. Where would he have experienced the chaos? Could he have seen random events such as thunder, and postulated gods to account for them? It is improper to speak of randomness here, but only of unexpectedness. But his experience of the world would have been such as to allow for unexpectedness. Besides, even if he created the gods to account for thunder, by virtue of this fact, he could not predict thunder. It would remain unexpected. In other words, the fact that he postulated gods does not render his world more orderly, so it cannot be that he postulated the gods to bring order into his world.

Or perhaps, one might assert, it was because of this very order that man created the gods. But why should he assume that it is in the nature of the divine to impose order? Why should it be self-evident to him that the principle of order is God? As a matter of fact, many pagan gods are known for their caprice. This assumption that God creates order is characteristic of religions based on the Old Testament. After the Flood, as the book of Genesis tells us, comes the guarantee of order and constancy in nature. Not only is God the guarantor, as the Genesis tells us, but He is also the principle of order separating light from darkness, and day from night. For those who grew up in such a culture it might appear obvious that before scientific theories came along the only way of explaining order was to say that it required a God or gods. This would not have been quite so obvious to the primitive man.

What about theories relating to the hostile environment of Early Man, or those that state that he experienced uncertainty because he lived in a world of scarcity while longing for security? A good deal of caution is called for when we begin to speculate on the psychology of people from other times, but let's examine these claims anyway. To assess the plausibility of the claim that primitive man experienced the world as scarcity we need to consider that his world gave him droughts and famines, floods and diseases, and plentiful supplies now and then. But it would have been in the nature of the world to be this way–both scarcity and plenitude would have been part of his experience. The world of a poor man is not the world of a rich man minus his wealth; the world of Early Man is not our world minus its wealth. Even if scarce seasons were more frequent than bountiful ones, he could not experience the world as scarcity. To the primitive man, that would have been the normal way of the world. For Early Man, the experience of the world includes being hungry most of the time. If you or I were transported back to *his* world, *we* would experience the world as scarcity. That is, his normal world would have been our world of scarcity.

As for Early Man's longing for security in an uncertain world, to provide a plausible answer we would have to refer to human psychological makeup. Is this not how we react in situations involving uncertainty? Perhaps. But this armchair psychologizing is much too speculative. The backward extension of our psychology onto the psychology of primitive man can be true only if cultural evolution has not had any impact on the nature and structure of human emotions. We would have to assume that human emotions are entirely biological in nature and therefore subject only to evolutionary development and not subject to the influence of cultural evolution. What, then, is the implication of this? It assumes that human beings have two distinct aspects, the rational which is subject to cultural change and the emotional that does not undergo change. This division of human beings into the rational and bestial is a centuries-old legacy, endorsed by the Bible. There are many contemporary scholars who are fervent critics of the "rational" and "affective" distinction, not to mention several ancient traditions that make no such distinction. In any case, the only point is that without accepting this assumption and its implication it is very difficult to see how the claims about Early Man's psychology can be plausible.

The same can be said of the great 'mysteries'. What is mysterious about birth or death? These are the most banal happenings. Primitive man would have accepted these events as the most natural things. In fact it is more plausible to say that both birth and death would have constituted one of the regularities of the world he lived in. They were part of the order of the world; instead of being mysteries that generated awe, they lent stability to his experience of the world. Whatever his emotional involvement, there is no psychological necessity why the phenomenon of birth and death should be seen as a mystery. Birth and death may be important facts for us, but why should this be equally true of Early Man?

To realize the flimsiness of the arguments that attribute religion to primitive man on the grounds of some alleged experience of nature, consider now a theory that neatly reverses this conclusion. The idea that man invented the gods when confronted with the terrors of nature or fear of death is centuries-old, stretching back to the Greeks. In the seventeenth century, Lessius, an influential theologian at Louvain University, argued just the opposite–fear lies not at the origin of religion but at the origin of *atheism*. Here is his argument briefly. Why, asks Lessius, does man want to deny religion? Quite obviously, he fears the punishment that will be meted out to him on the Day of Judgment. Unable to live with the fear, he invents atheism which denies the existence of God. Atheism, thus, alleviates his fear by removing the cause of fear. You can take your pick: the invention of gods removes fear and thus religion comes into being; the denial of gods removes fear, and thus atheism comes into being.

Clearly the problem with these theories is that 'chaos', 'hostile nature', 'mystery', and such other terms are not descriptions of some primal or primitive experiences, but rather concepts that go into structuring these theories. These concepts are the by-products of a culture that experiences the world this way. To appreciate the significance of this statement with respect to the hostile nature that primitive man allegedly confronted, let's look at one element within this experience: wildness. Our commonsense psychology tells us that the wild is something human beings are afraid of. This commonsense psychology is a matter of history too. The spread of Christianity in the West involved, among other things, a pacification of nature:

> Christianity...taught...that hills, valleys, forests, rivers, rocks, wind, storm, sun, moon, stars, wild beasts, snakes, and all other phenomenon of nature were created by God to serve man and were *not haunted (as the Germanic people believed) by hostile supernatural deities*, and that therefore it was possible...to *settle on the land without fear*. This was both preached and lived out in the fifth, sixth, seventh, and eighth centuries by tens of thousands of monks, who themselves settled in the wilderness... (Berman 1983: 62; emphasis added).

That is, until Christianity came to the Germanic peoples, they lived in fear and terror of nature. Nature was a hostile force populated by demonic powers and malignant spirits. The coming of religion removed this fear from man. Our 'secular' theories about the origin of religion continue this narrative. Could it be that the acceptance and popularity of the fear theory of religion reveals to us one of the basic trends in the contemporary intellectual scene, namely, a tendency to equate European history with human history? Perhaps the following story about the Buddha's conception will bring out the force of this question:

> Once it came to pass that a noble and beautiful woman...conceived. At this...moment, the elements of the ten thousand world systems quaked and trembled as an unmeasurable light appeared. The blind received their sight. The deaf heard. The dumb spoke with one another. The crooked became straight. The lame walked. Prisoners were freed from their bonds and chains. In hell the fire was extinguished. In the heaven of the ancestors all hunger and thirst ended. *Wild animals ceased to be afraid.* The illness of the sick vanished. All men began to speak kindly to one another as this new being was conceived in his mother's womb. (Herman 1983: 1; emphasis added).

Consider the italicized part of the story. Wild animals ceased to be afraid. Both in the commonsense psychology in India and in the innumerable stories about the sages who bring peace to animals in the jungle by their presence, the ideas are the same. The wild is what is afraid of man. In one culture, the wild is what man is afraid of; in another, the wild is what is afraid of man. In the first case, nature is experienced as a hostile force. But how can we make this claim in the second case?

The problem with the naturalistic paradigm is that the concepts it makes use of, namely, 'chaos', 'hostile nature', 'mystery', etc., are not the experiential presuppositions for the development of religion. Rather, they appear to be the results of the development of a particular religion.

By way of contrast, consider the tales told by the Ancient Greeks about their gods. Or those told by the Indians many thousands of years ago. Or even the tales of those tribes and groups, which anthropologists are so fond of studying, about gods and creation, thunder and lightning, birth and death. These are rich and enormously complex stories of a world filled with all kinds of beings and entities. There are intricate and devious plots clashing with unintended courses of events; divine and semi-divine beings vie with each other in choosing sides with mortals; often crudely and sometimes subtly they influence the course of a war, the fortunes of a people, and now and then even the banal actions of an unsuspecting person. In sum, these stories create another world which is even more complex than the events that they are supposed to explain.

Such pagan stories cast doubt on the naturalist theories which claim that religious explanations reduce fear by making strange events appear familiar to render them more manageable. In fact, by creating a whole pantheon of gods, people multiplied their fears. Not only was there thunder and lightning but a whole slew of deities (construed as causal forces) to interfere with his natural world:

> As Lucretius and Plutarch, in his treatise on superstition, make clear, fear of the intervention of the gods was a factor in ancient life which could not easily be ignored, *and many individuals appear to have lived their lives in constant dread...* It was a fact of life for many, and Epicurus...*regarded it as a matter of primary importance.* (Rist 1972: 177; emphasis added).

This kind of fear of the gods was superstitious (*superstitio* in Latin means the excessive fear of the gods), and one way of reducing this fear is to say that the gods *do not* interfere in the affairs of men. The naturalistic theories of religion rule out this option by claiming that the development of religion reduces the fear of natural events. To say that religion removes man's fear of natural events is another way of suggesting that 'true religion' replaced pagan superstition. Several authors claim that this is one of the major reasons for the triumphant spread of Christianity that eclipsed the pagan religions in the Mediterranean world. Even if we are willing to accept this as a historical truth with respect to the spread of Christianity, what does it have to do with Early Man? Nothing, unless you identify human history with European history. This is precisely what the fear theories of the origin of religion do. They effectively identify religion with Christianity and human history with European history.

The Psychological Speculations

If we shift our emphasis from the experience of nature to the result of that experience, we arrive at the second popular explanation about the origin of religion. The classic exponent of this theory is David Hume, the Scottish philosopher of the Enlightenment period. For him, too, fear was at the origin of religion:

> No wonder, then, that mankind, being placed in such an absolute ignorance of causes, and being at the same time so anxious concerning their future fortune, should immediately acknowledge a dependence on invisible powers, possessed of sentiment and intelligence. The *unknown causes*, which continually employ their thought...are all apprehended to be of the same kind or species. Nor is it long before we ascribe to them thought and reason and passion, and sometimes even the limbs and figures of men, in order to bring them nearer to a resemblance with ourselves. (Hume 1757, III: 317)

A careful reading of this citation reveals that Hume's claim is that we are ignorant of causes and that we are anxious about our future fortune. The result of this psychology brings about a *religious explanation*, which is characterized by five properties: (i) the religious explanation postulates invisible powers; (ii) it acknowledges the dependence of human beings on such powers; (iii) these invisible powers are construed as (unknown) causes; (iv) these causes are apprehended to be of the same kind; and (v) these causes are modeled after human beings.

Now, one of the features of a good theory is that there needs to be some logical relation between the explanation it provides and the facts that it tries to explain. That is, the theory must explain what it claims to be explaining, and not just explain any random thing. With this in mind, the challenge that Hume's theory must meet is this: On what grounds can it specifically claim to have explained the origin of religion and not the origin of something else, like philosophy, or proto-science, or ritual, or poetry, or mythology?

To go back to the five properties of the religious explanation listed above, it is obvious that any scientific theory too would have the first four of these properties: postulation of invisible powers and relations; the claim that we are dependent upon them; the idea that they are causal forces and powers which are of the same kind. Consequently, these four properties do not help us determine whether Early Man had come up with a religious, as opposed to a scientific, proto-scientific, or philosophical explanation. The burden falls entirely on the fifth property to transform this explanation into a religious explanation. Let us, therefore, look at it more closely.

Hume's claim is that ignorance of causes leads man to postulate the gods, which are modeled after his own image. There are two points here–one about the activity of forming the theory and the other about the end product, that is, the theory itself. The first point is methodological or procedural and the other is a semantic feature regarding theories–it relates to the meaning of the concepts in the theory.

The methodological aspect is this: Human beings constructed a theory which involved the activity of creating a model for their explanation. Alternatively, we could say that Early Man made use of analogies in the process of constructing a religious explanation. However, neither the activity of drawing an analogy nor of constructing models makes some theory into a religious theory. This point is hardly worth belaboring in a period where cognitive science, philosophies, and sociologies of science are studying the role of not just models but metaphors and analogies in the development of scientific theories. Thus, this alleged anthropomorphizing on the part of Early Man is in the best tradition of scientific theorizing and rationality. The only thing that Early Man had any knowledge about was himself. Consequently, when he developed an explanation about another domain, he cast it in terms of explaining the unknown in terms of the known. In this sense, how could the emergence of 'religion' show anything but human rationality? Bear in mind that Hume was an Enlightenment thinker who believed that religious explanations were the antipodes of rational explanations and was busy trying to figure out how this weakness of the human spirit could be made intelligible.

If we look at the leftovers of Hume's theory, it leaves us with just one possibility to explore: the causal forces operating in the universe are personalized entities, endowed with intention, "thought and reason, and passion". That is to say, divinity not only assumes a human form but it also regulates the universe according to its plans, intentions, goals and sentiments. This notion of divinity, however, is typical of the Semitic traditions but not of the Asian traditions. From Hinduism, through Buddhism to Shintoism, none of them suggests that the universe is held together by one or even several deities, let alone that their thoughts, reasons and sentiments regulate and govern the Cosmos. Thus, the conclusion is inescapable. Although Hume purports to be telling us how human beings could have discovered religion, what he is actually doing is explaining the origin of a religion like, say, Judaism. Or he does not consider religions in Asia to be religions at all.

As is clear from these arguments, even if these theorists believed that they were explaining the universality of religion, it is not evident from their explanations that they were indeed doing so. They could well have been explaining the origin of stories, of theories, or of philosophies. If we look at their explanations in terms of that which they are trying to explain, namely the universality of religion, there is no logical relation between this fact and the explanations they provide. We can draw the opposite conclusion on exactly the same grounds with equal plausibility. This means that these 'explanations' have not explained the claim about the universality of religion by the causes they identify in their theories.

We can try and recast the issue in a more general form. Why are these explanations supposed to be religious and not philosophical or anything else? In other words, the question is of (i) identifying or distinguishing religious explanations from other types of explanations; and (ii) determining what individual features distinguish one religious explanation from another. What are the possibilities open to us in answering this question? One possibility would be to state that their content makes them religious explanations. The same problem recurs: What makes some concept a religious concept as opposed to a proto-scientific or philosophical concept?

Suppose we say that concepts like 'God' are religious, and concepts like 'proton' are scientific. That could be helpful, provided we realize that not any kind of 'god' will do. To identify 'pif-paf' as a synonym for the notion of God, we need to be able to show that 'pif-paf' and 'God' refer to the same thing. We would need to establish that they both share the same properties. However, this does not appear to be a realistic course because it requires knowledge of God and many religions deny this to human beings, claiming that God is unknowable.

As an alternative, we could enumerate some properties that allow us to recognize the entity talked about. For instance, "that which created the Cosmos" could help fix the reference for the term 'God' without entailing a full explanation of the term. But then we would run up against the difficulty that there is an idea of a God who created the universe and is outside it, while there is also the idea of creatures that are creations of an uncreated Cosmos. Consequently, if the former idea of God holds, then none of the primitive religions qualify as religions and neither do Hinduism, Buddhism, Taoism, Shintoism, etc. Either we will have to acknowledge that there are no religions outside Judaism, Christianity and Islam, because they alone have this particular idea of God or we need to face up to the fact that these theories do not provide anything more than an *ad hoc* distinction between a religious as opposed to any other type of explanation.

Perhaps we can try and squeeze out of this difficulty in other ways. Van Baal, an anthropologist defines religion thus:

> all explicit and implicit notions and ideas, accepted as true, which relate to a reality which cannot be verified empirically. (1971:3).

In many writings on religion we come across claims that religion deals with the 'empirically unobservable', the 'scientifically unobservable', or with that 'which cannot be perceived by the senses', and so on. For our purposes it does not matter much whether the claim they make is that these 'unobservables' and 'imperceptibles' are terms like 'God' or 'sacred'. This attempt to distinguish the semantic content of these words by methodological means fails for two interrelated reasons. The first reason is that not all empirically unverifiable entities or terms are religious. Many basic concepts in theoretical physics as well as certain logical concepts are that too. Therefore, the problem of distinguishing a religious from a non-religious explanation is not solved. The second reason has to do with the development of both science and technology. Not only do they make perceptible some entities that were not so before, but what is more important is that our very notion of 'observability' changes as our knowledge of the world evolves. Therefore, there is no choice but to resort to the semantic meaning of these concepts, at which point, once again, we bump up against the fact that different religions contain different concepts.

So, what have people really been explaining when they thought they were explaining the origin of religion? Appeals to archaeological evidence such as burial sites is just icing on a rotten cake. They need to show that funeral practices are religious practices as well. Is this not the question at stake? Actually, even this is not enough. They would need to show that funeral practices can be nothing other than religious practices. The archaeological consensus on this is ambiguous:

> Neanderthal graves represent the best evidence for Neanderthal spirituality or religion...but, more prosaically, they may have been dug simply to remove the corpses from habitation areas. In sixteen of twenty well-documented Mousterian graves in Europe and western Asia, the bodies were tightly flexed (in near-fetal position)...which could imply a burial ritual or simply a desire to dig the smallest possible burial trench. Ritual has been inferred from well-made artifacts or once-meaty animal bones found in at least fourteen of thirty-three Mousterian graves for which information is available...but there are no Mousterian burials in which the "grave goods" differ significantly from the artifacts and bones in the surrounding deposit... In sum, the Neanderthals and

possibly their contemporaries clearly buried their dead, at least sometimes; but it does not follow that the motivation was religious... (Klein 1989: 328-329).

In sum, the naturalistic paradigm is riddled with several defects. It is hardly obvious what is being explained; nor is it clear what counts as evidence; the truth value of the assumptions made can be legitimately disputed; we could, with equal plausibility, argue for the opposite stance on exactly the same grounds; the theories have only trivial consequences; they transform Semitic theological ideas into the characteristic properties of religion; and all along they presuppose a theme while claiming to explain it.

What, then, do these naturalistic theories on the origin of religion amount to? On reflecting upon them, it appears that they see a tight relation between being a religion and being an explanation. To have a religion is to have an explanation. What do these theories try to explain? They explain many events and happenings–birth and death, the meaning and purpose of life and the Cosmos, the beginnings and ends of man and the world, etc. In short, these thinkers grasped the idea of religion-as-an-explanation. Even though this is not what they actually said, their insights consist in seeing religion not as this or that sort of explanation, but as explanation pure and simple.

The naturalistic paradigm is a latecomer in the field. Theological doctrines claiming that religion was God's gift to humanity had accounted for the origin of religion long before Bodin or Hume or Freud tried to do so. Therefore, if a choice has to be made between the two paradigms on the basis of their soundness, there are simply no good arguments for deserting the older paradigm. The reason for this is plain. The naturalistic paradigm makes theological assumptions too, although less explicitly and less honestly. In this sense, the naturalistic paradigm does not make a paradigm shift, no matter what is believed or said on its behalf. The harshest criticism of the naturalistic paradigm would be not that it is incoherent, but that it smuggles in theology as the science of religion. It is not a challenger to the supernatural explanation of religion. It has never been that. Therefore, the real question is not about the universality of religion but about the intellectual belief that it is so.

CHAPTER VI

SHALL THE TWAIN EVER MEET?

At the end of the 1890s, there emerged a movement in Germany called the *Religionsgeschichtliche Schule* (this translates clumsily into English as The History of Religion School). Note well that the word 'religion' appears in the singular. During this period, it was taken for granted that the word signified the same phenomenon all over the world and that it was possible to write a history of the various forms of religious experience. Although this School is not well known today, its ideas were to have a profound influence on twentieth century scholarship on religion and are therefore important to look at. To start with, its members had an openly declared religious affiliation, which was Protestant Christian. Their focus was on religion and not on theology. Doctrinal statements about religion interested them less than popular religion. They emphasized the unity of religion, which meant the ability to investigate relations between religions. Moreover, they did not speak in terms of true religion and false ones but rather suggested that the difference between religions is one of degree. All religions, they believed, form a continuum of the human response to the revelation of the Divine and the difference in degree is based on the adequacy of this response.

They explicitly recognized that even Christianity is historical. Before them, the Enlightenment and other thinkers too had developed the idea of a human history. The primary landmarks of the Enlightenment account of human history included that of a primal religion and its subsequent decay and degeneration. The account of the *Religionsgeschichtliche Schule* differed from this account in the sense that it claimed that religion itself has a history.

The history of religion evolves, they claimed, and this evolution is based on the evolving human responses to the revelation of the Divine. Thus, although their account transcends the idea that there is false religion in some cultures, it retains the idea of a developmental ordering of history.

They argued that religion is 'One', not by looking at this or that religion but by looking at living religion in its various manifestations as a response to divine revelation. This constantly evolving human response to the revelation of the divine constituted the *living* religion. Bereft of this, religion would freeze into a fixed set of dogmas and doctrines. They believed that this human response is universal and cross-cultural and the variety of responses accounts for the differences among religions. As these responses get articulated, this variety gets its Gestalt, or particular identifiable form. The dynamic of the evolution of religion, they claimed, is a result of the tension between the nature of the revelation of the divine and the way the different human responses are expressed.

The ideas of this school were very influential and brought about a change in the way religion was looked at from then on. The emphasis shifted from an organized entity–be it a set of doctrines, a movement, or a structure–to an experience which an individual could have. Concepts like 'holy', and 'sacred', became vital to denote a particular kind of experience which could be identified as typically religious. This appeal to the nature of religious experience appeared interesting because it could provide a criterion using which it would be possible to identify the 'religious' in terms of experience, and 'religion' by referring to the religious.

The ideas of this school were the result of the development of many historical and cultural events, chief among which was the rising specter of Atheism. A new movement of Free Thinkers had taken shape, beginning with the Enlightenment critique of religion. The firm grip that religious ideologies had had on social life began to loosen. An important shift occurred at this time as Christianity began to slowly transform into Theism, that is, rather than focusing on Jesus Christ as the fulcrum of Christianity, the emphasis shifted to God. However, developments such as Theism and Deism ended up reinforcing Atheism because with the diminished emphasis on the Christ figure, Christianity became less distinctively Christian. The roots of these problems lay within Christology itself, that is, in the study of the nature and person of Jesus Christ. It is worth devoting a couple of paragraphs to examine the Christological problem a bit more closely as it has not only kept scholars preoccupied for 2,000 years, but still continues to be of vital relevance.

The dilemma that Christian theologians had to grapple with was this. According to the Bible, God reveals Himself in Jesus uniquely. The two important elements to note in this statement are the 'Revelation' and the person of 'Jesus'. If we emphasize the *unique* character of God's revelation in Christ, it means that Jesus is the only way to God. On the other hand, if we emphasize the *revelation* of God as such, the figure of Christ becomes but one of the multiple revelations of God. Thus, not only does the Christ figure diminish in importance, but Christianity also ceases to be unique.

In the course of two thousand years, many solutions have been worked out to address the issue of the Christological dilemma, from rabidly exclusivist positions at one end of the spectrum to the extremely tolerant philosophical Theisms at the other end. The Christ-centered approach emphasizes the unique way; thus it focuses on the person in whom God reveals Himself–an exclusive Christology that makes theology irrelevant; the God-centered approach, by contrast, emphasizes God who reveals Himself–an exclusive theology that makes Christology irrelevant. The point, however, is that Christianity needs both but cannot have both.

This is the Christological dilemma. On one hand, it says that the person of Jesus Christ is the way for humankind. But precisely this claim has not only been the grounds for creating divisions within the Christian community itself, but also in dividing the rest of the world into believers and non-believers. The missionaries had repeatedly confronted the problem of communicating the exclusivity of an 'all-inclusive' Christ. With the emphasis on the uniqueness of Jesus Christ, Christianity could never become truly universal. This, of course, meant giving up its universalistic pretensions to being the 'true' religion.

On the other hand, if Christianity emphasizes God who reveals Himself, this allows for multiple revelations in human history. The world becomes literally a "universe of faiths," allowing for the possibility of knowledge of God outside Jesus. The uniqueness of God's revelation in Christ has to be sacrificed. If looked at cross-culturally, even the uniqueness of God will have to be sacrificed, because God refers to different entities in different traditions. God will merely become a Christian God, finding his place among other gods. Or he will be assimilated in other cultures as yet another member of the heathen pantheon. This assimilation may allow us to talk in the languages of other cultures, but at the huge cost of sacrificing the uniqueness of the Christian God. The alternative, of course, is to deny the multiple revelations and to emphasize the uniqueness of the God-Christ relationship. Such a stance, as already noted, becomes radically unintelligible to others, in exactly the same way it had been for the pagan Romans. It poses the problem of explaining what the "all-inclusiveness" of Christ is supposed to mean.

Thus, for Christianity, universal acceptance comes at the cost of no longer remaining distinctively Christian. This is the price extracted from Christianity for making itself universally acceptable. In a sense, this is the revenge of the pagans. What is even more significant is the heavy price that must be paid, in turn, for extracting this revenge.

A move towards Theism was one of the solutions to the Christological dilemma. Such a theism could talk about God in general terms understandable to others by giving up the Christ-centered approach. It tried to develop a 'universal' language. Doing so entailed a sacrifice of local colors and cultural variations since to talk about religion and God across cultures requires a general and abstract theism.

Towards the end of the nineteenth century, a new crop of scholars emerged, widely influenced by the *Religionsgeschichtliche Schule*, who attempted to reconcile the burgeoning problem of atheism with liberal Protestant beliefs. They laid emphasis on the subjective aspect of religion, that is, religious experience. This subjective religious experience was supposed to constitute the religious domain, demarcating and distinguishing it from all other domains of human experience. Some of the major proponents of this theme, which was to find wide currency in later times, were Schleiermacher, Otto, Söderblom, and William James, as well as phenomenologists like Mircea Eliade and sociologists like Emile Durkheim. A similar approach was taken up by a loose confederation of 'atheistically religious' scholars, suggesting the great popularity of this approach.

At first glance it appears as though this transformation of Christianity into theism would make it possible to talk about religion without having to appeal to a Christian God. The Christian God appears to have become so irrelevant to being religious that atheistic Christianity and atheistic religiosity appear to be reasonable options. However, if we seriously explore the relation between religiosity, i.e., the subjective experience of an individual, and religion, this is not quite the case. Let's begin this exploration with Schleiermacher.

Schleiermacher firmly believed in God and religion, although his emphasis was on intuition and feeling rather than on scripture and dogma. This led many to see in Schleiermacher a possible source for developing a characterization of religion that would: (i) demarcate religion from non-religion; (ii) guide cross-cultural investigation into religion; and (iii) defend religiosity independent of any beliefs.

Not everyone is swayed by Schleiermacher's emphasis on feeling and intuition. Some perceive it to be a defensive move to protect religion at all costs from the mounting atheism:

> (Schleiermacher)...is motivated in this project by two goals. The first is to present an accurate description of the religious consciousness...
>
> The second goal is more theoretical and apologetic. Schleiermacher hopes that by presenting religion in its original, characteristic form he will demonstrate the inapplicability of Enlightenment criticisms of religious belief... Religion is a sense, a taste, a matter of feeling and intuition. Consequently, it remains unscathed by Kant's contention that our experience is structured by the categories and thoughts we bring to it and thus that we produce rather than reproduce the world we think we know. As a sense that precedes and is independent of all thought, and that ought not to be confused

with doctrine and practice, religion can never come into conflict with the findings of modern science or with the advance of knowledge in any realm. It is an autonomous moment in human experience and is, in principle, invulnerable to rational and moral criticism. (Proudfoot 1985: 2).

The brunt of Proudfoot's objection is that Schleiermacher's project fails on conceptual grounds. A religious experience of the kind that Schleiermacher describes is an intentional state. An intentional state is one that relates to beliefs, hopes, judgments, love, hate, etc. All of these mental states require a specific object of thought, that is, they are about something. Therefore, a religious experience cannot just be a matter of feeling or intuition without some specific object that this feeling is directed towards. Consequently, Schleiermacher is not justified in speaking of a religious experience or religiosity that is independent of concepts that structure the experience. Let's see how justified Proudfoot is in his criticism of Schleiermacher by looking at a series of lectures that Schleiermacher presents in a book.

To begin with, Schleiermacher repeatedly makes clear throughout that his audience is a cultured one. It is addressed to the 'cultured despisers' of religion.

(D)o not relegate me without a hearing to those whom you look down upon as common and uncultivated as if the sense for the holy, like an old folk-costume, had passed over to the lower class of people... You are very well disposed to these our brothers... Do you then turn to them when you want to disclose the innermost connection and the highest ground of those holy sanctuaries of humanity? Do you turn to them when concept and feeling, law and deed are to be traced to their mutual source, and the real is to be exhibited as eternal and necessarily grounded in the essence of humanity? ...

I wish to show you from what capacity of humanity religion proceeds, and how *it belongs to what is for you the highest and the dearest...* Can you seriously expect me to believe that those who daily torment themselves most tiresomely with earthly things are the most preeminently suited to become intimate with heaven? That those who brood anxiously over the next moment and are firmly chained to the nearest objects can raise their eyes furthest to the universe? ...Therefore, I call *only you to me, you who are capable of raising yourselves* above the

common standpoint of humanity, you who do not shrink from
the burdensome way into the depths of human nature in order
to find the ground of its action and thought. (Schleiermacher
1799: 86-87; emphasis added)

This citation and others like it make it clear that Schleiermacher
speaks to a specific audience. Only the 'cultivated' can understand
him. His audience must be 'cultivated' in at least four senses of the
term. The first sense can be put in the form of a question: What is
he saying for this audience to understand? He is saying that
"Religion's essence is neither thinking or acting, but intuition and
feeling". Religion is "an insolent enemy against the gods" because
religion is neither art the way a practice is, nor speculation the way
science is, but a sensibility or a taste for the infinite. He entreats
his audience to become familiar with the formula of an intuition of
the universe, which is the highest and most universal formula for
religion.

> (T)o accept everything individual as a part of the whole and
> everything limited as a representation of the infinite is religion
> (*ibid.*: 105).

In other words, as we work our way through his speeches, we
begin to realize that this religious 'intuition' and 'feeling' is, in
fact, quite well-structured. It tells you what your object of
experience is supposed to be and how you should experience that
object. That is to say, you cannot have this experience if you do
not already have the concepts that help you structure it:

> But persons who reflect comparatively about their religion
> inevitably find concepts in their path and cannot possibly get
> around them. In this sense, all these concepts surely do belong
> to the religion, indeed, belong unconditionally, without one
> being permitted to define the least thing about the limits of
> their application (*ibid.* 132).

It must be noted that he happens to be talking about concepts such
as miracles, inspirations, revelations, feelings of the supernatural,
etc. These concepts, he tells us:

> indicate in the most characteristic manner human
> consciousness of religion; they are all the more important
> because they *identify not only something that may be in*

> *religion universally, but precisely what must be in it universally* (*ibid.*: 134; emphasis added).

He is talking about religion as an intuition but is explicitly identifying the presence of the above-mentioned concepts as an identifying mark of religion. Not only must his audience have these concepts, but it must also have already experienced the universe in such a way that:

> the universe is one pole and your own self is somehow the other pole between which consciousness hovers. The ancients certainly knew this. They called all these feelings "piety" and referred them immediately to religion, considering them its noblest part. *You also know them...* (*ibid.*: 130; emphasis added).

The above, then, indicates the second sense in which his audience must be cultured. There is also a third sense in which his public is required to be cultured and cultivated. To speak of this, Schleiermacher indulges in historical comparisons. The following long citation shows the extent to which Schleiermacher is a child of his culture:

> To the *unrefined person* who has only a confused idea and only a dim instinct of the whole and of the infinite, the universe presents itself as a unity in which nothing manifold is to be distinguished, as a chaos uniform in its confusion, without division, order, and law, and from which nothing individual can be separated except its being arbitrarily cut off in time and space... With this impulse his God becomes a being *without definite qualities*, an idol or a fetish, and if he accepts several of these, such beings can only be distinguished by the arbitrarily established limits of their realms. *At another level of formation (Bildung)*, the universe presents itself as a multiplicity without unity, as an indeterminate manifold of heterogeneous elements and forces... If the idea of a God is added to this universe, it naturally disintegrates into infinitely many parts...gods arise in infinite number, differentiated by the various objects of their activity, by different dispositions and inclinations. You must admit that this intuition of the universe is infinitely more worthy than the former; *Now let us climb still higher* to the point where all conflict is again united, where the universe manifests itself as totality, as unity in multiplicity, as system and *thus for the first time deserves its name*. Should not the one who intuits it as one and all thus

have more religion, even without the idea of God, *than the most cultured polytheist?* Should Spinoza not stand just as *far above a pious Roman, as Lucretius does above one who serves the idols? (Ibid.*: 137; emphasis added).

These are the different levels of cultivation or culture. In general, those at the lower level are unable to grasp the higher. The higher is not only better but it also expresses the 'most holy', the highest unity:

> However fortunate you may be at deciphering the *crude and undeveloped religions* of the distant peoples or at sorting out the many types of individual religions that lie enclosed in the beautiful mythology of the Greeks and the Romans is all the same to me; may their gods guide you. *But when you approach the most holy, where the universe is intuited in its highest unity,* when you want to contemplate the different forms of systematic religions–*not the exotic or the strange but those that are still more or less present among us*–then it cannot be a matter of indifference to me whether you find *the right point from which you must view them (ibid.* 211; emphasis added).

With ideas like this, how is it possible to assert that religion is some kind of an unstructured experience to Schleiermacher? Even this level of culture and cultivation is not enough to belong to Schleiermacher's public. You must find the right point of view. Which religion was believed to have achieved the highest unity *without* having the right point of view? Why, Judaism, of course. There, then, is a fourth sense in which you have to be cultured. You must neither be a polytheist, though that's better than being an idol worshipper, nor a primitive; it is not even sufficient that you are a monotheist, because Jews are that as well. You need to be a Christian. As he puts it in *The Christian Faith* (1830: 37-38):

> On the highest plane of Monotheism, history exhibits only three great communities–the Jewish, Christian and the Mohammedan; the first being almost in process of extinction, the other two still contending for the mastery of the human race. Judaism, by its limitation of the love of Jehovah to the race of Abraham betrays a lingering affinity with Fetichism... And so, this comparison of Christianity with other similar religion is a sufficient warrant for saying that Christianity is in fact the most perfect of the most highly developed forms of religion. (cited in Eilberg-Schwartz 1990: 74-75).

But does he mean any kind of Christian? Not quite, because he makes little of doctrines and dogmas. And who holds dogmas central to religion? The Roman Catholic Church, of course. Consequently, it is not even enough to be a Catholic in order to belong to Schleirmacher's club of cultured despisers. You must be Protestant.

In other words, Schleiermacher makes no bones about the fact that the public in whom he hopes to find the 'feeling' are Protestants. Those who can have this experience, and who have had such experiences, are Protestants as well. It is clear that this is indeed the implication of what he says if we reflect on two further considerations. Schleiermacher recognizes that Christianity is a tradition with a history and is different from other traditions. If indeed religion was merely, and only, a question of the experience of an individual then there is no way that there could be such a thing as Christianity, or Judaism or anything else. After all, the fact that they exist and have a history is dependent upon the fact that they are transmitted. If religion was about some intuition or some experience of the universe alone, then such a transmission is impossible.

The second consideration is that if you cannot teach this sense to others, how can anyone be expected to have this experience in the sense that Schleiermacher outlines above? Not a problem, says Schleiermacher, because everyone has an innate religious sense. This inborn religious capacity can be nurtured or destroyed depending on the tradition one is born into. Of course he believes that not all traditions can nurture it. Nor does he believe that a tradition which nurtured this feeling a thousand years ago can continue to do so today. The second Protestant theme emerges here–the corruption and degeneration of religion into dogmas, rituals, and priesthood.

Schleiermacher keeps insisting that religious experience can be had only within a religious tradition. In fact his most famous assertion on this score goes like this:

> (R)eligion can be understood only through itself and its special manner of construction and its characteristic distinction will not become clear to you until *you yourself belong to some one*

or other of them. (Schleiermacher 1799: 210-211; emphasis added).

This makes it clear that when he speaks about understanding religion through itself, he is not talking about some experience which can be understood only by having that experience. He is not providing us with a tradition-independent concept of the subjective experience of religion which we could use in classifying some unique experience as religious. He is telling us what it means to be a religious person with reference to a specific religion. In short, it is not an inter-traditional, comparative concept, which picks out a phenomenon like 'religion' by speaking about the experiential state of an individual. Rather, it is an intra-traditional concept that distinguishes a truly religious person from one who merely pays lip service to a set of doctrines. So much for Proudfoot's objections to Schleiermacher.

Another influential writer in this domain is Nathan Söderblom. Archbishop of Uppsala, he was a deeply and devoutly religious Christian. Most students of religion are familiar with his justly famous entry in the *Encyclopedia of Religion and Ethics* under the heading "holiness," where he distinguishes the 'holy' from the 'profane'. His liberal credentials are impeccable as he identifies both Buddhism and Hinduism as religions because they pass the test of 'holiness'. He talks about the 'original idea' of holiness, the phenomenon at the primitive stage of religion. To Söderblom, religious experience was something unique to which human beings had always been open. It had begun with notions like mana, the concept of an impersonal force or quality that resides in all things. He speaks of this experience as a fundamental one. That is to say, primitive man, wherever he lived, must have encountered this object which induces this experience, suggesting that God must have revealed himself to all human beings sometime during the course of human history:

> religion is not anything we do, nor is it anything we might think about God, but what God does with us; also that we can know God only to the extent he reveals himself to us. (In Sharpe 1990: 81).

Speaking of *The Problem of Religion in Catholicism and Protestantism*, Söderblom wrote:

> Something of revelation is to be found everywhere. In the
> higher religion it is purer. (*ibid.* 157).

Put differently, this characterization of religious experience is
dependent upon accepting some truth or the other with respect to
what is commonly accepted as religion. Thus, what is true of
Schleiermacher is true of Söderblom as well. The religious
experience which so many appeal to, the 'holy' or the 'numen', is
not some conceptually unstructured experience but a well-
structured one. In fact, Söderblom, talks about his perception of the
holy in the third person thus:

> One Sunday, he had held his service as usual. When he
> returned with a close friend to his room, there came over him
> what might be called a direct perception of the holiness of
> God. He understood what he had long felt indistinctly, that
> God was far stricter than he could imagine or than anyone can
> really comprehend. God is a consuming fire. This
> apprehension was so powerful, so shattering, that he was
> unable to stay on his feet. Had he not collapsed into a chair
> with his head on the table, he felt that he must have fallen to
> the floor. He moaned and groaned under this mighty grasp.
> Slowly he recovered and calmed down. But for the rest of his
> life, for decades these two experiences have been firm points
> of departure or, rather, irrefutable experiences, fundamental to
> spiritual life, incomparable in their meaning, the
> incomprehensible means of mercy: the cross, the miracle of
> God's mercy. Man's nothingness, broken-heartedness,
> trembling, his faith *quand même*. Since then he has been
> unable to doubt God in spite of everything (*ibid.*: 44).

From the above citation it is clear that Söderblom's Protestantism
as well as typically Augustinian themes are presuppositions of this
experience just as is the manifestation of the 'mana' of the Divine.

Another famous exponent of the experiential aspect of religion was
Rudolf Otto. In his book, *Das Heilige*, which formulated and
popularized the phrase '*mysterium tremendum et fascinans*'
(fearful and fascinating mystery), he says:

> It is essential to every theistic conception of God, and most of
> all to the Christian, that it designates and precisely
> characterizes the deity by the attributes spirit, reason, purpose,
> good will, supreme power, unity, self-hood... Now all these

attributes constitute clear and definite *concepts*: they can be grasped by the intellect; they can be analyzed by thought; they even admit of definition... Only on such terms is *belief* possible in contrast to mere *feeling*... We count this the very mark and criterion of a religion's high rank and superior value–that it should have no lack of *conceptions* about God; that it should admit knowledge–the knowledge that comes by faith–of the transcendent in terms of conceptual thought, whether those already mentioned or others which continue and develop them. Christianity not only possesses them in unique clarity and abundance, and this is, though not the sole or even the chief, yet a very real sign of its superiority over other religions of other forms and at other levels. This must be asserted at the outset with the most positive emphasis. (1917: 1).

As though this were not enough, Otto continues to speak throughout his book in terms of a developmental ordering of religion: from 'primitive religion' through the 'most perfect', the 'most advanced' religion, namely Christianity in its Protestant version. The experience–*mysterium tremendum et fascinans*–is an experience of the Deity, of God, of the Numinous. Other cultures, he avers, have vaguer conceptions because that is what, as we know by now, the Bible claims. Otto does not characterize religion on the basis of the non-rational elements of personal experience, but rather identifies the non-rational elements in religion and relates them to the rational. That is, he relates the *conception* of the deity to its experience.

Whether he speaks of a general religious experience or not, he too has a specific audience in mind. Speaking of the 'state of the soul' in solemn worship, Otto says:

As Christians we undoubtedly here first meet with the feelings familiar enough in a weaker form in other departments of experience, such as feelings of gratitude, trust, love, reliance, humble submission, and dedication (*ibid.*).

The book appears liberal in tone because it is tolerant of other religions, and does not dismiss them as Devil worship. This is indeed true, but what of it? When you talk about specifically Christian concepts such as an innate sense of divinity, when you periodize history in terms of the development of this sense of divinity, characterize your religion as the most perfect, most advanced form of expression, and on the grounds of its theology you are convinced that God reveals Himself to all men, what is so difficult about being both liberal and tolerant?

To the extent that liberal Protestants allowed *secular* values like tolerance and pluralism to infuse their discourse they were willing to appreciate the Hindus (who challenge their gods), or the Buddhists and the Jains (who deny the existence of any such entity). But they could do so only after presupposing that (i) these were religions; (ii) fitting them in some kind of developmental framework; and (iii) ranking them in a hierarchy which included Judaism, Islam and Christianity.

In fact, as Söderblom says, the conception of the 'Holy' disappears in Hinduism over a period of time to be replaced by the notions 'cleanliness' and 'uncleanliness', i.e., by hygienic concepts. This theme is familiar from the earlier chapters. The growth of non-Christian religions has always been a one-way street leading to degeneration. To put it in eighteenth century terms, 'popular Hinduism' is a degeneration of 'philosophical Hinduism'.

Thus, it is clear that none of these writers who popularized the strategy of characterizing religion on the basis of experience was able to speak of this experience independent of the traditions to which they belonged. Yet their work is considered to be a basis for the cross-cultural investigation into religion. But only on the presuppositions that the divine has revealed itself in the Universe, that this revelation has been understood differently by different peoples, that some standpoint is more adequate than others, and that there is some definite conception of divinity, were they able to speak of the religious experience in different cultures. These are all Biblical themes. Without presupposing the truth of the Bible, you cannot speak of the religious experience of the Hindus, or the Buddhists, or the Africans and the Native Americans. Schleiermacher, Söderblom, and Otto accept this. The same cannot be said of their successors. These later scholars picked up on the idea of religious experience, used the same concepts as popularized by these writers, but insisted on seeing in it a 'neutral' or 'universal' experience, independent of any particular religion.

Now, scholars can carry on all they want and formulate the concept of religiosity (seen as an experience) in 'neutral' or 'scientific' terms, but it does not mean that they actually come up with a neutral or scientific understanding of this experience. Instead, it is more likely that they smuggle in the same religious categories. One way of illustrating this point is to look at the conceptual difficulties that two secular characterizations of religion face in their quest to provide a neutral (i.e., non-religious) definition of the religious experience. The authors are Durkheim and Eliade.

Here is Durkheim's definition of religion:

> A religion is a unified system of beliefs and practices relative to sacred things, that is to say, things set apart and forbidden– beliefs and practices which unite into a single moral community called a Church, all those who adhere to them (Schneider 1964: 35).

Durkheim relates religion to 'sacred things', that is, to 'objects set apart and forbidden'. If we parse his definition carefully we can see that his claim suggests three distinct steps: first some things are recognized as sacred objects; then, relative to these sacred objects, beliefs and practices are formed; and subsequently, there is the crystallization of a moral community called a Church. That is to say, the sacred is not made up by religious beliefs or practices, but rather, beliefs and practices are formed around whatever is sacred. The moral community itself results from the adherence of individuals to these beliefs and practices.

Durkheim's definition relies on the fact that the terms 'sacred' and 'profane', strictly speaking, are not part of a religious vocabulary but in themselves are neutral terms. Etymologically, the word 'sacred' is derived from 'setting apart' which can just as well be related to anything neutral, such as military secrets or the formula for Coke. However, it is only when these objects are infused with religious beliefs that they qualify as terms that can be used in the definition of religion. If all cultures set apart the same set of objects, or if they constantly treated some set of objects as sacred, we could argue that these sets of objects are 'sacred' irrespective of the word used to describe them in different cultures. But since this is not the case, it is clear that the distinction between 'sacred' and 'profane' is drawn *within* a religion. In that case, it cannot be used to distinguish between religion and something else. A person inducted into a religious community learns to draw the distinction between the sacred and the profane as he is initiated into his religion.

At least in the case of Durkheim the problem can be posed sharply. The same cannot be said of the extremely prolific and influential writer, Mircea Eliade. He also alludes to the distinction between sacred and profane:

> Religious man assumes a particular and characteristic mode of existence in the world and, despite the great number of historic-religious forms, this characteristic form is always recognizable. Whatever the historical context in which he is placed, *homo religosus* always believes that there is an absolute reality, *the sacred*, which transcends this world but manifests itself in this world, thereby sanctifying it and making it real. He further believes that life has a sacred origin and that human existence realized all of its potentialities in proportion as it is religious–i.e., participates in reality. (Eliade 1961: 202).

Rather than getting into fruitless controversies, let us grant that *homo religosus* entertains all of these beliefs and sees manifestations of the sacred in mundane objects like stones and pigs. If someone sees energy or force as a 'sacred' foundation for life rather than simply as energy or force there is no sense in arguing about it. But, in return, it must be granted that this is not the way many other individuals, who may be lost to the devil, experience the world. This is just to reinforce the point that 'sacred' and 'profane' are not distinctions drawn from within a language that is common to both sets of individuals.

If categories such as 'sacred' and 'profane' are internal to a religion they cannot help us in distinguishing between religion and other phenomena. Or if the 'sacred' and 'profane' distinction is drawn *within* an initiation ritual, then the initiation ritual cannot be seen as drawing the distinction between the 'sacred' and the 'profane'. After all, all kinds of secret and not-so-secret clubs have initiation rituals. Nor can these words help in distinguishing one religion from another. Unless, of course, we take the easy way out and take refuge in the familiar theme about the hierarchy of religions. Some religions have "extra dimensions" while others get by with the bare necessities:

> (F)or the entire Paleo-Semitic world...a sacrifice...was only
> custom...in Abraham's case it is an act of faith. He does not
> understand why the sacrifice is demanded of him; nevertheless
> he performs it because it was the Lord who demanded it. By
> this act, which is apparently absurd, *Abraham initiates a new
> religious experience*, faith. All other (the whole oriental world)
> continue to move in an economy of the sacred that will be
> *transcended* by Abraham and *his successors*... Abraham's
> religious act *inaugurates a new religious* dimension. (1959:
> 109-110; emphasis added).

Of course it is possible for a person from within a religion to make
a distinction between his tradition and other phenomena–including
other religions. However, Durkheim and Eliade claim that they are
providing a general characterization of religion without using
categories that are specific to a particular religion. This is the part
that is objectionable.

The state of affairs seems to be this. On one hand, a particular
religion has become the framework to describe other cultures. On
the other hand, it cannot be said that all of these writers are trying
to perpetrate some kind of fraud. Their beliefs and reasons for
writing the way they do appear to be genuine. How can we try and
understand this state of affairs where gifted and brilliant minds are
blind to the theological nature of their claims and genuinely seem
to believe that they are being neutral? They simply cannot see the
forest for the trees because the religious experience itself is part of
a religious vocabulary and framework. The notion of religion is
part of a religious framework. Their 'scientific' investigations into
religion are conducted within this religious framework which is not
even noticed by them. This religion may be a de-christianized
Christianity, secularized to suit modern tastes, but it is no less
religious because of that.

Although the birth of Christianity was in a fundamentally pagan
milieu, it never really understood paganism. All it could do was to
transform paganism into a pale and erring variant of itself. It was
successful in its attempt, if for no other reason than the
disappearance of the Greco-Roman civilization. Its opponents were
vanquished. Nevertheless, the contemporary 'others', the pagans of
today, still remain and continue to resist description and defy
analyses.

This is where the Christological dilemma discussed earlier in this chapter becomes relevant. One horn of this dilemma was that Christianity could become universal only if it ceased to be specifically Christian. To put it in contemporary language, the more secular the world becomes, the less Christian it appears to be. The twin movements of Christianizing the pagan world and de-Christianizing Christian beliefs help us understand what is really happening. The secular world is itself in the grips of a religious framework. The 'sacred' has entered the domain of the 'profane'. What we observe is not the "illusion of religion" but an illusion of being free from it. This is the charge. The next chapter will help us find out if the secular world is really...

CHAPTER VII

GUILTY AS CHARGED?

Who is a religious person? This question admits of many answers. The aptness of the answer depends on who is asking the question to whom, the context of the dialog and so on. The question can be put to, say, a bishop, or it can be asked about the subjective state of a lay person. At the other extreme, this question can be completely unintelligible to some. A question that is apt in one context can become a category mistake in another context. A category mistake occurs when terms and concepts which are appropriate to some domain are misapplied elsewhere. Decisions about the appropriateness of categories are based on ontology (i.e., beliefs about what there is in the world), linguistic practices, and knowledge about the relevant domains. A classic example to illustrate a category mistake is the statement: "Do green ideas sleep furiously?" Here properties are ascribed to things that cannot possibly have these properties: ideas cannot have color and it is not possible to sleep furiously. It is a category mistake to use these qualifiers in this statement. Similarly, in some cases, the question "who is a religious person?" is a category mistake.

The relevance of this point can be illustrated by a brief examination of some of the claims of the missionaries, as well as standard text book claims regarding caste and religion in India. As we have seen, it is claimed that Buddha rebelled against the caste system and rejected Brahmanism. If this is the case, our minimal expectation regarding Buddha's teachings would be to find an unequivocal rejection of the caste system. By examining two Buddhist texts, The *Dhammapada*, a major text attributed to Buddha himself, and *Sonadanda Sutta,* a minor text recording

Buddha's dialogs, we will see what we can make of this claim. The last chapter of the *Dhammapada* is about Brahmins. Here are three from the fifty-odd verses on the issue:

> Not by matted hair, or by clan,
> Or by birth does one become a brahamana
> In whom is truth and dhamma
> He is the pure one, and he is the brahamana (§393; 78)

Again,

> And I do not call one brahmana
> Merely by being born from a [brahmana] womb,
> Sprung from a [brahmana] mother.
> He is merely a "bho-sayer"
> If he is a possessor of things.
> One who has nothing and takes nothing,
> That one I call a brahmana. (§396; 78)

Or again,

> Who, here, having abandoned the human bond,
> Has transcended the heavenly bond,
> Who is released from all bonds,
> That one I call brahmana. (§417; 81)

In tenor, theme, and substance, all the verses are of the same nature. Buddha tells us who or what a true Brahmin is. Unlike the missionaries, he does not say that being a Brahmin is to be a fraud, a cheat, or a liar; he does not call Brahminism or the caste system an abomination. Would we expect this from someone who rejects the caste system? In answering this question it would be helpful to consider some of the prominent figures in history who rejected some idea or the other. Marx rejected capitalism. He didn't say he rejected it because it was not 'truly' capitalist. Calvin rejected Catholicism. He didn't say it was because it was not 'really' Catholic but by calling it the Devil's church. However, he defended Christianity by saying who the 'true Christian' is. It was in the name of Christianity that Calvin rejected Catholicism.

If this is how we use words such as 'reject', Buddha appears not to be revolting against the caste system. Before we ask what exactly he was doing, take into account the following dialog with a Brahmin named Sonadanda about who a Brahmin is.

11. (The Buddha) said to him: 'What are the things, brahman, which the brahmans say a man ought to have in order to be a brahman, so that if he says: "I am a brahman," he speaks accurately and is not guilty of falsehood?

12-13. Then Sonadanda...drawing his body up erect, and looking round on the assembly...said to the Master: 'The brahmans, Gotama, declare him to be a brahman able to say "I am a Brahman" without being guilty of falsehood, who has five things. What are the five? In the first place, sir, a brahman has to be well born on both sides, on the mother's side and on the father's side, of pure descent back through seven generations, with no slur upon him, and no reproach in respect of birth. 'Then he must be a scholar who knows the mystic verses by heart, one who has mastered the three Vedic samhitas and other scholarly subjects...

'He must be handsome, pleasant in appearance, inspiring trust, with great beauty of complexion... He must be virtuous, very virtuous, exceedingly virtuous.

'Then he must be learned and wise...'

14. 'Of these five things, Brahman, is it possible to leave one out, and to declare the man who has the other four to be a brahman, so that he can, without falsehood, claim to be a brahman?'

'Yes, Gotama, that can be done. We could leave out colour. For what does colour matter? If he has the other four...

15. 'But of these four things, brahman, is it possible to leave one out, and to declare the man who has the other three to be a brahman...?'

'Yes, Gotama, that could be done. We could leave out the verses. For what do the verses matter? If he has the other three–good birth, virtue and wisdom...'

16. 'But of these three things, Brahman, is it possible to leave one out, and to declare the man who has the other two to be a brahman...?'

'Yes, Gotama, that could be done. We could leave out birth. For what does birth matter? If he has the other two–virtue and wisdom–brahmans would still declare him to be a brahman...'

21. 'Then', said the Master, 'of these two things, brahman, is it possible to leave one out, and to declare the man who has the other to be a brahman...?'

'Not so, Gotama!...Where there is morality, there is wisdom, and where there is wisdom there is morality...'

22. 'That is so, brahman. I, too, say the same...' (Ling, Ed., 1981: 42-45)

Sonadanda begins with five necessary criteria which a Brahmin should possess and in the course of the dialog, ceases to consider some of them as necessary properties. Some of his Brahmin friends are dismayed by the ease with which Sonadanda gives up the three criteria feeling that their color, learning, and birth are being undermined. In order to make them understand the reasonableness of his argument, Sonadanda says:

19'.My venerable friends...I do not depreciate our colour, nor our scholarship, nor our good birth'.

20. 'Venerable friends, you see this Angaka, our nephew?'

'yes, sir, we see him'.

'Well! Angaka is handsome, pleasant in appearance, inspiring trust...

'And Angaka, sirs, is a scholar who knows the mantras by heart, he has mastered the three Vedic samhitas...

'And Angaka, sirs, is born well on both sides...of pure descent back through seven generations...

'Now, sirs, if Angaka should kill living things, and take what has not been given, and become an adulterer, and tell lies, and drink liquor, what then would his colour be worth? what the verses? what his birth?' (*ibid.*: 44-45.)

Regardless of the above, there is little doubt that Buddha did criticize the Brahmins and perhaps even 'Brahmanism'. However, the question is, did he *reject* the caste system? This issue is important to demonstrate that 'being a Brahmin' picks out individuals belonging to a specific domain. Even if the criteria for being a Brahmin are formulated in terms of moral virtues, the range of application of these criteria is not applicable to all human beings but only to those persons belonging to the caste system. In other words, even if all 'true' Brahmins are moral and wise, not all moral and wise people are Brahmins. If Buddha's dialogs are to be intelligible at all, it is not possible to deny certain pragmatic considerations, such as who he was talking to and what topic he was talking about. The topic of conversation happened to be the caste system and from the above citations there are no grounds to conclude that he was rejecting it.

According to the textbooks (e.g., Warder 1971), two traditions co-existed in India for a long time–the Shramana and the Brahamana. Shramana translates as 'strivers' and this group opted out of life, or to use popular terminology, renounced the world. It is important to note that Shramana was not a protest movement, or one that rejected any particular form of social order. To them, renunciation of social life was the condition for achieving enlightenment. To seek it, individuals had to be free from personal, ethical, and social obligations that bound them to earthly life. From this tradition grew the Ajivikas, the Jain tradition, and later the Buddhist tradition.

Then there was the Brahamana tradition. This was oriented towards social life and developed an elaborate structure of rituals over a period. It also regulated social institutions, the structure of social interactions and did not consider opting out of society as the only means to enlightenment. From this tradition there developed many philosophical schools, elaborate ritual practices, and the caste system.

Indian culture evolved as an interaction between these two traditions. The Brahamana tradition recognized the legitimacy of opting out of society, and the Shramana tradition began to address itself to those who lived in society. In doing so, they had to face the question of the possibility of seeking enlightenment while living in society. Among other things, this meant paying the required attention to the issue of social regulation.

By virtue of having opted out of society, the Shramanas were outside the caste system. They were not outcastes, they just did not belong to the domain of the caste system. However, when they turned towards social life and began to build a following in society, they had both options: either to continue to live as renunciates or to become part of the social order and strive for enlightenment from within the social order. Since the Shramana tradition was neither a reformist nor a revolutionary movement, it did not propose any blueprints for an alternate social order. Their concerns were different. They sought to figure out how individuals can achieve liberation given the socio-psychological position that they find themselves in.

These were the terms of the dialog between the Shramana and the Brahamana tradition. Buddha, being part of the former, was faithful to his tradition. He teaches people that they too can follow the eightfold path, and that they can do so from the position they are in. And what positions would these be? Ones assigned by the caste system. Thus, one of the pragmatic presuppositions of Buddha's dialogs was this audience that he addressed his talks to, which was, as the history books tell us, divided into the four varnas: the Brahmins, the Kshatriyas, the Vaisyas, and the Sudras.

The above is a brief sketch of the context of Buddha's dialogs. To establish that it is not off the mark let us examine some of the scholarship on this matter. First, in the words of a hostile critic of Indian religion, Max Weber:

> So far as it actually took place, the disregard of Buddhism for status differences meant no social revolution. That members of the lowest strata were to be found among the adherents of early Buddhism is not traditional and very improbable. For it was precisely *Sramana* who came predominantly from distinguished circles of lay culture recruited from the city-dwelling Kshatriya patricians, somewhat as in the case of our Humanists, who constitute its membership. In fact, it appears certain that originally *Buddhism, exactly like Jainism, first firmly adhered to the conviction that only one born in the Brahman or Kshatriya castes was qualified for full gnosis...*

> A "struggle" against the Brahmans somewhat in the manner of Christ against the Pharisees and scribes cannot be traced in Buddha's preaching. He left aside the question of the Gods as well as *the meaning of the castes...* (T)o change the social order in this world neither early nor later Buddhism has attempted to do. (Weber 1958: 226-227; emphasis added).

Next, here is the testimony of a hostile critic of Brahmanism and a sympathetic admirer of Buddhism:

> According to the Buddha all four classes are equally 'pure', and what matters is their conduct. Although the Buddha thus rejected their special claims and sought to reform their entire ideology, he wished to do so by conciliating the Brahmins, by restoring them, according to his version of history, to their original condition. In effect his idea was to assimilate the brahmans to the sramanas: to establish that anyone could become a Brahman by adopting a simple life of meditation and virtuous, tolerant and gentle conduct. (Warder 1980: 180.)

At first sight, this appears ambiguous. To reduce the ambiguity we need to expand on at least one thread. In the *Agganna Sutta*, also called the 'Buddhist Book of Genesis', Buddha discusses the matter with two disciples: Basitha and Bharadvaja. As usual,

> both were brahmans and belonged to wealthy families; the former is said to have been an expert in Vedic lore, and to have renounced great wealth when he became a Buddhist bhikku. (Ling, Ed., 1981: 101.)

One day, discussing the claims of the Brahmins, namely that they were born from the mouth of Brahma and that "the Brahman class is the best", Buddha remarks that "the Brahmans have certainly forgotten the past when they say that sort of thing. "There are four social classes", continues the Buddha, "the nobles (Kshatriyas), Brahmans, tradespeople and work-people. Amongst all of them moral qualities are to be found." So begins this dialog. The first thing to note is that the nobles come first, followed by the Brahmins. Secondly, it is equally important to bear in mind that Buddha himself was a Kshatriya. The importance of these two statements will become clearer as we work our way through the dialog.

Buddha begins to tell a story about one evolutionary cycle of the world. After the previous world had disappeared, eons later, earth formed again. Many cycles later, human and other beings appeared too. As the world evolved further, more events took place, including the appearance of rice. Having discovered its edibility, human beings cultivated rice; stored the harvest in granaries; and, finally, divided the rice fields among themselves. Each distinguished his own plot from those of the others by marking its boundaries. A greedy person from the community, while guarding his own plot, stole the rice plot of another and made use of it. The others in the community took note of this and severely reprimanded the greedy person, who, despite punishment and warnings, continued to repeat the act. These people, continues the Buddha,

> gathered themselves together, and lamented what had happened; they said:

> "Our evil deeds have become obvious; stealing, censure, lying, punishment are now known among us. What if we were to select a certain person who should be angry when indignation is called for, who should censure whatever be censured, and should banish anyone who deserves to be banished? We will give him a certain proportion of the rice in return for these duties."

> 'Then,...they went to the one among them who was the handsomest, the best favoured, the most attractive, the most capable, and said to him: "We wish you to be the one who will be indignant at whatever one should be rightly indignant at, censure whatever should rightly be censured, banish him who deserves to be banished. And we will contribute to you a certain proportion of our rice."

> 'He consented, and did so, and they gave him a portion of their rice.

> 21. "Chosen by the whole people"...this is what is meant by Maha Sammata; [the Great Elected One]; this was how the name arose. "Lord of the Fields" is what is meant by "kshatriya"; *so kshatriya [noble] was the next title to arise*...(R)aja was the third title to arise.

> 'This...was the origin of this social circle of the nobles...Their origin was from among those same beings as themselves, and no others; and *it took place according to dhamma, fittingly*'. (*ibid.* 109-110; emphasis added).

From the above account, as a caste, kshatriya is the first and the king comes from this group. Not only does Buddha elevate the kshatriya but also declares that this took place according to *dhamma*–not the Buddhist dharma, but 'universal dharma' and that it is appropriate. However, let us not draw any conclusions yet, but listen to more of the story.

22. Now it occurred...to some of them as follows. "Evil deeds have become manifest among us: such as stealing, censure and lying. Punishment and banishment are also common. Let us put away evil and immoral customs." So they put away evil, immoral customs, and...thus it was that 'brahmans' became the earliest title for those who did so...

23. '...Such...was the origin of this social circle of brahmans. Their origin was from just those people [above referred to]; *[and it took place] according to dhamma [according to what ought to be]*' (*ibid.*: 110-111).

The origin of the second group is also appropriate. Among them, Buddha distinguishes further subgroups: those who meditated; those who took to writing books because they were unable to meditate; and those who learnt Vedic lore, being unable to accept the discipline the other two activities demanded of them. It is the last group, says the Buddha ironically, which now claims to be the best. Buddha speaks of the emergence of the next two caste groups, i.e., the Vaisyas and the Sudras. Both of them took place according to *dhamma* as well:

24. 'Now...there were some others...who, adopting the married state, took up various trades. The origin...of the social group called the vaisyas...took place in accordance with dhamma [according to what ought to be, justly].

25. 'Now...those of them who were left took to hunting...Thus...is the origin of this social group called sudras... [and took place] according to dhamma [according to what ought to be]' (ibid. 111).

Apart from these four castes, Buddha speaks of the Sramanas thus:

26. 'Now there came a time...when some kshatriya, misprising his own dhamma, went from home into the homeless life, saying "I will become an ascetic." Some brahman did the same; likewise some vaisyas and some sudras, each finding some fault in his particular dhamma. Out of these four groups the company of the ascetics came into being. Their origin was from just these beings like unto themselves, not different. And it took place according to dhamma, that is, fittingly' (*ibid.* 111-112).

In other words, Buddha finds that each of these caste groups and the Sramanas came into being correctly, appropriately, and according to dharma. This alone would be enough to reduce any ambiguity in Warder's testimony but there is something more to this story. The dialogue ends with a verse which Buddha attributes to Brahma. After having first recited it, the Buddha says:

> 32. 'Now this stanza...was well sung by Brahma the ever-youthful, well said, and full of meaning. And I too...say:
> *The kshatriya is the best among this folk*
> Who put their trust in lineage.
> But one in Wisdom and to virtue clothed
> Is best of all 'mong spirits and men'. (*ibid.* 113; emphasis added)

Buddha leaves little room for doubt, here, whether he is rejecting the caste system or not. After recounting this story, but without referring to this verse, Warder concludes:

> It should be noted that the Buddha's opposition is not total: rather he seeks to conciliate and win over the brahmans of his day to his new way of thinking. He flatters them that their class was formed originally from good motives and had good traditions. It is only more recently that it has become degenerate and its way of life harmful... (1980: 163).

The message is clear. Buddha's criticisms of the Brahmins cannot be seen as a *rejection* of the caste system.

Finally, the words of a skeptic, Frits Staal, Professor at the University of California, who has put in a lot of effort in 'seeking out the Buddha', tell us of the results of his search:

> If he preached that the true Brahman is not he who is born in the highest caste, but who is fearless, controlled, free from sins, etc.–the *Upanishads had already stated that a Brahman is only he who speaks the truth, or knows Brahman*...and the Jaina Uttaradhyayana-sutra had declared: "He who is exempt from love, hatred and fear, and who shines forth like burnished gold, purified in fire, him we call a Brahman..." (Staal 1989: 406-407; emphasis added).

In other words, whatever else Buddha might have been doing in these dialogs, it is difficult to suggest that he was rejecting the caste system. If he did not presuppose the caste system, and its continued functioning, his question would not make sense at all. Brahmanism is not identical to the caste system in Buddha's dialogs. Consequently, even if he rejected Brahmanism he was not doing the same with respect to the caste system. His question "Who is a Brahmin" picks out an individual belonging to the caste system. All human beings do not belong to the caste system–its domain is limited to specific traditions.

Let's now bring the speeches of Schleiermacher and Buddha sharply into focus to see what the analogy is. Sonadanda picks out Angaka, who is a Brahmin, to say that being a Brahmin does not consist of either color, or birth, or knowledge of the Vedic samhitas. His fellow-Brahmins agree that if a Brahmin were to indulge in certain actions, and be devoid of certain characteristics, he would cease being a Brahmin even if he possessed the other characteristics.

Schleiermacher talks to a Protestant audience. He tells them that being religious does not consist in believing in this or that doctrine, or in going to this or that celebration in church. It involves having a particular kind of experience. The word 'God' in Christian vocabulary designates a particular kind of experience, one of being "absolutely dependent on the totally other". As he expresses this point in *The Christian Faith*:

> As regards the identification of absolute dependence with "relation to God" in our proposition: this is to be understood in the sense that the whence of our receptive and active existence, as implied in this self-consciousness, is to be designated by the word "God," and that this is for us the really original signification of the word. (In Proudfoot 1985: 20).

His audience agrees that they, the Protestants, would not be religious without such an experience even if they were born into the religious tradition in question.

The question 'Who is a Brahmin?' makes sense to a Brahmin. The question 'Who is religious?' makes sense to a Protestant. Are these questions also intelligible to others? In the case of Buddha, the question 'Who is a Brahmin?' makes sense to his audience, which consists not only of Brahmins but also of other caste groups. His public could make sense of this question if, and only if,

'Brahminhood' and 'being a Brahmin' were experiential categories to them. Even though Brahmins are different from the other caste groups, this otherness cannot be something alien. It must be the case that Brahmins are constituted in the same way as the other caste groups are constituted, so that they, together, experience this constitution as a tradition. In other words, even if belonging to a different caste group, the category 'Brahmin' is not an alien category to the other caste groups.

The same holds good for religiosity as well. The Protestant religiosity of a Schleiermacher must be an experiential category to Catholics as well. Protestants are different from Catholics but cannot be totally the other. They are both constituted by the same tradition, namely Christianity.

Could either of these questions make sense to yet others as well? Could Catholics make sense of the question "are you a Brahmin?" They could not. Catholics fall outside and beyond the scope of both the question and the answer. To ask such a question to a Belgian Catholic or a German Protestant is a category mistake. The category of 'Brahmin' has individuals constituted by the caste system as its domain of application. Belgian Catholics and German Protestants do not belong to the domain of individuals to whom the category 'Brahmin' is applicable.

What about religiosity? It appears to be taken for granted that it is the experiential domain of all and sundry. It even seems to make sense to atheists because, after all, they do talk of an atheistic religiosity. Western anthropologists, philosophers, and theorists of religions, all talk about the religiosity of the Hindus, of the Africans, or the Native Americans, without feeling that they are committing a category mistake. We can fall in line with the majority and accept this, or we can choose to reflect upon it. The reason we do not feel the category mistake is because our language (the Christian language), and our ontology (the Christian faith) have become the universal language and ontology of humankind.

This is where the twain meet. Not in the East or West, but in the Christian and secular worlds. Christian ideas begin to sound so secular that we do not realize how Christian they are. We do not have to be Brahmins to make sense of the question 'who is a Brahmin', nor do we have to be Christian, or a theist, to make sense of the question 'who is a religious person'. Nevertheless, we have to be part of these cultures for the questions to be intelligible. 'Who is a Brahmin?' is a question internal to a culture and a tradition, which requires that the interlocutors share a set of presuppositions. This is also the case regarding the question 'Who is a religious person?' Take caste away from the first context and the question does not make sense; take religion away from the latter context, and it becomes unintelligible as well.

In India the case seems obvious. We are constantly reminded that the entire society is dominated by caste. In the West, it does not appear to be so. It sounds improper to suggest that the entire western society is dominated by religion, because the secular guise of religion makes the situation indistinct. The reason for this difference and for the illusion that the West is not dominated by religion goes back to the universalistic pretentions of Christianity which compel it to secularize its ideas.

In India, two distinct kinds of individuals have problems with the question 'who is a Brahmin?' The first are among the Brahmins themselves: educated, literate, reflective Brahmins, who, rightly or wrongly, think that the caste system is an evil in Indian society. Under the influence of some doctrine or the other about society, they reject their own Brahmanism. Normally this involves ceasing to participate in some rituals and practices; and assuming an explicit stance that the caste system is an evil monstrosity that ought to be abolished. However, despite this, many are driven to confess, as a famous writer from South India once did: "even though I have renounced Brahmanism, the latter will not renounce me".

Similarly, this is also how Brahmins are experienced among individuals from the second group: educated, literate, and reflective members of the so-called lower caste groups. For most, the criticisms never progress beyond the hackneyed criticisms from eighteenth-century Europe. Nevertheless, exactly the same realization pervades their perception as well. A vague sense that a rejection of this or that practice and an endorsement of this or that belief are not sufficient–either with respect to themselves or with respect to the Brahmins.

This must not be misconstrued as a point in favor of cultural determinism. Its purpose is merely to draw a parallel with the situation in the West. In western culture too, there is a two-fold dynamic when someone brought up as a Christian decides to cease being one. One aspect involves rejecting a set of beliefs (mostly, it involves just one belief, that is, the existence of God); and the second is to stop going to church. Atheism or agnosticism is seen as a solution to the problem they had, or as an option that better reflects their beliefs. But unlike their Indian counterparts, neither the individuals who take these steps nor those outside and around them seem to realize that they have an unresolved problem.

The point to consider is this. If the secular world is really the 'other' of the religious world, how can these people adapt so easily to it? How are they able to find their points of reference with such ease, if the secular world is alien to the religious world they once inhabited? If religion is an attitude, a feeling, a way of life–as everyone keeps insisting it is–how can they navigate with such skill in an entirely new world? People cease being religious because they believe that religion is an unsatisfactory solution to questions or problems they had. They believe that they would be better off finding other solutions to questions like the meaning of life, or in seeking the spark of divinity elsewhere. But 'meaning of life' questions are questions generated by religion. They stem from the Biblical belief that God regulates the universe according to his plans, intentions, and goals. These are not questions formulated to resolve problems, nor have they ever resolved the 'meaning' problem.   Nevertheless, these questions, although generated by religion, continue to persist in a secular framework. That is why, after a brief transition period, individuals who give up their religion are able to thrive in a secular world because it shares the same belief pattern as the religious world. Or else they continue in their search for new forms of religiosity. Keep in mind the assumption in this case: that human beings have a specific need that is supposed to be satisfied by religion. Churches might be the wrong answers, but they are considered answers nonetheless. Instead of a God-ordained religion, the solution is alleged to be found in some alternate form of spirituality, or a spiritual experience that will fulfill this supposedly innate religious need.

The 'secular', 'atheistic', world is a solution to the Christological dilemma. To find universal acceptance, Christian ideas must secularize themselves. The secular world is not the 'other'; it is not an alien world to Christianity. The religious world creates the secular world in its own image. The familiar reference points take on a secular form. Those who believe that they have ceased to belong to a religion, in effect, just move from one religious world to another. They merely encounter religion in a secular guise. Christian beliefs dominate the world by appearing to be increasingly less Christian. The process can be described in the following terms. Some beliefs are detached from the set of religious beliefs and practices with which they were once intimately bound. The detached beliefs progressively lose their religious bite in direct proportion to their universal acceptance. However, this does not make these beliefs secular. They remain religious no matter how one twists and turns the matter.

Consider Apostel's claims about atheistic religiosity. He tries to provide room for this experience by referring to the etymology of the word:

> The well-known etymological remark that brings 're-ligion' in connection with '*re-ligare*' (to tie together, to link) makes us see religious phenomena as instruments of connection, as modes of union. (1981:28).

There's no use arguing about whether the above sentiment helps the author in seeing religion the way he wants to see it, or that this remark is well known (implying, therefore, that it is also true). To what extent is this an etymological point?

In the literature, there are two attempts at deriving the Latin word *religio* from some or the other root. Neither of the proponents of the two etymologies was a trained linguist. The first etymological attempt is by Cicero in *De Natura Deorum* and the second derivation is by Lactantius in his *Institutiones Divinae*. Cicero lived about half-a-century before Christ; Lactantius was a Christian theologian, who lived around two hundred and fifty years after Christ. Balbus, the Stoic partner in the Ciceronian dialogue, argues thus:

> For religion has been distinguished from superstition not only by philosophers but by our own ancestors. Persons who spent

whole days in prayer and sacrifice to ensure that their children should outlive them were termed 'superstitious'...Those on the other hand *who carefully reviewed and so to speak retraced all the lore of the ritual* were called 'religious' from *relegere* (to re-trace or re-read), like 'elegant' from *eligere* (to select), 'diligent' from *diligere* (to care for), 'intelligent' from *intellegere* (to understand); for all these words contain the same sense of 'picking out' (*legere*) that is present in 'religions'. (*De Natura Deorum*, II: 72; emphasis added).

This etymological derivation of Cicero appeals to his culture and tradition. Given what we have seen about Roman *religio*, this stance appears both sensible and acceptable. *Religio* is almost synonymous with *traditio*. The idea of carefully reviewing, or retracing and picking out makes sense when religion is the tradition handed down by your ancestors.

About three hundred years later, Lactantius–who thought of himself as a Christian Cicero–in explicit opposition to his pagan counterpart reflected upon the etymology of *religio* in these terms (*Institutiones Divinae*, IV: 28):

We are fastened and bound to God by this bond of piety, whence religion itself takes its name. The word is not as Cicero interpreted it from 'rereading', 'or 'choosing again' (*relegendo*)... We can know from the matter itself how inept this interpretation is. For if superstition and religion are engaged in worshipping the same gods, there is slight or rather no difference...because religion is a worship of the true; superstition of the false. And it is important, really, why you worship, not how you worship, or what you pray for... We have said that the name of religion is taken from the bond of piety, because God has bound and fastened man to Himself by piety, since it is necessary for us to serve Him as Lord and obey Him as father... They are superstitious who worship many and false gods; but we, who supplicate the one true God, are religious. (Trans. Sister McDonald 1964: 318-320).

Coming from Lactantius, this remark makes sense. Christianity sees man as the servant of God; he is tied and bound to Him as His creature. After all, it is not sufficient that we merely worship–we have to worship God not the Devil. It is, therefore, perfectly plausible that Lactantius would speak of the bond between the individual worshipper and God as the defining trait of religion.

Lactantius' derivation, hardly surprisingly, became well known and famous. Many authors during the Renaissance reflected upon the nature and origin of religion and further popularized the etymology provided by Lactantius.

The contrast between the pagan and the Christian etymological derivations of the term *religio* is far too important to note only in passing. Cicero suggests that '*superstitio*' refers to excesses: "spending days in prayer and sacrifice in order that one's children outlive their parents." This is contrasted with *religio,* where one carefully selects from the inherited tradition. The function of criticism was to restrain excesses, i.e., the function of reason was to criticize *superstitio*.

In Lactantius, we see the extent to which paganism had already become incomprehensible to Christianity. The distinction between *religio* and *superstitio* is now seen as the opposition between "the true" and "the false". He complains that this distinction–which, note well, paganism does not make–disappears if one focuses merely on the modes of worship. He is both right and wrong. *Superstitio* was also *religio* to the pagans, but carried to extremes. Too much smoking and drinking are excesses; but they do not cease being smoking and drinking because of that. Complete abstinence from alcohol or cigarettes is the opposite of drinking and smoking and this is how Lactantius sees *religio* and *superstitio*. In this sense, he is right in saying that the opposition disappears in Cicero, but he is wrong to imply that pagans saw this distinction as an opposition.

Consequently, in the Christian definition, the focus of *religio* shifts to whom you worship, and not any God, if you please, but the One who is your Maker, Master, and to whom you are tied by bonds of obedience, piety, and so forth. If, as Lactantius observes, the word *religio* is derived from such ideas as these, then the very concept of *religio* depends on other theological concepts. The difference between the Pagan Cicero and the Christian Lactantius is indeed one of 'theologies'. Although both use the same word, its sense and reference shifts. In Cicero, it merely refers to following ancestral practices. Lactantius's definition, on the other hand, is acceptable only if we assume the truth of Christian theology.

The above reflection can help us draw two interesting conclusions. First, with respect to the way theological ideas get detached from their context and yet remain recognizably theological; the second with respect to the very concept of religion.

When we come to appreciate the relationship between *re-ligare* and Christian theology, Lactantius and his problems with Cicero become perfectly intelligible. But what happens when this "well known remark" gets detached from its context and penetrates the secular world? How does it become 'universal'? In Lactantius's definition, God and Man are the two elements in the relation. In secular terms we can speak of these two elements of the relation in whatever terms we like without feeling restricted by Christian theology. It can be the 'finite' or the 'infinite'; the 'cosmos' or the 'universe'; 'humanity' or 'life'; 'individual' or the 'society', etc. Yet the idea that being tied or linked is a religious experience is recognizably Christian. The background of Christian theology makes it intelligible; otherwise, it is not.

To appreciate this point more fully, consider the oft-made (partially true) claims about the Indian traditions. These 'religions' it is said, aim at liberating men from their bondage, i.e., from the ties and bonds that link men to the world. These religions do not aim at severing this or that bond, but all links, bonds and connections human beings have in the world, with the world, and with the Cosmos. As a consequence, if religion is *re-ligare*, Indian religions cannot be 'instruments or modes of connection'. A religion whose explicit aim it is to free you from links cannot be said to provide you with an experience whose zenith consists of developing a feeling of dependence. In other words, that which sounds perfectly absurd in the Indian (Asian) context sounds perfectly sensible in western culture. This is because the concept 'religion' (*re-ligare*) is itself tradition-bound; it is theological; it is intra-traditional and not inter-traditional. This has nothing to do with what word we use to say 'religion'. The thesis is that 'religion' expresses some concept; this concept, enunciated by the word 'religion', is Christian-theological. It is not, it cannot be, an inter-traditional concept. There's no use saying that the Indian traditions are different. There is simply no other way to conceive of religion except as handed down by Christian theology.

'Religion' is how Christianity (to speak only of this tradition) described itself when demarcating itself from the traditions of other peoples and cultures. It is the self-description of Christianity. It is the outer-boundary of Christian self-consciousness and not its internal core. That is, Christians, when they talk to each other, may or may not talk in terms of their religion. Externally, when they talk to 'others', it is their self-identity:

> The Christian group, to verbalize the new life that they were experiencing and proclaiming, introduced in addition to ecclesia other elements of a new vocabulary... In addition, however, they of course took over also a great many terms from the older religious life... Among these was the word *religio, which appears richly in the Christian writing in Latin from the beginning.*

> Actually, until the fourth century it was used more than later. It would seem that there is perhaps a correlation between the frequency of the usage of this word and the historical situation of religious pluralism and rivalry... *By the fifth century, when the Christian church had virtually eliminated its rivals, the term was less actively in use, and in fact almost disappeared.* (Smith 1962: 24-25; emphasis added).

Of course, they took over the word. They did so by radically shifting its reference. But this is not a mere taking over of a vocabulary. Christianity fashioned a new vocabulary. *Religio* lost its roots in paganism when the Christians took over the word. Henceforth, it would flourish in new soil until the only connection between it and the old concept would be the word alone. 'Religion', in this sense, is rooted in the Christian appropriation of the Old Testament.

In the chapter on Roman *religio*, I made the claim that "Our intellectual world happens to be a Christian world." "Whether a Jew, a Dinka or a Brahmin; whether a theist, an atheist or a Muslim, our questions have a common origin." Now it should be clear why we all share a Christian world. In the name of science and ethnology, Biblical themes have become our regular stock-in-trade. The idea that God gave religion to humankind turns up in a secular guise in the idea that all cultures have religion; the theme that God gave one religion to humanity has metamorphosized into the belief that all religions have something in common; that God revealed himself to humankind is sanctified in the claim that in all cultures and at all times there is a subjective experience of religion which is fundamentally the same; the idea that God implanted a sense of divinity in Man is now a secular truth in the form of an anthropological, specifically human ability to have a religious experience. And so the list goes on, and on. Theme after theme from the pages of the Bible has become the 'but of course!' of intellectuals–whether Jew, Muslim, Dinka or Brahmin. We've all become Christians precisely to the degree that Christianity has become less distinctively Christian in the process of its secularization. We may not recognize Jesus as the Savior but the retribution for this pagan challenge to Christianity is in direct proportion. Pagans no longer have access to their pagan roots or the pagan experience. All their dogmas are Christian. We could stop here, but the Divine retribution goes far, far deeper. Let's take a look at the far reaches of this retribution.

The questions 'Who is a religion person?' and 'Who is a Brahmin?' can be understood in two ways. Firstly, they can identify individuals from within a particular group. That is, they can point to an individual within a tradition as an exemplary specimen of that tradition. They can, thus, distinguish between two individuals who belong to the same tradition or group. Secondly, these same questions also provide the criteria for belonging to a particular group. That is, they specify the conditions under which someone can be identified as a Brahmin or a religious person. Here, Brahminhood and religiosity are general properties of the group that give it its identity.

Now, although religiosity can provide the criteria for belonging to a particular group, it cannot distinguish religion from other phenomena. It can only be used to distinguish one human being from another. Thus, religiosity, or the subjective experience of God, cannot be used as a criterion to point to different traditions and say that is what identifies something as a religion. The reason for this, as already discussed, is that the concept of religiosity is based on Christian theological presuppositions, and is therefore inapplicable in other contexts.

However, in spite of the fact that there are no criteria to properly identify religion in other cultures, it happens to be the case that academic discussions about other religions are mostly conducted within the framework of Christian theology. Almost all the concepts used in the discussion of religion, whether it be the 'religion' of the Native Americans or the Dinka, use words like 'prophetic', 'sacramental', 'revelatory', 'liturgy', 'worship', 'sacrament', 'eschatology', 'soteriology', 'sacred', 'profane', 'God', 'Devil', 'transcendent', 'immanent', 'holy', 'absolute', 'faith', 'piety', 'blasphemy', 'apocalyptic', 'salvation, 'sin', and so on and so forth. These concepts form a cluster and this concept cluster picks out certain practices. Directly, they pick out the linguistic practices of a community of believers, and indirectly they refer to the cultural practices of a community with a history.

The issue is not so much about the meaning of specific words. The issue is whether, in the absence of a background set of beliefs, it is possible to pick out what these words refer to. Is it possible to distinguish something that constitutes a 'totality' due to the interrelationship between these concepts? For example, the whole story of the Bible, God, Jesus, sin, salvation, worship, etc., are some of the concepts that form the 'totality', or the Gestalt, of the Christian religion. For an intelligible interpretation of individual words, the 'totality' which these concepts refer to is essential. In cultures where these words are native and these terms are applicable at the level of daily language, in a way that people are able to relate incidents from their own history to clarify the meaning of these words, it does not present a problem. Where there is a shared history of practices these concepts are readily intelligible.

When we transport these terms to a culture lacking these practices and a language lacking these words, however, it poses a problem. Yet we come across hundreds of books and articles that speak of "Buddhist Soteriology," "Hindu Eschatology," "Taoist Liturgy," the "Sacrament of the *Vedas*," and so on. These writers do not question the presumption of sameness. This, of course, has a double advantage. Such writers sound terribly profound to the ears of those not trained to speak in a theological language; after all, how many Indians are trained in Christian theology? The effect is exactly the same as in using technical vocabulary from a specialized domain while having a perfectly normal conversation in English with a nonprofessional. The only reason it sounds profound is because it is unintelligible to most. This generates the second advantage, which is pernicious to any intellectual enquiry–the very possibility of questioning such a writer is ruled out. You cannot challenge these writers unless you master this way of describing the world.

This should draw our attention to two problems. In the first place, the mere use of theological concepts in describing traditions like, say, Hinduism, does not establish that Hinduism is a religion. After all, each of these concepts faces those very problems that the concept 'religion' faced. How can you argue that the *Vedas* are scriptures; that the Indian temples are akin to churches; or that *Bhakti* is piety? There is a second problem, which is more damaging. It is the way in which Indian scholars have taken to speaking about Indian texts. In expounding on The *Bhagavad Gita*, for example, it is standard fare to come across gibberish scholarship that speaks of its 'theological contradictions', 'soteriological ambiguity', 'liturgical inconsistencies', or 'canonical ambivalence'. Each of these concepts comes from the Christian tradition to talk about Christianity. These are theological concepts and parts of Christian religious life. If the same framework is used to talk about either Hinduism or the Gita, then it means that this framework is being used in the same standardized way that we use scientific theories and their categories. That is, we identify Christian theology as the science of religion–something that not all Christian theologians themselves would consent to.

Why have so many brilliant and distinguished writers been unable to see how ridiculous this approach is? A partial answer has already been provided. The assumption that all cultures have religion is a historical legacy. Due to its long currency, it has become an unexamined piece of trivia and over the course of history it has come to sound progressively secular. It is therefore hard to grasp the import and significance of the suggestion that our secular world is actually a Christian world. Let's see if we can further outline the contours of this argument.

Suppose that we define religion (i.e., we explain our pre-theoretical notion about religion) as involving a belief in the existence of God. Although our intuitions tell us that Buddhism and Jainism are religions, they, as we well know, deny the existence of God. Consequently, we must conclude that Buddhism and Jainism are counter-examples to this definition and hence this definition is not a good one. A pre-theoretical notion simply means that the notion in question is not yet part of any accepted theory. That is to say, it is a notion that you and I have. It is not a part of the theoretical discourse; rather, it is a part of our ordinary language use. Our definition, then, is good only as long as it is able to explain the notions underlying our use of the word 'religion'. Therefore, any explanation will have to rest on the ultimate authority of our linguistic practice and a counter-example would mean that the given explanation is contradictory to our linguistic practice.

But *whose* practice and *which* language are we talking about? Shall we say the practice of the West and languages like English, Dutch, German, French, and such? Linguistic practices are those of a community that speaks this way and not any other way. It is in this way that practices have a cultural history. The cultural history of the West happens to be, among other things, a history of Christianity as well. Are we to say that all cultures have religion simply because the linguistic practice of one cultural community allows that all cultures have religion?

If it is merely a dispute about using the word 'religion', the problem is easily settled: none of the Asian languages has the word 'religion'; therefore, one cannot use this word in identifying Asian traditions from Hinduism to Shintoism. If Asians do not have this word (or any other word from the concept cluster), they do not have a pre-theoretical intuition related to the use of this word or any other word from the concept cluster either. Now, in discussions such as this, at this point people begin to object that even though Asians may not have a word for religion, they have the concept anyway, suggesting that it is up to the theorists to come up with a good definition to explicate this concept. It is inconceivable to most people that they do not have religions. But why is it inconceivable? What makes it inconceivable?

It is because thinking about religion takes place within the framework of a linguistic practice which itself is religious. The network of practices referred to by 'religion' molds the pre-theoretical notion of what religion is. We learn to use the word 'religion' as we participate in, and become a member of, the linguistic practice of a community. It is important to realize that this linguistic practice refers to that of using a theological language and not to the practice of using a natural language (like French, German, or Dutch).

The concept cluster which gives Gestalt to religion has assumed the status of being an integral part of natural language-use. As an example, consider such sentences as 'It is raining', 'Het regent', 'Es regnet', from English, Dutch, and German, respectively. We understand these sentences to be saying the same thing–they express the proposition that it is raining. Whenever they are enunciated, such natural language sentences are understandable by those in whose language such sentences are uttered. The reference or the meaning of such a sentence is guaranteed by its background, namely, a particular linguistic practice. Not only do speakers of a particular language understand such sentences in their language, but the possibility of accurate translation depends on the fact that the propositions expressed in these different languages are the same. The point is this: the Christian way of talking about itself (i.e., as a religion) appears as natural a way of talking as talking about the weather. To say that 'it is hot', 'it is dry', 'it is raining', does not presuppose any specific vocabulary but merely a shared, common world. The world we live in, the experiences we have in it, and a competence in some natural language, are the requirements to utter and understand such sentences. Exactly the same status is accorded to concepts like 'religion', 'sacrament', 'liturgy', etc., while describing other cultures and their so-called religions. Without batting an eyelid people say things like Shintoism involves ancestor 'worship'; or they speak of the 'theology' of Buddhism; the 'gods' of the Hindus; and so on. Having a religion has become as natural as the rain and harvest–a precondition of human existence.

If we stop for a second and reflect on the fact that western culture has been dominated by Christianity for over eighteen hundred years, the implications of this will be apparent. With respect to language, it is this: theological vocabulary does not appear to be tied to any specific religion. Religious language does not seem to possess a recognizable Gestalt because it has faded into the background. In part, this is what it means to say that Christianity has gone secular. Its language, its vocabulary, its concepts, are all part and parcel of daily language, daily practice, daily vocabulary of even those in the West who have been brought up as 'atheists', 'free thinkers', 'heathens', or however they feel like describing themselves. Today, it is not possible to talk about religion without using the language and vocabulary of Christianity.

This also explains why travelers from sixteenth, seventeenth, or eighteenth century Europe were able to see idolatry, devil worship and heathen immorality when they visited India. Their religious concepts granted that to them. That is how their thinking was structured. Heading into the twenty-first century, with the legacy of centuries of descriptions of religions of other cultures behind us, this way of thinking is even more deeply entrenched. We may declare ourselves to be atheists, we do not know much about the Bible and still less of its theology, but our daily language is saturated with theological terms specific to Christianity. Not only does this language allow us the assumption that other cultures have religions, but it also threatens to make some sets of practices radically unintelligible if they are not described as religions. Buddhism and Hinduism appear as different forms of religion. To say that they are not religions appears to make these practices unintelligible. Their apparent unity is itself threatened. It is only by linking practices and construing them as a unity—as 'Hinduism', as 'Buddhism', etc.,—that phenomena are saved from the threat of total unintelligibility.

But this threat is only an apparent threat. In exactly the same way that religion generates but one kind of linguistic practice, members from other cultures might well be able to describe their traditions differently without having to deny intelligibility or unity to their traditions. From within one description, a Japanese is simultaneously a Buddhist and a Shintoist. From another point of view, a different description of the Japanese may be possible which provides an alternate unity to their traditions. What is at issue here is the extent to which this argument helps in making sense of the unexamined and deeply rooted belief that all cultures know of religion in some form or another.

When we look at a Japanese bowing before the portraits of his ancestors; or at a Thai putting garlands on the statue of the Buddha; or at a Hindu prostrating in a temple; the only way we can save these phenomena from the threat of unintelligibility and lack of unity is to call them religious observances. We are compelled to tie such practices with other ones, and these practices with some texts, and so on, until we can see them as constituting a unity. However, note well: the unity we create, the descriptions we provide are necessities for us and to those who share our religious vocabulary. For those who do not share our language, in all probability, the unity that we generate will appear chaotic; our intelligibility conditions are their opacity; our obvious and self-evident truisms are their esoteric and the exotic.

We can now better understand why we have had to create Hinduism, Buddhism, Shintoism, and all of these other religions. Our language, and the practice of the community we are a part of, threaten to render phenomena chaotic if they are construed any other way. At the same time, we feel that the world is not quite how we describe it. Hence the unease, the inconsistencies, and the dilemmas.

Our 'secularized', modern world is closer to Jerusalem than it is to Athens. We are indeed travelling further and further away from that grand old pagan city. Now we can see why the creation of religions in India has to do with the conceptual compulsion of a religious culture. If we are already certain that Buddhism and Jainism are religions even when they deny the existence of God, what are we talking about when we talk about religions? If belief in God is irrelevant to being religious, how are we to begin making sense of all those centuries of bitter struggle between atheists and theists, all those tortures, persecutions and executions? Are we supposed to believe that this was a linguistic, etymological misunderstanding? Could we blithely imply that the horror of religious persecution could have been avoided if only the participants knew their Latin well and had sat down to discuss the meaning of '*re-ligare*' instead of chopping each other's heads off? How can we possibly characterize as identical a set of structures where the existence or nonexistence of God is an intelligible question, and another set of structures where such questions cannot even be formulated?

The historical and the linguistic aspects relating to the above questions have already been addressed. The following chapters will look at the conceptual aspects of the problem.

PART III

How can a secular world be a religious world in disguise? Building a theory of religion will help solve these and the other problems noted so far. A characterization of religion, its reflexive nature, and its inherent dynamic explain how religious themes are secularized.

CHAPTER VIII

HUMAN TRAGEDY OR DIVINE RETRIBUTION?

Discussions about the origin of religion that preoccupied eighteenth-century thinkers are hardly of interest to scholars today. To most, the universal existence of religion is a fact–not a phenomenon in need of an explanation. Contemporary thinkers are more interested in the history, development, and structure of specific religions than in developing theories about the necessity of religion in human societies.

The characteristic form for the study of different religions in the twentieth century was that of comparative studies. However, once the novelty of the other religions wore off, this trend began to exhibit its sterility and emptiness. Instead of a rejection of this approach, however, what began to happen was a super-imposition of further 'isms' in the hope of yet being able to squeeze something out of the comparative approach: structuralism, functionalism, symbolic interactionism, Marxism, phenomenology, etc. Books, journals, articles, and Societies multiplied by their hundreds, each doing comparative studies: a mega-comparison of science with religion; maxi-comparison of Buddhism and Christianity or Confucianism with Christianity; a point-by-point comparison of 'Trinity' with 'Trimurti', or 'Dharma' with 'religion'.

The different combinations within each of the above-mentioned 'isms', and the explosive growth of the different domains of investigation have made it impossible for any one individual to have a global view of the field of religious studies. Be that as it may, this book attempts to tell a different kind of a story–a conceptual one. Being a conceptual tale, it will answer one single question: if the secular world of today is, in fact, a religious world in secular clothing, what consequences does this have for the field of religious studies?

I have argued in the previous chapters that investigations into 'religions' in other cultures were carried out within a religious framework, suggesting that Christian theology is the framework within which these investigations have taken place. This is how I have tried to account for the 'discovery' and creation of religions in India. Further, I have argued that this theological framework has universalized itself under a secular guise. In the process, the framework has faded into the background, obscuring the fact that this seemingly secular world of today is, in fact, a religious world. Such a characterization is not without consequences. In the following sections I will endeavor to demonstrate some of these consequences.

The Consequences

If religion is a pre-theoretical concept, disputes about the concept are bound to exhibit certain problems. For example, some of the consequences of not having a theory about religion are: (i) It remains unclear whether or not some entity can be called a religion or not, but also, more importantly, we don't know how to go about settling disputes when they arise; (ii) A dispute, say, about whether Hinduism is a religion ends up becoming very much like a conflict of tastes since there's no strategy for testing its claims; (iii) in the absence of a theory, all we can do is direct our objections towards a definition. Not only is it fruitless to target definitions but it also leads to interminable discussions as these discussions take the form of classificatory problems. That is to say, instead of providing knowledge about the object under investigation, (i.e., telling us what the object refers to) they merely tell us whether a particular object belongs in this or that category; thus, (iv) a referential problem ends up getting a classificatory answer. Let's explore these consequences in some detail now.

What is the Dispute About?

Consider a scientific theory, say, the theory of black holes. Such a theory is able to specify (a) what object it is talking about; (b) what distinguishes black holes from white dwarfs and pulsars; (c) what the properties of black holes are; (d) how black holes come into being; and many such things. In such a theory you can ask several knowledge-seeking questions that are both precise and that can be answered. By contrast, the disputes in the field of religious studies do not appear to take this form. The discussions appear purely terminological.

> It is apparent that a universally useful "all-purpose" definition is difficult if not impossible to attain, its intellectual desirability being, in any case, by no means self-evident. Secondly, it is clear that religion may logically be defined from any number of specific vantage points, none of which need presuppose the ontological accuracy or inaccuracy of religious knowledge in general or particular terms. (O'Toole1984: 10).

Having said this, O'Toole spends the next 30 pages discussing various definitions of religions. Another sociologist declares that:

> (an) adequate definition of anything as complex and variable as religion is, however, difficult to provide. Some prefer not to make such a definition, feeling that religion can be described more adequately than it can be defined. (Vernon 1962: 43).

Nevertheless, a chapter on a 'sociological definition of religion' is indispensable to his book. Thus we can build a huge list of authors who (i) insist on being unable to give an adequate definition; (ii) provide their own definition; (iii) accept the permissibility of other definitions; and yet, (iv) spend a great deal of time and effort in criticizing others' definitions.

Some philosophers even make a virtue of such disputes. By calling some concepts 'essentially contested', they render the dispute senseless and sensible at the same time. It is sensible because our disputes appear normal–after all, the concepts are 'essentially contested'; it is senseless because, being essentially contested, there's no possibility of a resolution. Why not simply stipulate a definition and get on with the more serious job of building a theory?

Both the importance they attach to the questions and the way they end up trivializing the problem can be illustrated by the following example:

> If you cannot define something, how do you know what the "something" is? A definition is essential, in any meaningful discussion and to avoid confusion and argument. (Vernon 1962: 43).

There are three points that Vernon is making here: (i) to know something we need to define it; (ii) when we say what some phenomenon is, we avoid confusion with respect to the reference of the term; (iii) this prevents argument. These are all reasonable suggestions. But then, look at his definition:

> Religion is that part of culture composed of shared beliefs and practices which not only identify or define the supernatural and the sacred and man's relationships thereto, but which also relate them to the known world in such a way that the group is provided with moral definitions as to what is good (in harmony with or approved by the supernatural) and what is bad (contrary to or out of harmony with the supernatural) (*ibid.* 55-56).

This hardly helps us understand what phenomenon Vernon is talking about–a shared set of beliefs and practices that abound in terms like 'supernatural' and 'sacred'; 'harmony' and 'out of harmony'; 'known' and 'unknown' worlds. The problem with this definition is that it's even fuzzier than the term 'religion' as used in normal day-to-day conversations. Instead of eliminating confusion about the reference of the term, this definition makes it cloudy. The same considerations hold good elsewhere in the literature. Geertz, a famous anthropologist, defines religion as:

> (1) a system of symbols which acts to (2) establish powerful, pervasive, and long-lasting moods and motivations in men by (3) formulating conceptions of a general order of existence and (4) clothing these conceptions with such an aura of factuality that (5) the moods and motivations seem uniquely realistic. (1966: 4).

While Geertz spends the rest of the article in unpacking his definition, which pretty much makes paranoia sound like a religion, another scholar, Williamson, concludes his with a 'universal' definition:

> Religion is the acceptance of...a set of beliefs that exceed mundane matters and concerns; the commitment to a morality

or the involvement in a lifestyle resulting from these beliefs; and the psychological conviction which motivates the relation of belief and morality in everyday living and consistent behaviour (1985: 30-31).

Such, then, is the fetish about definitions in the field of religious studies. Of course we must strive to provide clear and unambiguous definitions to improve upon our day-to-day discourse. But none of the definitions cited above do this. This is hardly a way "to avoid confusion and argument." In fact, such definitions invite article after article on 'definitional' questions. This might be a good way to make a living but it hardly brings us any closer to an understanding of religion.

A Matter of Taste

If we look at the procedures that scholars adopt in the course of formulating their definitions of religion, we see that they are tailored to accommodate the personal tastes of the author himself. They believe that certain practices are religious and seek a definition that will do justice to what they accept to be true. Durkheim, for example, is dissatisfied with the 'minimal' definition of Tylor ("Religion is a belief in supernatural beings") because he sees that Theravada Buddhism falls outside the scope of such a definition. Consequently, he provides a definition that would make Buddhism fit into the category of religion, while excluding magic. Söderblom feels that magic is also religious and looks around for a definition that would include the former. There are those who think that Football and Nationalism are religions; thus, they fish around for definitions that will include them. Yet others, more conservative or less imaginative as the case may be, are quite satisfied to provide a definition that would grant 'religious experience' or 'religiosity' or just plain old 'religion' to groups and cultures from the Apaches to the Kayapo Indians; from the Hindus to the Maoris; from the Bantus to the Bhils. By virtue of this, conflicting definitions are very much like a conflict of tastes; some think that magic is also religion, some do not. So what do we do about it? Some may find it unpalatable to call football a religion but, quite obviously, others find it perfectly apt. How do we go about arguing?

Interminable Disputes

One of the ways to challenge the adequacy of a definition is by using the strategy of providing counter-examples. However, this strategy only works if it is used within the framework of a theory. In the absence of any theoretical framework, the only avenue open to counter examples is to appeal to counter-intuitive consequences of a definition, the way Melford Spiro, an anthropologist, does. But, how do we settle the problem when intuitions conflict?

> Since 'religion' is a term with historically rooted meanings, a definition must satisfy not only the criterion of cross-cultural applicability but also the criterion of intra-cultural intuitivity; at the least it should not be counter-intuitive. For me, therefore, any definition of 'religion' which does not include, as a key variable, the belief in superhuman…beings who have power to help or harm men is counter-intuitive. (1966: 91).

Spiro settles for a "minimal" definition based on consensus. Whose consensus though? To begin with, 'religion' is not a technical word with standardized usage. Consequently, the consensus cannot be about the use of the word by a group of theorists. Nor can there be a consensus among the majority of human beings, because most people on earth have never heard of the word 'religion'. Besides, why should we rest content with a consensus? After all, we want to know why Buddhism is a religion and not something else. A mere consensus that it is a religion does not settle this matter.

Spiro's minimal definition, as quoted above, is the following: "Belief in super-human beings". It's as easy to criticize this definition as it is for him to meet the criticisms. Suppose that I believe in the existence of extra-terrestrial beings with the power to help or harm human beings. According to Spiro's definition, I am religious because of this belief. I could say that this is actually a counter-example to his definition; but all Spiro has to do is deny that this is a counter-example and simply call me religious because of this belief. Given that neither of us has a theory, the only court of appeal left to both of us is our intuition as language speakers. Why should the intuitions of either of us be wrong? Why should the 'intra-cultural intuition' of Spiro count for either more or less than my intuition? Spiro appeals to the "historical rootedness" of the meaning of the word 'religion'. But both the meaning of religion and the meaning of the word 'religion' have changed over the course of the last two thousand years. Thus, the "intra-cultural intuitivity" that Spiro talks about is neither constant nor homogeneous. On what possible grounds can we propose a resolution of this question? All we can say about this dispute is that what is counter-intuitive to some need not be so to others.

A Confusion of Issues

Since human discourse is inter-subjective, that is to say, our interactions with each other are based on shared meanings, others must know what we're talking about. When a problem of definition is discussed within a theory, the idea is to provide an answer to a referential problem, that is, 'what is one talking about?' In the absence of a theory the problems lead to disputes about the ways of classifying the facts at our disposal. Is Voodoo magic or religion? Is Confucianism a religion or not? Is magic an earlier form of religion or a phenomenon of a different kind? This type of a disagreement is interminable, because it is endemic to the classificatory activity.

When we speak of knowledge, we need to allow for the possibility of a classificatory system that orders facts, concepts, and theories without itself being part of any specific theory. For instance, this is the case with an encyclopedia or a dictionary. Here, ordering or classifying knowledge is distinct from acquiring knowledge. In disputes about religion our problem arises at the level of the facts we want to classify. Assembling these facts is dependent on the classificatory systems we use. We could have a classificatory concept of religion that includes sub-concepts like 'initiation rites', 'burial practices', 'worshipping modes', and so on. In such a case we might assemble facts about the initiation and funerary rituals in other cultures; or about practices of going to temples, mosques, or churches, and claim that religion is a set of such practices. We might regard both the *bar mitzvah* of the Jews and the 'sacred thread' ceremony of the Hindus to be initiation rites; we might see a Thai garlanding a statue of Buddha and a Muslim praying in a Mosque as different modes of worship.

In such cases we can always question, say, the legitimacy of considering puja–which is what the Thai is doing–as being equivalent to worship. One might want to claim that *puja* has nothing to do with worship. Then either the disagreement is about the choice of words, in which case the dispute is arid, or it is about the facts. To one, it is a fact that the Thai is worshipping because he is garlanding a statue; to the other, it is equally a fact that he is not worshipping because he is garlanding a statue. There's no agreement about what constitutes 'facts' in such a case.

In light of this, consider the following two citations, both of which speak of the importance of definitions. John Hick, an extremely prolific writer, says that a definition would help us determine whether "Marxism...(and) Christian Science...(are) religion(s)." Hardly something to lose one's sleep over, one would think. Alston, however, has deeper grounds for being concerned even though his argument exhibits the characteristic confusion present in such discussions.

> An adequate definition should throw *light on the sorts of disputes and perplexities that typically produce a need to define religion*, such as disputes over whether communism is a religion, and whether devotion to science can be called a man's religion. (1967: 142; emphasis added).

There are two ways of interpreting the "disputes and perplexities" that Alston talks about. Either they involve difficulties with our classificatory systems or they have to do with our knowledge of the phenomenon. Let's take, for example, the discussion about classifying 'Science' or 'Hinduism' as religions. If we say it depends on our definition of religion, then, at best, it is a debate about our classificatory systems. Such disputes are arid, and lead to endless unproductive discussions without increasing our knowledge in any way. The more reasonable response is to say that the resolution of this dispute depends on our knowledge. That is to say, what do we know about 'Science', 'Hinduism', and 'Religion'? If this question is settled, more often than not, our "disputes and perplexities" disappear as well. Therefore, to resolve this type of problem we need to acquire knowledge about these phenomena.

An Alternate Description

The above, then, are the problems that have faced and continue to face the field of religious studies. However true this portrayal may be, it makes the authors–both contemporaneous and those from yesteryears–appear to be stupid. This is not a conclusion we can rest with easily. In fact, making their actions intelligible has constituted one of the dominant concerns of this essay. Therefore, we need to consider an alternate account that portrays these writers as being both reasonable and consistent. This alternate description hinges on the claim that, in the background, and guiding their investigations, is the presence of a Christian theological framework. In other words, the only way to make sense of their discourse on religion is to assume the truth of Christian theology. Take Christian theology away, and we're left with scholarship that sounds like nonsense. Let's see if by employing this strategy we can make the scholarship on religion appear to be more reasonable and consistent.

What can we make of the extraordinary fixation on finding a definition for religion? The questions about what religion is, or whether entities such as Buddhism are religions, are extremely important issues within a religious tradition like Christianity. If Jesus were to be no different from Buddha; or that God in Christianity were to be the *Atman* of the Hindus; or if it made no difference to human salvation whether Christianity is true or Jainism is, the threat that a religious tradition like Christianity faces is obvious. The same consideration, with appropriate modifications, applies to Islam and Judaism as well. Therefore, the question about what religion is, or whether the religions of other cultures exemplify religion, are important questions for theological enquiries within these traditions. These are questions within Christian theology, which theology also provides some kind of a theoretical framework. What happens when this theological framework 'disappears' into the background?

The following thought experiment answers this question beautifully:

> Imagine that the natural sciences were to suffer the effects of a catastrophe. A series of environmental disasters are blamed by the general public on the scientists. Widespread riots occur, laboratories are burnt down, physicists are lynched, books and instruments are destroyed... Later still there is a reaction against this destructive movement and enlightened people seek to revive science, although they have largely forgotten what it was. But all that they possess are fragments: a knowledge of

experiments detached from any knowledge of the theoretical context which gave them significance; parts of theories unrelated either to the other bits and pieces of theory which they possess or to experiment; instruments whose use has been forgotten; half chapters from books, single pages from articles, not always fully legible because torn and charred. Nonetheless all these fragments are reembodied in a set of practices which go under the revived name of physics, chemistry and biology. Adults argue with each other about the respective merits of relativity theory, evolution theory and phlogiston theory, although they possess only a very partial knowledge of each...

In such a culture men would use expressions such as 'neutrino', 'mass', 'specific gravity', 'atomic weight' in systematic and often interrelated ways which would resemble in lesser or greater degrees the ways in which such expressions had been used in earlier times before scientific knowledge had been so largely lost. But many of the beliefs presupposed by the use of these expressions would have been lost and there would appear to be an element of arbitrariness and even of choice in their application...What would appear to be rival and competing premises for which no further argumentation could be given would abound... (MacIntyre 1981: 1-2).

In a world such as the one described above, discussions would pretty much be guided by whatever takes one's fancy. For instance, in the scientific cosmology of today, insofar as physicists have some kind of a theory, 'black hole' is a concept within that theory. This concept allows us to discuss whether a particular stellar object can be considered a black hole or not. Suppose we come across a stellar object which behaves like a black hole–distortion of light and gravitational field, for example–but turns out not to be one, such an event will challenge a specific *theory* of black holes. It will not be a counterexample to the *definition* of black hole. Definitions do not allow for counter-examples–only theories do. The reason for this is simple. Definitions have no consequences, only the theories that embed them do. That is why substantive problems cannot be solved by definitional means.

Similarly, the disputants in the debates about the definition of religion feel that some sets of questions are related, that they are important, and that they must try to find a resolution to these questions. The importance they attach to issues like what religion is, or whether Hinduism or Marxism are religions, attests to the presence of a framework that compels them to ask such questions. This framework has faded into the background and, in any case, is not accepted explicitly. Consequently, it appears that there's no background framework guiding these questions. Yet, there is: this framework is basically provided by Christian theology even though its religious themes have faded into the background. This religious framework then serves as the general 'theory' within which these authors work. Thus, when studying Buddhism or Hinduism, for example, they consider these to be religions even before they set out to seek a definition. Their belief that such traditions are religions is backed by the enormous literature produced about them. If we look at the scholarship produced by these thinkers in this light, we can see how they appear more consistent. We can account for their preoccupation with religion and the need to come up with definitions. They are elaborating upon accumulated knowledge. Of course, this accumulated knowledge is based more on theology than empirical investigation, but at least this renders their effort more meaningful than it would otherwise seem.

If you are willing to entertain the idea presented throughout the course of this book that religion has secularized itself to become our common background, then it's easy to see why discussions about Marxism or Buddhism involve disputes about whether these entities can be called religions too. It is Christian theology that provides us with the concepts against the background of which we make such a determination. In this sense, 'religion' is a concept in theology analogous to the way 'black hole' is a term within physics. As a concept within theology, using this concept involves doing theology in the same way as a discussion whether some star is a black hole or not involves doing physics. In one case it is transparent; in the other it is opaque.

However, this opacity does not mean that such a theology is absent in the background. Christianity's status as a religion permits it to have a diversity of theological positions with respect to the others: from the position that all others worship the Devil to the position that grants a primal religion to other cultures. Underlying this diversity is the single idea, fundamental to Christian theology, that all cultures have religion. Disagreements about whether Marxism and magic are also religions express ongoing discussions of an unsolved problem stemming from this theological conviction. The fact that the problems remain unsolved makes the discussions appear interminable.

As an example, consider, once again, Spiro's claim that any definition of religion minimally includes a belief in superhuman beings with the power to help or harm men. It is a matter of established consensus that Hindus 'worship' trees, serpents, various animals, books, bicycles, images, and idols. Are we supposed to consider these people religious because of this? Coming from a Christian perspective, this is more a question about the hierarchy of life on earth. Humans are supposedly at the summit of creation and animals well below them in the ladder of life constituting the 'infra' or 'sub-human' species. Consequently, and only because of it, can gods be 'super-human'. There are cultures that do recognize the differences between species, but do not recognize any hierarchy of life on earth, even if human life is considered to be a desirable or privileged form of existence. In fact, one of the problems of the Christian missionaries with the Brahmins had to do precisely with this issue, as Rogerius records it:

> You cannot make them admit that Man outstrips the beasts and that he is a nobler creature than the animals because he has a superior soul. If you try to remonstrate with them on this, they would say, animals also have a similar kind of Soul. If you try to demonstrate this by the workings of the rational soul, which is evident in Man and not in the beasts: you may expect an answer...that the reason why the animals do not exhibit the kind of rationality and understanding that human beings can show, why they cannot speak as man does, is because they are not given a body capable of exhibiting the qualities of their soul... (1651: 110).

In other words, to the Christians, Man was at the summit of creation. To the Hindus, it was not so. Where does this take us with respect to Spiro's definition? His definition cannot be useful to us unless we presuppose at least a diluted amount of Christian theology–gods are superhuman, which is why they are worshipped; humans are at the top of the hierarchy of life with animals well below them, and so on. This 'minimal' definition, which appears reasonable, merely expresses a linguistic and historical intuition of a Christian culture and is just another example of secularized theology.

In simple terms, this is what my alternate description claims: the disputes about definitions indicate that Christian theology continues to serve as a background theory. Without such an explanation, the scholarship on religion appears to be outrageously silly.

Switching Tracks

So, what are we to do if we want to acquire knowledge about religion? To begin meeting this challenge, certainly, we first need to specify what religion is. To do this would require defining religion, but as we've seen this hasn't been particularly productive. This does not mean to imply that the task of providing definitions is unimportant. Wherever possible, it is advisable to fix the reference of a term as clearly as we can. We've seen in the course of this chapter that the definitional issue has two aspects: a referential aspect and a classificatory one. The former provides knowledge about the object; once we have such knowledge, more often than not the classificatory problems disappear.

Because we are looking at the task of defining the concept of religion as a *referential* and not a *classificatory* issue, the best way of providing a reference to the word is to point to the entities that this word picks out. We can begin our investigation of religion by using the word 'religion' in an intuitive way, that is to say, in the way in which we would use the term in our daily discourse. By and large, our intuitive notion of religion generally picks out a variety of entities from Christianity through Shintoism. It is important to emphasize that by saying this we do not mean to classify Christianity or Shintoism, etc., as religions yet. This is merely to say that the word 'religion' intuitively picks out entities like Christianity and Shintoism.

One of the accepted procedures for defining a concept is by an ostensive gesture, i.e., we define a category by pointing to an example. A child acquires the category 'cat', for example, not by being taught that a cat is a furry, four-legged feline, but by pointing to a cat. An ostensive definition merely picks out an example. A question such as 'what is religion so that we may know what it is?' can get a satisfactory description to help fix the reference of the term without suggesting that fixing the reference is the same as providing knowledge of the phenomenon. The 'is' in 'what is religion' is a request for identification. The ostensive definition fixes the reference and provides identification. The 'is' in 'so that we may know what it is' is a request for acquiring knowledge about the object. We can begin acquiring knowledge once we fix the reference.

What would be a good example of the category 'religion' and which religion can we study in order to build our theories? To revert to the example of a mother teaching the category 'cat' to her child, the first problem would be about which animal to choose to fix the reference for the term 'cat'? The second problem would be which cat to pick–the grey one, the black one, or the one with the white streak?

So, what example of the category 'religion' can we pick? Voodoo? Football? The Association for the Advancement of Science? Our linguistic and other constraints help us answer this question. All of the above can be considered examples of religion only by reference to what we've already learned from a few other examples of the category 'religion'. That is, we've learned to include certain entities in this class, such as Judaism, Christianity, and Islam; Hinduism, Buddhism and Jainism. In other words, whether Football is a religion or not, as per our linguistic practice, Judaism and Jainism are. Even though, in principle, we can choose any object as an example of the category 'religion' it is advisable to pick out a more characteristic example of the term.

Now, we can use the same argument with respect to even this restricted group. Irrespective of whether Hinduism or Buddhism can be considered religions, Judaism, Christianity, and Islam are religions if 'religion' refers to anything at all. That is, we can say that religion is what Christianity, Islam, and Judaism are. These three entities are exemplary instances, i.e., prototypical examples of the category 'religion'. 'Prototypes' is a concept from cognitive psychology and cognitive linguistics which signifies individual instances of a term which are also seen as its best examples. The human ability of categorization can be explained on the grounds of precisely such typical examples. Most of our natural language categories are not defined in the way that mathematical sets are.

There are no clear criteria for set-memberships, and being a member of a set is not an all-or-none affair. These natural language categories allow for graded membership, and are uncertain in borderline cases. How, then, do we learn such categories, and use them with the ease that we do? One of the answers has to do with the notion of prototypical examples. We choose a very typical example and judge the membership of other instances in relation to such an example.

By fixing the reference of the term 'religion' in this way, no avenue or answer is shut out prior to an empirical enquiry. It doesn't rule out the possibility that there may be many other religions besides the above three that might be less prototypical than these exemplars. Equally, once we determine what religion is, we might end up saying that these three are not as prototypical as we thought they were. By the same token, it does not necessitate that there exist other forms and other kinds of religions either. All that this definition does is to help us begin our investigation with minimum prejudices.

It is important to emphasize that choosing Judaism, Christianity, and Islam as prototypes of the category 'religion', does not entail that there exist no significant differences between them. Some may object that these religions are not monolithic entities, but are themselves differentiated internally. Is a cosmopolitan Sunni as much of a Muslim as a radical one? How can we consider both a cardholder of the Likud party of Israel, and a thoroughly secularized individual, whose only title to being a Jew is that his mother was one, as members of the Jewish religion? What is common to both a Unitarian and a Catholic that makes them Christians? Which group shall exemplify these religions, and for what reasons?

To find out how genuine this difficulty is, and whether we can overcome it, it would be best to specify what precisely a problem of this type is. Consider, to begin with, three individuals: let's say that one of them attends Catholic mass every Sunday; the other is a member of the Unitarian church and participates in some activities (including dancing), and yet another refers to himself as a Baptist. Let's further grant that our Catholic believes that transubstantiation occurs during the mass; and even further assume that our Unitarian listens to political speeches only–which is why he goes to his church every Sunday; and that our Baptist believes that Jesus went to America. If religion is what Christianity is, our problem in this example is to specify what Christianity is so that we may know what makes these three into Christians.

In answering this question, it's important to bear in mind that we're trying to find out what makes something a 'religion' and not what makes something 'Christianity'. We are not studying the nature of Christianity but are only identifying it as an example of religion. Consequently, the internal question of Christianity, namely, "who is a 'true' Christian?" is not a problem that we need to solve. Determining which of these three individuals should be called 'Christian' and for what reason is an *internal question* of this tradition. Moreover, neither of these individuals have any doubt that they are Christians. They do not call themselves Jews, and you are not likely to mistake them for Lingayats either. In fact, each one of them represents a movement within Christianity and this is how we describe them when we write sociological and psychological tracts about these groups. At the outer boundary of their religious self-consciousness, internal theological dilemmas play no role. Each one of them is an instance of the term 'Christian'. They are that for both themselves and for us, and we are not confronted with a classificatory but a referential issue. 'Who is a Christian?' can be interpreted, as we've already seen, either as a request for identification or as a demand for classification. There is no problem of identification, whereas the problem of classification is internal to Christianity. There's no single theology that all Christians accept; hence, they dispute about classification internally. However, this is neither your problem nor mine. What is true for a Unitarian, a Catholic, and a Baptist can be generalized and thus the identification of Christianity, Judaism, and Islam as examples of the term 'religion' does not create referential problems.

There's yet another rationale for choosing these three religions as exemplary instances. Since we're investigating that which is designated by the term 'religion', if we were to pick entities from other cultures and languages where the term 'religion' itself does not exist, it would require taking an epistemic decision. We would have to provide a justification for the grounds on which we can claim that the entities in these other cultures are examples of the term as well. Such a decision is not justifiable at this stage because that's what we're setting out to investigate.

Now to answer the second question (which religion shall we pick?) we can say that whether Judaism and Islam are religions or not, at least the term picks out Christianity. That is, when we use the category 'religion', we minimally refer to Christianity. If someone refuses to recognize that Christianity is an example of the category 'religion', then he would have to deny that the concept 'religion' has any reference to any entity in the world at all. He would then be running counter to our linguistic practice because the word does have a reference. If Christianity is not an exemplary instance of religion, then we have no other examples of religion.

Once we accept that the term 'religion' refers to Christianity, the definitional task is completed because the referential problem is solved. From this stage on, our task consists of studying the entity that religion is and not studying the concept 'religion'.

It is at this stage that a temptation might rear its ugly head. It consists in the belief that we can answer the question about the existence or non-existence of religion in other cultures by simply looking at the properties of Christianity. We might think that because some properties characteristic of Christianity are absent from traditions elsewhere like, say, in Hinduism or Buddhism, the latter cannot possibly be religions. However, this position can only be justified if we're able to show that the properties of Christianity are also the properties of religion. In the absence of such an argument, all that we can do is notice that Christianity and some other tradition differ from each other. Therefore, unless we have established what religion is, and what properties make Christianity a religion, we would not be justified in seeking comparisons with Christianity to make claims about the existence of religion in other cultures.

From a Simple Answer to Complex Queries

What, then, is our concern when we take Christianity as a prototypical example of religion? Clearly, the concern is not to study the nature of Christianity, but to begin a study of religion. That is to say, to study Christianity as a religion so that we can make some headway in understanding the nature of religion. How can we go about studying religion, and not Christianity? What makes Christianity a religion?

In the process of secularizing itself, Christianity does not disappear. It continues to remain Christianity and continues to distinguish itself from other religions, *including the secularized variant of itself.* The question is where do the dynamics of this double movement of Christianity come from? Is it an intrinsic dynamic of Christianity to retain its own identity as a religion and simultaneously secularize itself as its 'other'? Is this what religion is? That is, does religion consist precisely in this double movement?

Christianity is both a religion and a de-Christianized religion. It is both an 'encounter with the sacred' and a 'profane' variant of itself. It is within religion that the 'sacred' (itself as a religion) and the 'profane' (its own secularization as the other) distinctions are drawn. Thus, to study religion requires studying both religion and its externalization of itself as the 'other' and to study this process as constituting the very motor of religion. Can we establish that this is what religion is? This is the challenge that needs to be met head-on.

CHAPTER IX

BLESSED ARE THOSE WHO SEEK

What is religion? We are now in a position to appreciate why attempts at defining the term have not been able to shed much light on the matter. Therefore, in the next step of our investigation we'll leave our concerns with both the word 'religion' and the associated concepts behind and embark on building a theory about the object that religion is.

Theory construction involves generating a hypothesis under certain constraints. The constraints we face in this case are twofold: historical and phenomenological. Any theory of religion must be consistent with the facts as seen from a historical perspective; further, the theory should be able to account for the various aspects of religion as they appear to those who are religious.

Religious Intolerance and What It Can Tell Us

Today it has become almost banal to observe that Christianity was an intolerant religion. Not many believers these days would support the way in which Christianity persecuted both heretics and heathens. Closely connected to its intolerance is the missionary activity of Christianity. Intolerance and proselytization were, of course, not the unique prerogatives of Christianity. Islam shares these properties too, as did Judaism in the early centuries during the Common Era. Whatever our moral standpoint on intolerance and conversion might be, these two attitudes contain a solution to the problem of understanding what religion is. In other words, these attitudes can help us in our quest to unearth the necessary characteristics of religion.

Christianity was intolerant of both heretics and heathens. It persecuted beliefs and practices that ran counter to those of its own. The fact that the Church persecuted at all indicates that Christianity saw certain others as its rivals. Rivals of what kind, though? Over the course of the centuries, the Christian Church has confronted several different kinds of rivals. The Catholic Church, for instance, was regularly embroiled in competing with the monarchy for political power. The same Church also fought both against authoritarianism and in favor of military dictatorships. Nevertheless, it did not regard either democracy or monarchy as competing religions. In other words, the church has met with several rivals during its history but has regarded only some of them as rival religions. The same applies to the mass of Christian believers: they fought the Roman *religiones*, the Jews and the Muslims, and the schismatic movement within Christianity as rival religions. They also fought for or against democracy, Fascism, etc., as rivals, but not as rival religions. Therefore, one way for us to begin studying the nature of religion is to identify those traditions which our prototypical religion saw as its competitors. Because Christianity saw itself as a religion, the manner in which it drew the battle lines between religions will tell us something about what Christianity thought religion was.

Historical Framework

Since Christianity refers to itself as a religion and recognizes itself as one, the terms in which it does so give us its concept of religion. This concept not only enabled Christianity to describe itself as a religion, but it also helped it in recognizing some of its rivals as religious rivals. Therefore, to study Christianity as a religion is to study those properties by virtue of which Christianity thinks of itself as a religion. This is the first step of the argument that merely allows us to establish the terms of description.

Judaism, Christianity and Islam are historical movements. Historically they have each seen the other as rival religions. Whatever goals they're competing for, they're doing so as religions. The second step of the argument establishes that the terms under which Christianity recognized itself as a religion are also the terms under which Islam and Judaism recognize themselves as religions (using whatever word they use). Therefore, the Christian concept is not just Christian. It cuts across the three

Semitic religions. It is not my concept or your concept, but self-descriptions of these religions. Consequently, what we have on our hands is the only reasonable concept of religion that does not presuppose what religion is. At the same time, it suggests that the concept 'religion' is itself part of a religious framework and vocabulary. This lends greater probability to the claim that whether or not Judaism and Islam use the word 'religion', they too are religions.

The third step of the argument picks out two important facts. First, the terms under which Christianity regarded Islam and Judaism as rival religions also make Judaism and Christianity rivals to Islam, and Islam and Christianity rivals to Judaism. Second, each of these three religions singled out other rivals under the same description elsewhere every time. Judaism had singled out the Roman *religio* as its rival before Christianity was even born. Centuries before the European Christians launched their massive evangelizing activities in India, Islam had picked out precisely those Indian traditions as its rivals that Christianity was later to identify.

The fourth step of the argument examines the pagan response to the Semitic religions. Roman *religio* and the Indian traditions did not recognize themselves in the description provided by the Semitic religions. Nor did they perceive religious rivalry between themselves and the latter. Roman *religio* found the Semitic terms of description incomprehensible. "How could only your religion be true and ours false?" they asked uncomprehendingly. The Indian traditions expressed an indifference to Christianity. "There are different roads to heaven", they said, shrugging their shoulders. Even under persecution, this tone did not change.

These four steps constitute the historical constraints under which we must generate our hypothesis about religion. On one hand, the hypothesis must capture the self-description of the Semitic religions; it must also show why 'Hinduism' or 'Shintoism' appear to be religions to them. On the other hand, the same hypothesis must also show why neither the Hindus nor the Romans recognized themselves as religions.

To sum up, we need to find out what Christianity's concept of religion is, and how is it possible to show that its concept is also that of Judaism and Islam. If we can generate a description of religion and show that Christianity, Judaism, and Islam recognize themselves in such a portrayal, then we've answered this question. That is to say, by developing a hypothesis about religion; by arguing that the presence of 'something' makes Christianity, Judaism and Islam religions; by showing that this hypothesis captures their self-descriptions we can argue backwards to their concept of religion.

We will then be in a position to answer the following questions: (a) how to account for the fact that these religions see religions everywhere they go; and (b) why neither the Roman *religio* nor the Indian traditions recognized themselves in the Semitic descriptions.

At this stage we have to accept the self-description of the Semitic traditions. Does the nature of religion entail that it must describe itself as one? This is a matter that requires investigation. If it turns out that a self-description as religion is a necessary property of religion this will imply that a science of religion can only be a theology.

Religion and Doctrine

The lines along which Christianity drew a distinction between religious rivals and rivals of other kinds was by isolating a set of beliefs and attacking these beliefs. It did this with the pagan *religio* and repeated the same feat more than a thousand years later with the heathens in India. How could Christianity possibly argue that the difference between religious communities resides in the different beliefs they hold? They could do so only by believing that human practices are embodiments of beliefs–a theme that Protestants made much use of.

To put it succinctly, the features by means of which the others were seen as rival religions by Christianity were the following:

(a)   To begin with, there was a rivalry with respect to doctrinal aspects. That is, the Christians noted differences in beliefs.

(b)   They believed that the difference between communities had to do with these doctrinal aspects.

(c)   They saw the practices of individuals as expressions of different religious beliefs because they believed that the actions of the faithful are embodiments of their beliefs.

(d)   Consequently, conversion from one religion to another meant a rejection of one set of beliefs and embracing another on the grounds of *truth and falsity*.

Christianity construed others as rival religions along these lines. Both Judaism and Islam also transformed other traditions into rivals along the same lines. These three religions did the same thing to each other and to traditions elsewhere.

The attitude of the others—both the Romans, and, much later, the Indians—was fundamentally different. Galen had compared the figure of Moses not with any priest but with Plato the philosopher. Lucian, the satirist from the second century, described Christianity as a philosophical school competing with the Stoics, Cynics, Skeptics, and such others. Christianity, on the other hand, did not consider philosophical schools as its rivals. Rather, it considered the several cults which flourished in Rome and elsewhere as its rivals. Judaism too had worked out a compromise with the Romans precisely with respect to Roman cultic ceremonies as these were in conflict with its religious observances. The Indian traditions were *indifferent* to the doctrines and practices of both Islam and Christianity. This indifference shows that the Indian traditions did not see either Christianity or Islam as its rivals.

Thus, we arrive at the first stage in the characterization of religion. It involves an emphasis on doctrines or beliefs, and it regards actions as embodiments of these beliefs. This is merely one aspect of the three Semitic religions that we can isolate purely on historical grounds. With respect to Judaism, even though it is widely held that practical observances are of greater importance than beliefs, this is only so when compared to Christianity and Islam. It may be true that beliefs are relatively secondary in Judaism. However, the presence of a doctrinal core is crucial to this religion. Such a core consists, for example, in beliefs that the Mosaic Law was handed down by God; that the anointed one will come to liberate the Jewish people; that the God of Abraham, Isaac, and Jacob is the true God, and so on. The importance of doctrines to Judaism is also evident from the fact that no Jew could accept the view that Jesus is the Messiah. By way of contrast, consider the fact that in India there would be little problem in accepting Jesus as an *avatar* much like any other *avatar*. Thus, the central point being made here is simply that a doctrinal core or belief system appears to be an important component of religion.

What kind of doctrine are we talking about? Doctrinal differences are seen to constitute religious distinctions if in one way or another they have to do with God and His relationship to humanity. In the struggle of the Semitic religions against the pagan or heathen 'religions', one of the doctrines in dispute involves the nature of the pagan gods. In their struggle against each other, the Semitic religions disagree about the revelation of God. We can empirically observe that these three prototypical religions dispute about God and that this issue distinguishes religions from each other. Thus, our quest also entails that we answer the following question: what makes some doctrines into religious doctrines? Any hypothesis about religion must shed light on three aspects: religious rivalry, importance of doctrine, and the necessity of God to religion. These are the preliminary constraints on generating a theory about religion. They tell us where to look, narrow down the search-space and hence are productive.

Reasons and Causes

As a starting point in building our hypothesis, it would be helpful if we looked at a problem that confronts the social sciences in their quest to gain knowledge about human beings. Something seems to be the matter with the social sciences. For some reason, a strange disquiet reigns in these disciplines. There is dissatisfaction that the rate of progress in acquiring knowledge about human beings is far too slow in proportion to the input. By contrast, the natural sciences have made phenomenal progress. In moments of honesty or perhaps despair, proponents from the fields of the social sciences admit to a feeling that, in fact, no progress is being made.

Many hypotheses try to account for this state of affairs. One of the sub-issues spawned by this debate concerns the relation between reasons and causes. The questions are these: what should the social sciences look for in their attempt to account for human behavior? Should they appeal to causes in explaining human behavior, or can they make human actions intelligible by appealing to reasons? For example, consider alcoholism. Can it be explained by causal factors such as genetically-based predispositions, or does it have to do with social or psychological factors that may indicate the reasons for it. In fact, the difference between the natural sciences and the social sciences has often been described along these lines. The natural sciences provide us with explanations by identifying causal laws; the social sciences render human actions (rationally) intelligible by appealing to the reasons (beliefs, desires, mental states etc.) for actions.

Perhaps a very simple example might help illustrate both the difficulty and the issue in this discussion. Consider a non-smoker who objects to others smoking in the room. Why does he object if others smoke in his presence? Let's look at the two kinds of accounts that answer this type of question (i) an explanatory account—one that explains the causes; and (ii) an intelligibility account—one that provides the reasons. We could make the reaction of the non-smoker *intelligible* by appealing to rationally justifiable beliefs held by him. Perhaps he believes that smoking is injurious to health; or he does not wish to indulge in passive smoking. Thus, we can understand his behavior by appealing to his belief-states (or intentional states). We look at this behavior as an intentional act. It is important to note that his actions are connected to his beliefs by principles of reasoning.

Now let's suppose that this non-smoker is not particularly concerned about passive smoking but the fact is that he cannot stand the smell of smoke. His behavior has nothing to do with his beliefs but rather can be explained by the *cause* that he is allergic to smoke. Thus, we have two kinds of accounts, an intelligibility account and an explanatory account, each of which focuses on different kinds of questions.

On one hand it appears impossible to speak of human actions without taking desires and beliefs into consideration. But if we do so, it reduces the predictive power or the problem-solving capacity of the accounts. This is because there's a knowledge gap between the actions we perform and our belief states. Even such a trivial action as opening a door cannot be said to be the result of a particular belief state. Perhaps I feel that the room is stuffy, perhaps I want to let the cat in, or perhaps I want to eavesdrop. Thus, intentions cannot be inferred by looking at actions. On the other hand, a search for the underlying causal laws governing human behavior has not yielded much fruit either. Such is the impasse in the social sciences.

Our Father, Who Art in Heaven

Now consider an account that promises to give us both. It offers a causal as well as an intelligible explanation rolled into one. This account claims that actions are intelligible, that is, they can be understood, because they express beliefs. It further suggests that the relationship between intending and acting is constant and that nothing interferes between the two. Normally, 'the world' happens to get in the way between our intentions and our actions. This account promises us that this isn't the case and that looking at actions is sufficient to draw inferences about the reasons for actions. There is only one condition: a complete and accurate description of the actions is required before we can know the reasons for the actions.

Now suppose we have a doctrine that says the following: A being exists, who is God. His actions are the universe (i.e., He is the cause of the universe). The reason for the universe is His will, or purpose. But we can never provide a complete description of the actions and purposes of such a being because we cannot possibly observe all His actions. This being has communicated His purposes to us, but our ability to understand His message is limited by the descriptive possibilities open to us. However we have two sources of knowledge: a set of actions that we can try to understand, and a message that we can try to make sense of. The set of actions is all of God's creation, i.e., the Cosmos. The message is His Revelation.

We now have on our hands what we can call a 'religious doctrine'. This doctrine makes the Cosmos an *explanatorily intelligible* entity, that is to say, it regards the Cosmos as being explainable and intelligible. It does so by a fusion of causes and reasons: God is the cause of the universe; He is also the reason for the universe. The universe is the will of God and expresses his purpose. In a deep and fundamental sense, to grow up within a religious tradition is to grow up with this experience where the Cosmos has an explanatory intelligibility. To have a religion is to have such an experience. Note well, this doctrine does not provide us with an account that actually explains the Cosmos or makes it intelligible. Rather, it merely affirms that the Cosmos is explanatorily intelligible. To better grasp this claim, it may help to contrast it with the Indian concept of *leela* which suggests quite the opposite–that it is futile to look for intelligibility in the events in the Cosmos.

Further, this religious doctrine not only claims that the Cosmos is an expression of God's purpose, but also that this religious account itself is an expression of God's purpose. Consider what religion does. First, it makes a truth claim by saying that the Cosmos is the expression of the purposes of God. Because this is what the world is, knowledge of the world must take the form of an account that is explanatory and can be made intelligible. That is to say, we would need to understand God's creation; and we would need to make sense of, or find intelligibility in, the purposes of God. The religious account claims such explanatory intelligibility in the world by bringing causes and reasons together in an extraordinary way. Because this is what it claims, the religious account too must exemplify the purposes of God. Thus religion makes both the Cosmos and itself explanatorily intelligible–it not only tells us why God made the world, but also why He gave religion to mankind.

This, then, is what makes an explanation a 'religious' explanation. It is an explanation of the universe, which *includes itself* as part of the explanation. God revealed His purposes by telling us about them. Religion need not prove the existence of God; the existence of religion is the proof for the existence of God. In this sense, religion is God's gift to humanity and not a human invention.

Let's draw upon the Bible to further illustrate this idea. As a being with goals and purposes, God brought forth the entire Cosmos for some purpose. What we human beings see are the phenomena; but underlying them, and expressed in them, is the will of God. The same God, the Good Book further tells us, has manifested His will to us in two ways: through the Revelation as captured in the scriptures, and in His products, i.e., Nature. We can study His works and through such a study learn about His will.

Now, as we know, it isn't possible to infer the reasons for an action by looking at the action. This being the case, how can we know God's will by studying His actions? The answer must be obvious.

God is perfectly good and perfectly consistent. His actions perfectly express His intentions. His will is not arbitrary, but perfectly constant. Because he is a Being who is perfectly trustworthy His works do not deceive us.

Consider, by contrast, the gods of the so-called religions like those of the Greeks, the Romans, or the Hindus. The only thing constant about these gods is their unpredictability. They constantly interfere in the affairs of human beings in ways that are both unpredictable and mysterious. By contrast, the Bible inculcates an experience of the Cosmos as a particular kind of order. This order consists of the fact that phenomena express a deep, underlying constancy. This constancy is the will of God that governs the world.

To accept this is to accept that everything in the universe has a purpose. Since our birth and death occur in the Cosmos, consequently these events have a purpose as well. To be part of a religion is to believe that human life and death (and everything in between) have significance, a meaning, and a purpose. A religious doctrine need not specify the purpose of any individual life or death; it is enough that it merely says that there is one. Consequently, to accept that life, including your life, has a meaning and purpose is to accept this doctrine. It means believing in the fact that your life itself can be explained and made intelligible. As an individual, you do not know what the purpose or meaning of your birth or death is. However, because you believe that they have a meaning and purpose, your actions appear to constitute the meaning of your life.

Clearly, the difference between religions will revolve around the specification of these purposes. What makes them into rival religions is their specific characterization of this explanatory intelligibility of human life and death (at a minimum). What makes them into religions is their affirmation that the Cosmos is such an entity.

This does not imply that any particular religion must have a specific statement to the effect that the Cosmos is an entity that can be explained and made intelligible. This is, nevertheless, the affirmation provided by religion. It makes the world explanatorily intelligible by structuring the experience of the world accordingly. That is to say, we view the world from within such a framework.

Order, Explanation, and Religion

Now we are in a better position to appreciate the insight of Hume and some of the other Enlightenment thinkers. They grasped the idea that religions are fundamentally explanatory in nature. Under this interpretation, the prototypical model of an explanatory framework is the phenomenon that we designate by the term 'religion'. It is not the case that religion explains this or that specific phenomenon. Nor is it the case that it is a class of explanations alongside which exist other classes of explanation like, say, the 'scientific' and 'philosophical' explanations. Rather, religion is the basic model of explanation. All other explanations, including scientific explanations, are inspired by and modeled after this explanatory model.

Religion and the Meaning of Life

One of the oft-heard claims about religion is that it helps human beings find meaning and purpose in their lives. Equally often heard are claims that suggest that one of the problems in the secularized societies of today is that people experience 'anomie' or 'alienation' by virtue of not being able to find such meaning; or by feeling that life is meaningless. This question about the 'meaning of life' is supposed to be *the* existential problem to which religion provides answers.

However, it is not always clear what this claim amounts to. Are the various religions so many different attempts to find solutions to the question of the meaning of one's life and death? Some would say no. Yet others would say yes. Gazzaniga, one of the founding fathers of cognitive neuroscience, speculates on the origin of religion by speaking about "the inevitability of religious beliefs". Based on the work of anthropologists, he considers religion to be universal in human societies. Assuming that it has something to do with the structure of the human brain, he invites us to:

> (c)onsider the world ten thousand years ago. Throughout the entire world there were at most only ten million people. Of these, half were under the age of ten and the oldest and wisest in the village was typically only thirty. There is no reason in the world not to think that this inference-capable human did not experience a dash of existential despair. "What," he might ask, feasting on roast gazelle, "does it all mean?" His dilemma

must have been grave. Everything this organism did had meaning. If he didn't get up and go hunt, he didn't eat. If he didn't build a hut, he was cold. If he didn't domesticate wild grain, his diet was boring. Finally he asked, "I know why I do all those things, but *why am I here?*"(1985: 169; emphasis added).

Some would find this 'explanation' of the origin of religion absurd for the simple reason that it is not clear that religion answers this question at all. What religions have done is to assert that life and death have a meaning and purpose. No religion has been able to answer a specific individual's 'existential question'.

In fact, if you talk to people who believe that they have found the meaning and purpose in life, you get the following reply as an explication of the said meaning of their lives: they describe what they are doing, and inform you that this description is the meaning of their lives. In other words, they merely assert that the meaning of life is the life that they are leading. Thus, for example, people may say that they pursue the arts, or use their skills to help the needy and this brings meaning to their lives. Even though what we have on our hands is a mere re-description of their actions, which we can observe for ourselves, this account makes it intelligible. As Davidson formulates it:

> (T)here is no denying that this is true: when we explain an action, by giving the reason, we do redescribe the action; redescribing the action gives the action a place in a pattern, and in this way the action is explained (in Davis, Ed., 1983: 64).

A re-description of an action by giving reasons for it appears to place the action in a pattern–thus making it intelligible. Neither you nor I is any the wiser for this re-description but we can see that it has the structure of an intelligibility account. They make their actions intelligible not merely by describing the pattern in their actions, but by re-describing the pattern they place it in a bigger pattern accessible to us. To those on the outside, the bigger pattern appears to be absent. But to those to whom their own lives appear meaningful, a pattern appears to be present. They feel that their lives are placed in a pattern and not merely that their lives have a pattern. Of course, they cannot tell us what this pattern is.

To put it in general terms, the answer to the question of the meaning of life cannot be sought by trying to answer this question. The problem lies elsewhere, namely, in the belief that enables the formulation of such a question in the first place. Why don't we come across such answers in any of the religious tracts if religion was really invented as an answer to such questions as 'Why am I born?', 'Where am I going?', 'What is the meaning or purpose of life?' and so on. Why, if religion was an answer to these questions, have religious figures (like Christ or Muhammad) kept silent about it?

The answer is simple. Religion does not answer these questions nor has it ever answered them. However, what it does is enable us to *raise* such questions because it is the only framework where such queries can be formulated. Religion was not invented to answer questions about the meaning and purpose of life. These questions come into being within the framework of religion. These problems do not antedate religion; they are generated by religion. Having done this, the religious framework tantalizingly hints that the problem is solvable. Take religion away and these questions will go away too.

Saying this does not mean to imply that life is either meaningless or that it is absurd. Even this answer is given within a framework which makes either meaning attribution or its denial sensible with respect to an individual or collective life. Rather, my claim is that the questions about the meaning of life are internal to religion. They are religious questions no matter what your answer is. They are not questions that a 'primitive' man raised 10,000 years ago. They are not the questions of the 'modern' man but those of a religious man–a *homo religiosus*. Religion claims that the world is intelligible, and promises to relate us intelligibly to the world, hence the search for meaning.

The Phenomenological Constraints

A good way to find out whether we are on the right track in investigating the phenomenon of religion is to see the extent to which we can accommodate some of the basic intuitions that believers and practitioners of religion have. The more this description approximates how religious practitioners have described and experienced religion, the closer we are to outlining the object of our study.

Let's begin with the following problem: is this characterization of the nature of religion too 'intellectual' or 'cognitive'? Can this account do justice to the experiential side as well? Is this characterization able to capture the phenomenological dimensions of faith, religious experience, and practice? These questions constitute some of the adequacy tests which this portrayal of religion must pass.

Earlier we observed that some of the philosophical schools in the Greco-Roman civilizations also disputed about the nature of the gods. However, Christianity did not consider these philosophical schools as competing religions. It considered only the various Roman cults as competing religions. Clearly something more is required before a dispute about God becomes 'religious'. This crucial component is the dimension of faith. To be religious is not merely an act of assenting to the proposition that 'God exists'. It requires seeing your life as a part of the purposes of God. In terms of this hypothesis, it means experiencing the world as an explanatorily intelligible entity.

The New Testament, for example, says:

> What doth it profit, my brethren, though a man say he hath faith, and have not works? Can faith save him?... Faith, if it has not works, is dead, being alone...Thou believest that there is one God; thou doest well: the devils also believe, and tremble (James 2: 14-26).

The Catholic Bishops of Belgium address this in similar terms, in a book directed towards their flock:

> Have you ever considered how our credo begins? Not with: I believe that something is true, that there is a God. It begins with: I believe in Someone, I believe in God. If you believe in someone, obviously, you also believe what he says. But believing in him is primary. Thus also with respect to God: No belief (the content) without believing (the attitude). (Geloofsboek, De Bisschoppen van België, Tielt: Lannoo, 1987: 12.)

This, then, is how Christianity has posed the issue of faith. It is not enough to merely assent to the existence of God but we must trust and believe in Him. The issue involves a tension between a knowledge-claim (the belief about God's existence), and a relation (personal, emotional, attitudinal) between a person and God. The nature of this tension has two dimensions: one involves individuals within a religious tradition, and the other oriented towards those outside of it.

The Two Dimensions of Faith

The first dimension points to the distance separating one individual from another, both of whom belong to the same religious tradition. For example, it could take the form of an exhortation that, say, Christians ought to have faith in God and that it is not sufficient for their salvation to merely believe in the proposition 'God exists'. Consequently, the problem of faith to a Christian, or a Muslim, or a Jew takes the form of understanding how to be a devout practitioner of their religion.

By contrast, the second dimension of faith is relevant at the outer boundaries of contact between two traditions. Depending upon the kind of tradition we're talking about, the problem may take several forms. A deeply devout Christian may look at a Jew and a Muslim and feel that even though all three of them worship God, the other two are deficient in their worship. Whether or not this Christian would characterize this religious difference in terms of 'degrees of faith', he would have no hesitation in using the idea of an 'absence of faith' when describing an unrepentant pagan like me. This is because at the point of contact between two traditions–say Christian and Jewish; or Christian and pagan–the problem of faith takes the form of the question of *truth*. For instance, why would Jews or pagans not accept the Christian doctrines? It's because faith in Jesus depends upon the truth of the claim that Jesus is The Savior.

Isolating the question of faith along these two dimensions does not mean to suggest that these dimensions are independent of each other, and that answers to one question are irrelevant to the other. We can appreciate the nature of their mutual dependence properly only when we appreciate the difference between these two dimensions. Therefore, let's begin with the issue of faith within a religious tradition.

Consider, for instance, a baptized, church-going Catholic. He attends Mass regularly and participates in most activities organized by his parish priest. Despite this, his fellow-Christians suspect that he is not 'truly' religious and merely acts as though he is. His actions appear mechanical, his assent to doctrines formal, and he does not appear to be guided by the state of mind that the believers call 'faith'. As a result, this individual's fellow-Congregationalists suspect that he does not 'really believe'.

The tension between the acts of this Christian and his state of mind arises not because there's some mysterious, additional something called faith which only the 'truly' religious have, but because of the nature of religion itself. Religion does not merely explain the origin of the Cosmos or of human life by postulating God as the cause. It also makes the world intelligible by making the will of God the cause of the universe in such a way that the world expresses His purposes. One cannot possibly accept that everything–including one's own life–has a purpose, which is God's purpose, and still be without faith in Him. Faith consists precisely in accepting His purpose. To accept such an account as true is to have faith in Him.

In the case at hand, this is how we can make sense of this particular Christian. Indeed, he does not 'truly believe'. Maximally, he perhaps believes that God created the universe (he sees God as the cause) and, in believing this, grasps religion as an explanatory account. However, he does not see that it is also an intelligibility account. Simply believing that God exists and that He created the universe does not make a person religious. It's only when a binding link between the cause of the world and the will of God is postulated that an explanatorily intelligible account comes into being. This is what makes something religious.

Why does this Christian not see the intelligibility in the religious account? Better put, what is involved in seeing it also as an intelligibility account? We need to appreciate the relation between reasons and actions. Our Christian is willing to accept the statement that God is the cause of the universe, but he is unable to see that this cause is God's purpose. That is to say, he does not see that God is a person. To him, God has become a vague entity, an abstract conception, some kind of a primordial power. His God, if you like, is not Allah, the Holy Trinity, or Jehovah. It is the de-Christianized God, the truly 'universal' God, the God who progressively loses His form as He is generalized to include and incorporate all the 'manifestations of the divine' across all cultures and at all times. His God is the answer to the Christological dilemma. This person is a truly tolerant Christian, one who is willing to concede that all religions are equally true. The price he pays for this admission is in direct proportion: he ceases being a Christian. He does not believe in God as a personal entity, as someone whose purposes are expressed in the Cosmos. In short, he does not 'believe'. To him, God has become a variable capable of different interpretations, all of which are equally true.

Does this suggest that intolerance and Christianity are necessarily related to each other? The answer is both a 'yes' and a 'no'. The 'yes' is evident, but the 'no' is more important. Intolerance is not a necessary property of Christianity but one that accrues to it by virtue of being a religion. That is to say, one cannot be 'religious' without being intolerant of those who are not. Faith and intolerance are two faces of the same coin. You cannot have one without the other. The historical record makes evident that the best exemplars of faith in each of these three traditions, depending upon the milieu they lived in, have also been the most intolerant regarding other traditions. What we need to demonstrate is how the nature of religion necessitates intolerance.

To have faith in God is to accept His purpose. Because the entire Cosmos and all human beings exemplify His purpose, the commitment of any one individual or group does not suffice as an exemplification of God's purpose. Considering the type of account that religion is, it can only be universal and unrestricted by space, time, or culture. The three exemplary religions we are looking at specify these purposes differently. Not merely in the sense that God will send the faithless to Hell and the faithful to Heaven, but the likelihood of finding yourself in either of these two places depends upon your getting His purposes right. You do not get that purpose right just because your name happens to be Bernstein, Thomas, or Abdullah but because you are a human being. Your choice is the right one because it is the only right choice for human beings. In other words, it is simply not possible to have faith in God and at the same time claim that all religions are equally true, and that each religion is a 'manifestation of the divine'. In this sense, intolerance of others arises because of the acceptance of God's purposes for mankind, i.e., because of faith in Him.

Intolerance, then, is necessary to being a religious person. This does not mean that intolerance needs to express itself in persecution, even though it has often done so. The relation between intolerance on one hand and persecution on the other is mediated by many different circumstances, including power. In this sense, intolerance does not entail that each believer must either be a missionary or a persecutor. However, it does entail that there's no question of accepting other religious views as equally true. Jesus or Muhammad might have spoken to those around them out of infinite love and compassion for humanity but that does not suggest that they were tolerant of other faiths. A believer who believes in the truth of his doctrine and thus in God cannot be a tolerant person with respect to religion. Religious tolerance is either a grotesque hypocrisy or an expression of an absence of faith.

Perhaps this is a good place to make a related point. The resurgence of Islam in the Arab world is often described as the growth of fanaticism and fundamentalism. Shaking their heads sadly, western commentators note that the Arab world has yet to undergo its 'enlightenment' and learn 'religious pluralism'. There's an exquisite irony to this situation when we see religious figures from the Catholic Church proclaiming this idea precisely when they're busy seeking a "second evangelization" of the West. The irony must be evident: you can have 'religious pluralism' only when you've lost faith and do not believe. The ferocious attack against Muslims, when launched by the Church functionaries, boils down to this feeling: Muslims have faith and we do not. How dare they believe, when we don't do so anymore? It could be true that an 'enlightened' person doesn't have faith in God, but this has nothing to do with religious pluralism.

Thus, the fact that Christianity, Islam, and Judaism competed with each other as religions does not merely appear as a contingent property that these three religions share. It is a necessary property of a religious account. To understand even better why this is so, we need to examine the second dimension of faith–the philosophical or theological aspect of faith.

The controversy, briefly formulated, involves the relationship between faith and reason. As these religions put it, human salvation depends upon accepting some doctrines as true. However, the evidence for accepting these doctrines as true is, at best, inconclusive. These doctrines include such things as the Covenant God made with the people of Israel, or the resurrection of Jesus Christ, or God speaking through Muhammad. These religions make it praiseworthy to hold on to these beliefs in spite of the absence of justifying evidence. At the same time, many feel that holding on to a belief when there's a lack of evidence for it is a kind of self-deception.

Extremely ingenious attempts have been made over the centuries to reconcile the issues of faith and reason. The strategies chosen have been wide and varied. At one end of the spectrum, there are attempts to show that these doctrines are very reasonable. Some suggest that certain beliefs are "properly basic", which do not require further justification and that the existence of God is one such. At the other end of the spectrum, there are the early Christian figures who make it emphatically clear that Christianity is to be "believed because it is absurd", and that Christ was "buried and rose again; the fact is certain because it is impossible". None of them is saying that the absurdity of a claim is evidence for its truth or that one ought to believe in something because it is absurd. Rather, their point is that it is not a proper question to ask of faith that it be justified on grounds of evidence. Faith is not a matter of facts; it involves something quite different altogether.

The question of truth remains unsettled and continues to cause problems for religion. With human beings, everything we believe as true of the world depends on other things we know about the world. Religion, by contrast, claims to be the truth about the world while being radically independent of any of our other beliefs about the world. Whatever else we may hold to be true, the message of a religion is not affected since God reveals himself to aid us in seeing the truth. This truth does not depend upon human knowledge and what we at any given moment believe to be true.

What we have on our hands, then, is an account that has no other parallels in the domain of human knowledge. Religion alone is both an explanatory and an intelligibility account not of this or that individual phenomenon, but of the entire Cosmos and of itself. Correspondingly, the question of truth takes a radical form. The problem is not whether religion is true the way our beliefs about Brussels or Paris are true. The truth about these cities depends on many of our other beliefs being true as well. This is not the case with religion at all. Religion is the truth in the specific sense of not being dependent on the truth of any other belief we hold about the world.

We can now appreciate why the problem of faith becomes a question of truth. Firstly, it is because we have to believe that we have a true explanatorily intelligible account. Secondly, we have to accept the truth of this account on its own say-so. The very existence of this account is the proof of its truth. In no other sphere of human thought would we possibly countenance such a move. Nevertheless, we need to do precisely this in the case of religion because its yardstick is not human.

Because what we believe to be true (possible) or false (impossible) depends upon other beliefs that we hold about the world, what appears 'impossible' given one set of beliefs might turn out to be commonplace given a different set of beliefs. To Tertullian and other believers, the resurrection of Jesus might appear 'impossible'. How would it have appeared in India two thousand years ago, if Jesus died there and was resurrected subsequently? Let a European scholar report a discussion he had with a citizen of twentieth-century India:

> A Tantric scholar, a man of shrewd intelligence and wide-ranging knowledge, made the following observations on the passion and resurrection of Christ. He explained the first by the evident fact that Christ, like many ascetics, has obtained siddhi (instanced both in his 'knowledge' and in his miracles), in consequence of which he suffered no pain on the Cross; and the second as a *typical example* of the burial and later disinterment of an ascetic in meditative trance, *a phenomenon of common occurrence throughout the subcontinent.* (Piatigorsky 1985: 211; emphasis added).

Note the italicized portion well. Holding a belief about the resurrection of Jesus is not absurd in the Indian context because such beliefs are related to a whole host of other beliefs in the Indian traditions. The same cannot be said within the European context where belief in the resurrection must be taken on faith alone.

By noting this relation between faith and truth we can better understand why religion is an intolerant account. Its truth is divinely inspired, not human at all. To acknowledge other claims as true in the same sense in which religion is true is to acknowledge the falsity of religion. Further, we can also understand why doctrinal content is so important to religion. We have to accept the doctrinal account of the Cosmos as the truth. Some vague notion of God is no substitute for it.

On Religious Experience

This characterization of religion also enables us to come to grips with authors like Schleiermacher and Otto who speak of religious experience. As we've seen, both argue that having a religious experience presupposes that one belong to a religion. To accept a religious account is to feel as part of the purposes of God and depend on His being. Without accepting such an account, there is no possibility of experiencing the 'absolute dependency' that Schleiermacher talks about; at best, a kind of relative dependency upon each other is all we can experience. To have the experience that Schleiermacher talks about, we need to attribute explanatory intelligibility to the Cosmos and accept such an account.

That is to say, we cannot substitute the idea of 'world' or 'Cosmos' for God and generate an atheistic religiosity. A person might feel "one with the Cosmos" or feel "totally dependent" on all objects that exist. Despite this, we cannot call such an experience 'religious' (whether atheistic or not) for at least two reasons. The first has to do with the nature of dependency. Maximally, in the best of cases, a person might feel as a part of the Cosmos. Let's grant this with goodwill, even though it's difficult to imagine anyone feeling dependent on, or being one with, objects in another galaxy. The second reason is even weightier and relates to a distortion of the linguistic meaning of concepts, and an inability (or unwillingness) to pay heed to what religious figures say. When we speak of 'the world' or 'the Cosmos', what do we refer to? Consider David Lewis' answer to this question:

> The world we live in is a very inclusive thing. Every stick and stone you have ever seen is part of it. And so are you and I. And so are the planet earth, the solar system, the entire Milky Way, the remote galaxies that we see through telescopes and (if there are such things) all the bits of empty space between the stars and galaxies. There is nothing so far away from us as not to be part of our world. Anything at any distance at all is to be included. Likewise the world is inclusive in time. No long-gone ancient Romans, no long-gone pterodactyls, no long-gone primordial clouds of plasma are too far in the past, nor are the dead dark stars too far in the future, to be part of this same world. May be, as I myself think, the world is a big physical object; or may be some parts of it are entelechies or spirits or auras or deities or other things unknown to physics. But nothing is so alien in kind as not to be part of our world, provided that it does exist at some distance and direction from here, or at some time before or after or simultaneous with now. (1986: 1).

The actual world embraces the universe as a whole. An atheistic religiosity that would like to describe itself as a feeling of dependency or oneness with the world must be able to account for feeling dependent on, or one with, all that was, is, and will be. With a generosity that breaks the limits of imagination we can conceive of a person feeling dependent on the past that includes the primordial cloud of plasma and the present that includes spirits if they exist. How to conceive of a similar feeling of oneness with respect to what does not as yet exist?

Controversies Illumined

This hypothesis, thus, captures both inter-religious disputes and the relation between intolerance and faith. It also sheds light on yet another dispute. Very often believers make the claim that you cannot investigate the nature of religion unless you are a believer yourself. Brilliant and reputed thinkers have argued for this point of view. Their opponents accuse such people of bad faith or dogmatism, contending that any phenomenon can be scientifically studied, including religion.

But can we study religion scientifically? The scientifically-oriented may claim that one does not have to be a stone to describe its fall, any more than one has to be neurotic to discuss the nature of neurosis. Therefore, why should one have to be religious to investigate religion scientifically? The point to consider is this. A person can judge the adequacy of one religion against another only from within the framework of a religion. That is, you have to accept some or the other account of the Cosmos as provided by religion itself. Consequently, religion can be investigated only by being religious. This point stands to reason because religion is a reflexive entity–it refers to itself or includes itself as part of the religious account. Consider the claim that the Bible is the word of God. How do we know this? We know this because the Bible says so. If you do not accept this account and embark upon a study of the Bible not as a religious text but as a piece of literature, the object of your study is no longer religion but literature. Thus, the believers are not being dogmatic when they say, as Söderblom did, that the only science of religion can be theology.

This does not mean to imply that any specific doctrine within a specific religion–say, for example, the doctrine of trinity–is either immune to criticism or beyond discussion. After all, there are many believers who criticize this doctrine. But, as noted earlier, we are not interested in finding out what makes some tradition into Christianity, but rather are seeking to find out what makes Christianity into a religion. As a non-believer, I cannot say what makes this account an explanatorily intelligible account of the Cosmos; why it is this only to some and not to the others; or what its intelligibility consists of. These issues require investigation. To be sure, we can ask the believers to explain themselves. In such a case, we study what it means 'to believe' for these people. If we understand their answers to the 'meaning' of the Cosmos and life we will have some idea about what it means to be religious.

"The Heathen in his Blindness…"

A hasty reader of this chapter might say that my story about religion is trapped within the Semitic framework; as a result, nothing is easier than to argue the absence of religion elsewhere. The point to consider is this. According to the Semitic religions, 'Hinduism', 'Buddhism', etc., are also religions (whether false ones or not). In other words, according to the Christian concept of religion, Indians also have religion. The hypothesis under development, then, has to account for two facts: first, why is it that the Semitic religions identified religions elsewhere; second, why is it that the pagans and the heathens reacted in total incomprehension. If it can be shown how both these facts are necessary, then the charge that this account is imprisoned by western monotheisms loses its credibility.

In the historical chapters constituting this work, we noticed that Christianity failed to understand the pagan traditions it encountered. Let's take a look at the reverse side to this. Did the heathen and pagan traditions understand Christianity? Examining this question will enable us to shed light on the vital theme of the mechanism of the domestication of the pagans.

Students of Antiquity are very familiar with the Response of Quintus Aurelius Symmachus, the last pagan prefect of Rome. This document dates back to the fourth century and is often seen as an example of an early plea for religious tolerance. There is, however, another interpretation which is more in line with my story. Symmachus is not pleading for religious tolerance. In fact, his plea at the end of his Response tells us that he does not understand religion at all. Let's listen to him again:

> Grant, I beg you, that what in our youth we took over from our fathers, we may in our old age hand on to posterity. The love of established practice is a powerful sentiment... *Everyone has his own customs, his own religious practices; the divine mind has assigned to different cities different religions to be their guardians.* Each man is given at birth a separate soul; in the same way each people is given its own special genius to take care of its destiny... If long passage of time lends validity to religious observances, we ought to keep faith with so many centuries, we ought to follow our forefathers who followed their forefathers and were blessed in so doing... And so we ask for peace for the gods of our fathers, for the gods of our native land. It is reasonable that whatever each of us worships is really to be considered one and the same. We gaze up at the same stars, the sky covers us all, the same universe compasses us. *What does it matter what practical system we adopt in our search for truth? Not by one avenue only can we arrive at so tremendous a secret.* (Barrow, Trans., 1973: 37-41; emphasis added).

If we place the last two lines in context, the drift of his argument is clear. To him, *religio* is a human search for truth. It is a human product, an expression of human striving, and a practical system. It is *tradition*–the ways, customs, habits and ceremonies as developed by a people. Just as there are different people, so are there different traditions. Hence, there cannot be only one avenue for arriving at a tremendous secret. Multiplicity of traditions indicates that *religio* is a creation of human communities (ancestral practices) to be venerated because of their antiquity. As an individual who is part of a community, you continue the practice of your forefathers. However, because of the very reason that it is a human practice, you can always ask: what does it matter what practical system human beings adopt in their search for truth?

By speaking of 'divine assignment', Symmachus appears willing to grant the following: Christianity is the practice of a people. That is, he is prepared to accept that Christianity is also a tradition. However, if Christianity is also a tradition, he cannot understand why the Christians continue to deny others their tradition. Symmachus is caught in this quandary. He is unable to see the gulf separating the two: *religio* as the tradition of a people and religion as God's gift to humanity. By classifying Christianity as another practical system, as one more expression of the human striving for truth, Symmachus is doubly blind. He is blind to the claim that religion is the truth as revealed by God; and he is blind to the existence of religion as an explanatorily intelligible account. He does not see religion as the 'true' explanation underlying God's creation or the meaning and purpose it conveys.

How could the last pagan prefect of Rome, evidently an intellect of no mean standing, not understand what every Christian writer had been saying for nearly three centuries? A random citation from the period of the Apostolic Fathers should give the reader a flavor of *how* the Christians were describing their own religion. In *The Epistle to Diognetus*, thought to have been composed about 124 C.E., in "reply to an inquiring heathen's desire for information about the beliefs and customs of Christians", an anonymous writer explains thus:

> The doctrines they (the Christians) profess is not the invention of busy human minds and brains, nor are they, like some, adherents of this or that school of human thought…

As I said before, it is not an earthly discovery that has been entrusted to them. The thing they guard so jealously is no product of mortal thinking, and what has been committed to them is the stewardship of no human mysteries. The Almighty Himself, the Creator of the universe, the God whom no eye can discern, has sent down His very own Truth from heaven, His own holy and incomprehensible Word, to plant it among men and ground it in their hearts... (Translated by Staniforth 176-178).

Symmachus might have been paying Christianity the greatest tribute that his culture possibly could in recognizing that Christians too had their own practical system. To Christian ears any such pagan tribute would have sounded like blasphemy.

Nearly 1,400 years later, in another place and by another people, a similar tribute was paid. The Brahmins of the coastal town of Malabar assured a Lutheran missionary during the early eighteenth century,

For as Christ in Europe was made Man, so here our God Wischtnu was born among the Malabarians; and as you hope for Salvation through Christ; so we hope for Salvation through Wischtnu; and to save you one way, and us another, is one of the Pastimes and Diversions of Almighty God (*Ziegenbalg Papers*, excerpted in Young 1981: 23).

The heathen, as a famous hymn tells us, is blind. Blind to what? To *the truth*, of course. Not merely are they blind to the truth, as revealed by the scriptures and as announced by the coming of The Savior, but to its very existence. If the Christians did not understand the pagans, the pagans too did not understand the Christians. What you can see in my hypothesis about religion is why people like Symmachus had to be blind and talk the way they did.

As shown earlier, religion is a reflexive entity, that is, its truth rests on its own foundation. It is what it says about itself, and what it says about itself is the truth. As such, it is accessible only to those who are a part of such an account. Heathens and pagans cannot testify to the truth of religion because this truth is not accessible to those outside it. It's in the very nature of religion that those who do not have it are blind to its existence.

Because heathens are blind to the existence of religion, it is obvious how they treat it: as merely one of many avenues to a 'tremendous secret'; as another tradition–just as acceptable as any other system in the search of truth. Both the Indians and the Romans were blind to religion, because they knew of no such phenomenon. Knowing only human certainties, how could they recognize an account that made both the Cosmos and itself explanatorily intelligible? Possessing only human knowledge, how could they recognize the divine truth? Knowing only of human striving, how could they grasp God's gift to humanity?

Nevertheless, religion has a way of getting through to those who are blind to it. If it didn't, it could not spread at all. It has spread and continues to spread. The empirical circumstances of conversion do not concern us. We need to identify the mechanism of conversion as it is relevant to our story.

Blind to the divine truth, the heathen knows only of human certainties. His certainties regarding his tradition reflect the character of traditions as such–customs handed down with their origins lost in time; folklore, legends, and myths. An individual located in a tradition is always fallible. There is no cognitive certainty that he is continuing the tradition in the proper manner. When confronted with 'the true' religion these uncertainties are amplified. The imperfections of tradition are highlighted since there is no guarantee that it has been accurately passed down from generation to generation. The collection of accumulated stories and legends are contradictory and conflicting. The 'true religion' plays upon the very nature of tradition with the result that it ultimately succeeds in *erasing its otherness* as tradition.

In which way is tradition the other of religion? The predicates 'true' and 'false' are inapplicable to a tradition because it is a set of practices. Religion transforms the very terms of description by characterizing tradition as a belief-guided and theoretically founded set of practices. Practical certainties are provided with something they never had or ever needed–a theoretical foundation. The very same stories and legends that surrounded the collective practices of a tradition are now seen to form a theoretical basis for the tradition. The predicates 'true' and 'false' begin to become applicable. Practices that were carried on simply because they were handed down from generation to generation are now seen as requiring reason, justification, meaning and purpose.

The otherness of the tradition is effectively wiped out by transforming it into another. Another what? Another religion, of course. When transformed into another religion, this tradition (which is both uncertain and fallible) acquires a property it never had before: reflexivity. That is to say, it begins to refer to itself in search of a 'deeper' foundation. The inconsistent myths and legends, or the practices that have been preserved from times immemorial, are seen to express a deeper truth. Religion forces tradition to recognize that it had hitherto entertained false beliefs. To be aware of this fact is to recognize in it a thirst for the 'truth'. The fallibilities of the transformed tradition are seen as a testament not only to its falsity but also to the awareness of its own falsity. In short, what was incomprehensible to the heathens before–the idea that they have a false religion–now begins to make sense. In the subsequent phase in the mechanism of conversion, not only is one's own tradition made to appear false, but also those of others.

These are the abstract, logical moments of the mechanism of conversion. This is also how Christianity grew: by absorbing the Roman cultic deities and transforming them into demons (as minions of the Devil), by disputing the "absurd tales of the poets", or by developing its theology. In simple terms, the basic mechanism in the spread of religion works by erasing the otherness of the other. The other is transformed into an image of itself, i.e., into a religion. There is no 'other' to religion–there is merely another religion.

Erasing the otherness is possible if, and only if, there's a framework which does not allow an otherness. A universal human history is this framework. Having transformed the real or imaginary past of a people (the Jews) into the universal history of mankind, Christianity developed its own theology that enabled the transformation of the other into another of itself. The theology of Christian faith began to take shape in its polemics with the heathens because of the mutually reinforcing relationship between the creation of a universal history and the transforming of the other into another.

This is how the heathens and the pagans–peoples without religion–are incorporated into theology. Religion is invisible to the pagan as long as otherness is a practical certainty. It is a practical certainty as long as he remains within the folds of a tradition. When he enters the process of 'conversion'–whose cognitive steps are described above–the otherness of traditions becomes a kind of 'anotherness'. When this happens, the scales fall from his eyes. He is now a member of a religion.

The otherness of traditions thus disappears within the framework of the reflexive entity that religion is. Being the word of God, religion is convinced of its certainty. It is convinced that God gave religion to all human beings. There can be no 'other'. Having no other, religion merely postulates other religions. It is impossible to think that India does not have religion; it merely has another religion. It is impossible that pagans do not worship; the "heathen in his blindness", as bishop Reginald Heber's hymn says, "bows down to wood and stone..."

Worship and Idolatry

Imagine the image of a woman kneeling before the cross or a statue of the Virgin Mary in an attitude of supplication. This is a classic example of religious practice if ever there was one. Why have religions emphasized the worship of God so much and, equally importantly, decried idolatry? Why does faith in God express itself in worship? Is this a necessary property of religion or merely a contingent one? This is one of the phenomenological adequacy tests which this hypothesis has to pass. On one hand, faith must express itself in worship. On the other, worship is a gesture made to false gods.

Religion does not exist in a vacuum, but is a part of *human* communities. Given the kind of beings we are, religion on earth will acquire certain contingent properties. That is to say, the conditions for the existence of religion will depend upon our nature as human beings. In principle, a religion could exist even if it lacked prophets, churches, belief in God, or holy books. However, because religion 'explains' and 'makes intelligible' the Cosmos, there are some anthropological constraints that must be taken into consideration. These conditions relate to the nature of human beings, their modes of learning, their mechanisms of transmission, etc. It isn't as if we could just remove the word 'God' and generate an 'atheistically religious' account. We must be able to specify the conditions for the growth and transmission of such an account. This adds force to the argument I made earlier that we cannot say much about religion merely by looking at the properties of the Semitic religions, unless we can also show that these properties accrue to them by virtue of being religions.

The points to consider are who provides the religious account and to whom it is provided. The religious account offers intelligibility, and, as human beings, if we want to make something intelligible we look for reasons or purposes. The religious account claims that both the Cosmos, and religion itself, embody the reasons or purposes of God. It further claims that God himself has handed down this account to humans, who are capable of acting according to His reasons and purposes. In this sense, the first contingent property that religion acquires amidst human beings is the existence of God.

The second contingent property that religion acquires is that it makes a claim about the beings to whom such an account is provided. It claims that human beings fulfill some or the other purpose handed down by God. It must be possible for them to achieve that purpose otherwise there would be no intelligibility to the account. This message also tells these beings what that purpose is: it is accepting God's purpose. This means that they must seek and achieve the purpose that God has given to mankind. God's purposes are not exhausted by the act of any particular individual or community at some place or time. Hence, an eschatology or a goal for humanity as a whole is part of such a message.

In the above sense, religion postulates a relation between human beings and God's will. Human beings are there for a purpose; their nature is such that they can achieve that purpose. Accepting the purpose of God lends intelligibility to human life because human beings can find meaning to their lives by trying to achieve that goal. Thus, the third contingent property of religion is that it must postulate a relation between God and human beings.

Not merely must religion speak of God's purposes, why human beings are here, and what their goal is, but also how this goal can be achieved. This, then, is the fourth contingent property of religion. As an account that makes the Cosmos explainable and intelligible, religion must specify the means through which the Cosmos continues to be explainable and intelligible. Such means must itself be part of that account. Worship, is the means through which an explanatorily intelligible account continues to retain its character to the believers. Worship sustains and expresses faith. True worship requires and strengthens faith. Without faith, one cannot truly worship. In worship, man expresses his faith in God; that is, affirms that he is using the means required to be a part of the purposes of God.

Thus, we can also appreciate why doctrine is a crucial component of religion and why it is not that at the same time. It is a property that religion acquires by virtue of the fact that it exists among human beings. This is the fifth contingent property that religion acquires. Because the means through which God's purposes can be achieved are themselves rooted in doctrines, this hypothesis captures the attempt of the believers to find scriptural grounds for worship. As Samuel Clarke expounds in *A Discourse Concerning the Being and Attributes of GOD, The Obligations of Natural Religion, and the Truth and Certainty of the Christian Revelation*:

> In *what particular Manner,* and with *what kind of Service* he [God] will be worshipped, cannot be certainly discovered by bare reason...*what Propitiation* he will accept, and *in what Manner* this reconciliation must be made; here Nature stops, and expects with impatience the aid of some particular Revelation. The God will receive returning Sinners, and accept Repentance instead of perfect Obedience. *They* cannot *certainly know*, to whom he had not declared that he *will* do so. (Excerpted in Pailin 1984: 175-76; emphasis in original).

The concrete specification of the purposes of God, and consequently, the means for fulfilling the purposes of God, depends on the doctrine in question. Each religious account defines that for itself.

Thus we can see why worship is a concept internal to religious life and religious doctrine. Worship involves seeing the Cosmos as part of God's reasons and purposes and doing what is required in order to continue to experience the Cosmos in this way. It is the means for the reproduction of religion. At the same time, worship appears as an attitude and a feeling: an expression of trust. One who worships is being religious within a tradition, carrying out the act, as his religion requires it. If we now return to the image of the woman kneeling in an act of worship, we can see how she is affirming the relationship between herself and God by using the means provided by her religion.

The Sin of Idolatry

Worship, of course, means worship of the true God. Do those who worship false gods really worship? We've seen how religion effaces the otherness of tradition by transforming it into another religion, albeit a false one. Such a religion,

> ...finds the devil or its own concept of God, ruled by the devil. So there is a vast difference between knowing that there is a God and knowing who or what God is. (*Luther's Works* 19, 55; cited in Harrison 1990: 8 and note 13 to that page.)

This pseudo-mechanism for the reproduction of religion is attributed to false religions. Needless to say, Devil worship was condemned as idolatry. In the early periods, it connoted false worship, or the worship of a false god. However, as Christianity expanded, so did the concept. It now incorporated many things including the worship of animals and images.

In a way, the last sentence is preposterous. Despite what is written about other people, it's always difficult to write off entire cultures as stupid. I mean, which Indian worships (as the notion of worship has just been explained) the cow? Which pagan ever worshipped images? How did he ever 'bow down to wood and stone'? Anthropology had to wait until the beginning of the twentieth century to realize that:

> no people worshipped material objects simply as material objects; that animals, plants, and inanimate objects were simply symbols. Thus Taylor initiated a symbolic approach...to magico-religious phenomena. (Morris 1987: 102).

Exaggeration or not, this demonstrates the problem that has been tackled at length throughout this book. 'God', 'worship', 'prayer', 'eschatology', etc., are concepts internal to religion. Use them and you're forced to do theology because you're forced to accept that the heathen worships cows, monkeys, serpents, tractors, bicycles, books, and images. In today's politically correct climate, it is no longer possible to sing Bishop Heber's hymn openly in church. Thus, a symbolic approach seems necessary to explain as worship an act that is not worship at all. We could almost rewrite the history of Christianity, Judaism, and Islam in terms of their hatred of idolatry. Given their theology, such an attitude is perfectly understandable.

A Summary

This portrayal captures the self-description not only of Christianity but also that of Judaism and Islam. What makes them religions also divides them, and this dispute is *unsolvable*. Each is a specific religion, that is, each is an explanatorily intelligible account. To those who accept this account the experience of the world is structured by this framework. An individual may switch from one religion to the other but only on the belief that one religion is better than the other and they can only do so after another religion has succeeded in making the Cosmos explanatorily intelligible to them.

This hypothesis also captures both inter-religious disputes and the relation between intolerance and faith. It brings together the emphasis on doctrine and the importance of faith by showing their interrelationship. Further, it cannot be accused of being merely intellectualistic because it can account for faith, religious experience, and worship–the three subjective dimensions of religion. Finally, it also explains why the pagans and heathens did not recognize themselves in the descriptions provided by Christianity.

CHAPTER X

IMAGINE THERE'S NO RELIGION

We can now appreciate why we can't study religion as an explanatorily intelligible account of the Cosmos without ourselves entering into that framework. It is the religious account that tells us what God is, what it means to experience the divine, and what constitutes faith or worship. In the definitions provided by religion we appeal to notions that belong to the domain of theology; using these concepts forces us to accept some or the other variant of theology as the framework for our study. While there's no objection to the study of religion, say, as in Christian theology, this does not help those who wish to undertake a scientific study of religion.

However, any object can be described at various levels. If we cannot study an object at one level of description, it doesn't mean that we cannot study that object at all. A human being, to give but one example, can be studied at the level of cell-biology, at the level of physiology and anatomy, at the psychological level, or at the social level. At each of these levels, we can give an accurate description of the creature that a human being is, without necessarily being clear about the relation between the different levels of description.

Exactly the same point holds for religion too. Since we are forced to do theology if we use the concepts handed down by religion, it would be best to look at religion from another level of description. Can we solve this problem if we describe religion in terms of worldviews? Even though religion is 'more' than a worldview and a worldview is different from religion, let's examine whether this concept can legitimately replace the concept of religion.

What exactly does the proposal to replace 'religion' with 'worldview' amount to? At first glance, it doesn't make much sense to define religion in terms of worldviews because then we would be defining the obscure in terms of the more obscure. Moreover, our arguments should not depend on any particular definition since changes in the definition make the investigation useless. Thirdly, as I've been at pains to argue, we should avoid terminological and definitional disputes as much as we possibly can.

Whatever the truth about religion may be, that is, whether it is God-given or fabricated, whether divinely-inspired or neurotically-induced, we merely need a general term to pick out this object without having to take recourse to theology. For this reason, 'worldview' must not be taken as an explicit definition of the concept of religion. Yet this does not mean that the introduction of this term is arbitrary. There are several adequacy tests we can subject this concept to that would justify our decision to allow 'worldview' to substitute 'religion'. The first is to find out whether 'worldview' and 'religion' could refer to the same entity. The second is to see whether any additional advantage accrues to us by virtue of this substitution.

Religion and Worldview

Scholars in the field of comparative religious studies have been championing the idea that we need to view both secular ideologies (like Marxism and Nationalism) and religions as different species of worldviews. In this sense, many have suggested that there is an intimate connection between worldviews and religions, and that we may profitably use the notion of 'worldview' even in religious studies. Consider what Paul Tillich, a Christian theologian of some stature, has to say about the nature of religion. Speaking to the lay public, he characterizes the "predicament of western man" as one of having lost depth by losing religion.

> The decisive element in the predicament of western man in our period is his loss of dimension of depth...What does it mean? It means that man has lost an answer to the question: what is the meaning of life? Where do we come from, where do we go? What shall we do, what should we become in the short stretch between birth and death? Such questions are not answered or even asked if the "dimension of depth" is lost...I

suggest that we call the dimension of depth the religious dimension in man's nature. Being religious means asking passionately the question of meaning of our existence and being willing to receive answers. (1958: 41-42).

Consider now what Olthuis, another Christian theologian, of somewhat lesser stature, has to say when he waxes eloquent on the subject of the "ultimate questions of life":

The ultimate questions of life lie deep within the heart of everyone. Who am I? Where am I going? What's it all about? Is there a god? How can I live and die happily? Everyone formulates some answer to these questions about the human condition, if only partially and implicitly. The answer we give may be referred to as our worldview, or vision of life. It may or may not be thematized or codified, but it makes up the framework of fundamental considerations which give context, direction, and meaning to our lives. (1989: 26).

From this citation, it would appear as though these 'fundamental' questions, including whether there is a God, are questions innate to the human species. The difference in worldviews appears to reside in the different answers to this set of questions. When he warms up to his subject, the claims take on a more radical form:

A worldview (or vision of life) is a framework or set of fundamental beliefs through which we view the world and our calling and future in it. The vision need not be fully articulated: it may be so internalised that it goes largely unquestioned; it may not be explicitly developed into a systematic conception of life; it may not be theoretically deepened into philosophy; it may not be even codified into creedal form; it may be greatly refined through cultural-historical development. Nevertheless, this vision is a channel for the ultimate beliefs which give direction and meaning to life. It is the integrative and interpretative framework by which order and disorder are judged; it is the standard by which reality is managed and pursued; it is the set of hinges on which all our everyday thinking and doing turns. Although a vision of life is held by individuals, it is communal in scope and structure. Since a worldview gives the terms of reference by which the world and our place in it can be structured and illumined, a worldview binds its adherents together into community. Allegiance to a common vision promotes the integration of individuals into a group (*ibid.* 29).

The invitation to contrast these two writers has mostly to do with the subject matter they're talking about. One is talking as a believer about religion and the other, again as a believer, about worldviews. Important for us to note is that we could switch the word 'religion' or 'worldview' in both these descriptions without noticing the difference.

Moving on from theologians to anthropologists and sociologists merely reinforces this impression. Suppose we say that a worldview involves a "quest for unity in a disordered life" (Gordon Allport); or that having a worldview entails "a conviction of harmony between ourselves and the universe at large" (John McTaggart). Would you find it particularly disturbing? Most probably not. However, in both of the above cases the authors are talking about religion and not worldviews. This situation is indicative of the probability that we're talking about the same phenomenon whether we use the word 'religion' or 'worldview'.

Reflexivity in Religion

I have argued that religion is an explanatory intelligible account of both the Cosmos and of itself. It is its own justification, its own truth, founded on nothing that is human. Given the nature of this object, we need not wonder that we have to take recourse to religious vocabulary in order to explicate the concept of religion. Nevertheless, we can attempt a study of what the believers call 'religion'. The concepts, the categories, the methods we use in such a study will appeal to the merely human, the merely fallible, and the merely conjectural. That is, we cannot claim that the object of our investigation is what religion "really is" because what religion "really is" includes what religion says about itself.

Until the advent of secular ideologies and scientific theories, the only candidates for the term 'worldview' were religions. For more than 1,600 years, religions fulfilled the role of worldviews. Therefore, the decision to take the latter as a good example of the former is not arbitrary. Instead, the argument must go the other way: if religions are not the best examples of worldviews, what else would be? Not merely do both concepts appear to pick out the same object but, more importantly, the properties of religion are carried over into a description of Christianity, Judaism and Islam as worldviews as well.

One of the reasons to try an alternate description, instead of subscribing to the self-description of religion, was that it wasn't possible to talk about religion without ourselves being religious. Now the following citation makes it appear as though we cannot speak about worldviews without ourselves having one.

> Philosophies and theologies are explicit logical systems. They can be studied in the same manner as mathematical propositions and their consequences. *Religions are implicit worldviews. They can be studied only through implicit worldviews.* (Drobin 1982: 273; emphasis added).

Is this merely a disguised way of saying that we cannot study religion without ourselves being religious? We are almost intuitively convinced that worldviews differ from religions even though we're unable to say what constitutes the difference. The properties of religion are retained in the description of a worldview. It appears possible to study religion without subscribing to the religious self-description; yet to say that we can study a worldview only from within a worldview does not make sense. Why this difference?

The scholarship on the subject seems to indicate that to navigate successfully in the world we need to have an adequate worldview. To investigate this intuition, let's formulate it as a problem at a level one step higher than at the individual level: (a) Do all cultures have a worldview? (b) Do all cultures need a worldview? (c) Could we describe a community and its boundaries by describing the outlines of their worldview?

When we formulate the problem in this way, we see that it leads us back to one of the central questions of this essay: Is religion a cultural universal? This time though, the question is sharper: we have a preliminary characterization of religion; we have identified the latter also as a worldview. Consequently, we are better equipped to tackle the issue now than we were before. Our questions are relatively well defined, and, more importantly, they restrict the space in which to look for answers. Let's turn our attention to answering these questions. The culture that we will look at is India.

Does India have any indigenous religions or worldviews? You might wonder how this question can be answered in anything but the affirmative considering the mountains of ethnographic data about the 'religious' practices in India. To begin with, I'm going to let the facts stand as they are, without calling into question the truth of any ethnographic work. Secondly, I will accept the constraints imposed by most works in Indology, anthropology, and so on. Working within these boundaries, I will provide you with the strongest species of argument that one could ever use in scientific discussions, namely, the *impossibility argument*. I will argue that no matter what the facts are, there simply cannot be religion in India. I will then formulate a proposal that might help us see the 'facts' in a different light.

An Epistemological Point

Before we get started, I would like to seek your agreement on a general point concerning one of the ways in which we determine the validity of what we know. Whenever we want to distinguish phenomena from each other, we can use a particular kind of test. It consists of taking a paradigmatic or classic example of something and testing it for *necessary properties*. If something could not possibly belong to some category in the absence of some properties, then those are the necessary properties for that category. We may consider it either as an essential property of the object, or as a criterion used in our classificatory systems. For instance, to take the famous example of Plato's beard: "No collection can be a beard, unless it is a collection of hairs". You could say that it is a necessary property of a beard that it have hairs, or you could say that we classify some collection as a 'beard' based on the criterion whether or not it has hairs. Of course, while 'having hairs' is a necessary property of a beard, that does not mean that it is any more or any less important than any other property that we might wish to consider.

The ability to execute such a test depends on our knowledge of the world. There's no guarantee that we will be able to specify a set of relevant properties in all cases. Nevertheless, if and where we can, it would be useful to do so. If you agree with this epistemological point, then we can go ahead and apply this test to our knowledge of religions. We will make use of both what has been said about religion so far, and what we know about those entities that we have identified as religions, namely, Christianity, Islam, and Judaism.

The Structure of the Argument

Let's focus on two properties that any religion must possess. The first is that religion must make claims about the origin of the world. This is because religion 'explains' and makes 'intelligible' the Cosmos as an expression of the purposes of the entity called God. Since these purposes are causal relations, such an account must take the form of a creation account that speaks not merely of the 'how' but also of the 'why' of the Cosmos. In the three religions, which are our prototypical examples, this is indeed the case. God gave us religion by telling us that He made the world, and that it embodies His purposes.

The second property is more general and is applicable to everything said by religion. The message must be true; or, better put, it must be believed to be true. Religious claims must be seen as items of knowledge. In other words, the claims made by religion have the same status as other 'true' knowledge claims about the world (such as that the earth revolves around the sun). For the sake of identification, I will refer to these two properties as the 'metaphysical' conditions that must be met by any candidate for the position of religion. This is the first part of my argument.

The second part of my argument will examine the sociological aspects relating to the existence of religion. I will argue that religions could not possibly survive in the absence of certain social conditions of transmission.

The Metaphysical Impossibility

Given that a claim about the origin of the world is a necessary property of religions, the Indian traditions could not possibly be religions because they do not properly raise the issue of the origin of the world. To be sure, there are innumerable creation stories in the Indian traditions. An examination of a few of them will put into perspective what they really amount to. To begin with, consider the following creation hymns from the *Rig Veda*: There is, first, the hymn (10.121) about the golden embryo, which is itself born. The waters appear to have been there before the embryo, while also suggesting that the latter generated the former:

> In the beginning the Golden Embryo arose. Once he was born,
> he was the one lord of creation. He held in place the earth and

the sky...When the high waters came, pregnant with the embryo that is everything, bringing forth fire, he arose from that as the one life's breath of the gods...

Let him not harm us, he who fathered the earth and created the sky... who created the shining waters (O'Flaherty, Ed., 1981: 27-28).

Second, there is a hymn (10.90) about the 'sacrifice of the primal man': from the *Purusa* comes the world. Again, the gods, the sages, and some other creatures exist before him.

It is the Man who is all this, whatever has been and whatever is to be... When the Gods spread the sacrifice with the Man as the offering...With him the gods, Sadhyas, and sages sacrificed (*ibid.* 30).

There is also the 'original incest'. Here, the father lusts after his own daughter and commits incest, which might account for creation. However, other creatures exist before this act: among others, Agni, the lord of fire. Fourth, there is the hymn (10.72) that becomes another creation story about the birth of gods, as O'Flaherty remarks:

It is evident from the tone of the very first verse that the poet regards creation as a mysterious subject, and a disparate series of eclectic hypotheses (perhaps quoted from various sources) tumbles out right away... (*ibid.* 37-38).

Then, there is a hymn (10.81-2) about the artisan of the gods, who is

imagined...as a sculptor, a smith, or as a woodcutter or carpenter, but also as the primeval sacrificer and the victim of the sacrifice, assisted by the seven sages. Finally, he is identified with the one who propped apart sky and earth, the one who inspires thought and answers questions but is himself beyond understanding (*ibid.* 34-35).

The origin stories thus go on and on. Some recur in several contexts and are retold in different ways. However, the point to note is their multiplicity. There is leeway to speculate as much as you want about the beginnings of the world. Ultimately, the following *Rig Vedic* hymn (10.129) makes it clear that it does not appear to matter all that much:

There was neither non-existence nor existence then; there was neither the realm of space nor the sky which is beyond. What stirred? Where? In whose protection? Was there water, bottomlessly deep? ...

Who really knows? Who will here proclaim it? Whence was it produced? Whence is this creation? The gods came afterwards, with the creation of universe. Who then knows whence it has arisen?

Whence this creation has arisen–perhaps it formed itself, or perhaps it did not–the one who looks down on it, in the highest heaven, only he knows–or *perhaps he does not know* (*ibid.* 25-26; emphasis added).

Consider now some stories from the *Brahmanas* and the *Upanishads*, where some of the earlier motifs reappear in a characteristic form:

Prajapati approached his daughter; *some say* she was the sky and *others* that she was the dawn. He became the stag...as she had taken the form of a doe. *The gods saw him* and they said, 'Prajapati is now doing what is not done'. They wished for one who would punish him, but they did not find him in one another. Then they assembled in one place the most fearful forms, and these, assembled, became the deity Rudra. (O'Flaherty, Ed., 1975: 31: emphasis added.)

This deity kills Prajapati and from this body many other things, including man, emerge. This story, told in the *Aitareya Brahmana*, takes a different form in the *Kausitaki Brahmana*. The latter text says that Prajapati desires progeny and practices asceticism (tapas). During this process, he heats up and thus fire is born. Following it, the wind, sun, moon and the dawn are also born. He instructs his children to practice asceticism and while they are doing so, his daughter assumes a seductive form. Looking at her, the brothers have an orgasm. They beg their father to save their seed, which he does. From this is born the thousand headed god. The *Satapatha Brahmana* tells another story altogether: Prajapati does penance, and begets *agni* (fire) from his mouth. The hungry fire wants to devour him. He offers oblation to the fire, and from this oblation many things are born. How was Prajapati himself born? (XI, i, 6)

Verily, in the beginning this (universe) was water, nothing but a sea of water. The waters desired, "How can we be reproduced?" They toiled and performed fervid devotions, when they were becoming heated, a golden egg was produced. The year, indeed, was not then in existence: this golden egg floated about for as long as the space of a year.

In a year's time a man, this Prajapati, was produced therefrom; and hence a woman, a cow, or a man brings forth within the space of a year; for Prajapati was born in a year. He broke open this golden egg. There was then, indeed, no resting place: only this golden egg, bearing him, floated about for as long as the source of a year. (Sproul, Ed., 1979: 184-185.)

In the *Brihadaranyaka Upanishad*, a mortal, the primal man, creates the world, which includes the immortal gods. In the *Chandogya Upanishad*, the idea of the origin takes the following forms. First,

(i)n the beginning this was non-existent. It became existent, it grew. It turned into an egg. The egg lay for the time of a year. The egg broke open. The two halves were one of silver, the other of gold. The silver one became this earth, the golden one the sky, the thick membrane (of the white) the mountains, the thin membrane (of the yoke) the mist with the clouds, the small veins the rivers, the fluid the sea. What was born from it that was aditya, the sun... (Müller, Ed., 1879: 54-55.)

Second, this apparently is not how it went at all. As a father instructs his son:

'In the beginning', my dear, 'there was that only which is, one only, without a second. Others say, in the beginning there was that only which is not, one only, without a second; and from that which is not, that which is was born.

'But how could it be thus, my dear?' the father continued. 'How could that which is be born of that which is not? No, my dear, only that which is, was in the beginning, one only, without a second.

'It thought, may I be many, may I grow forth. It sent forth fire. That fire thought, may I be many, may I grow forth. It sent forth water...

'Water thought may I be many, may I grow forth. It sent forth
earth (food)... (*ibid.* 93-94).

The stories go on, from the epic *Mahabharata* through the
Puranas, in a similar fashion. The Jains deny any creation of the
universe or the possibility of a creator god, as the following ninth
century piece from the *Mahapurana* (4.16-31, 38-40) shows:

Some foolish men declare that Creator made the world.
The doctrine that the world was created is ill-advised, and
should be rejected....
No single being had the skill to make the world–For how can
an immaterial god create that which is material?
How could God have made the world without any raw
material?
If you say he made this first, and then the world, you are faced
with an endless regression.
If you declare that this raw material arose naturally you fall
into another fallacy,
For the whole universe might thus have been its own creator,
and have arisen equally naturally.
If God created the world by an act of his own will, without any
raw material,
Then it is just his will and nothing else–and who will believe
this silly stuff? ...
Know that the world is uncreated, as time itself is, without
beginning and end,
And is based on the principles, life and rest.
Uncreated and indestructible, it endures under the compulsion
of its own nature, divided into three sections–hell, earth, and
heaven. (Embree, Ed., 1988: 80-82.)

The Buddhists are not far behind. In the *Digha Nikaya* (3.28), a
discourse attributed to the Buddha, we find:

There are some monks and brahmans who declare as a doctrine
received from their teachers that the beginning of all things
was the work of the god Brahma. I have gone and asked them
whether it was true that they maintained such a doctrine, and
they have replied that it was; but when I have asked them to
explain just how the beginning of things was the work of the
god Brahma they have not been able to answer, and have
returned the question to me. Then I have explained it to them
thus:

> There comes a time, my friends, sooner or later...when the world is dissolved and beings are mostly reborn in the World of Radiance. There they dwell...for a long, long time.

> Now there comes a time when this world begins to evolve, and then the World of the Brahma appears, but it is empty. And some being, because his allotted span is past or because his merit is exhausted, quits his body in the World of the Radiance and is born in the empty World of Brahma, where he dwells for a long, long time. Now because he has been so long alone he begins to feel dissatisfaction and longing, and wishes that other beings might come and live with him. And indeed soon other beings quit their bodies in the World of Radiance and come to keep him company in the world of Brahma.

> Then the being who was first born there thinks: "I am Brahma...the All-seeing, the Lord, the Maker, the Creator, the Supreme Chief, the disposer, the Controller, the Father of all that is or is to be. I have created all these beings, for I merely wished that they might be and they have come here!" And the other beings...think the same, because he was born first and they later...

> That is how your traditional doctrine comes about that the beginning of things was the work of the God Brahma (*ibid.* 1988: 127-128).

In addition, there are several creation stories among the many tribes that populate India. The mere presence of this multiplicity of stories in India is not what makes the case interesting. After all, they could each be believed by different groups separately, giving us a picture of Indian culture as one constituted by distinct communities. Rather, it is the case that most individuals believe in all of these ideas! It is neither abnormal nor exceptional to hear the same individual repeating several of the above-mentioned ideas with respect to the origin of the Cosmos in different contexts. Taken together, these ideas allow one to say just about anything and everything–we could even dismiss the question about the origin of the Cosmos as an illegitimate problem. That is to say, depending on the context, an individual may refuse to advance claims about the origin of the Cosmos, or consider it a purely speculative exercise lacking all truth content, or argue that all claims are equally true, or even that the Cosmos has no origin at all, suggesting that it is always present.

An Objection and an Illustration

At this stage of the argument, you might raise the following objection. Doesn't the belief that the Cosmos was always there itself count as an answer to the question of the origin? Whether you believe that God created the world, or that the Big Bang did, or even that the world always was, is, and will be there, each of these beliefs is an answer to the question about the origin of the Cosmos. I would like to emphasize that the issue of the origin of the Cosmos is only a necessary property of religion. It requires more than a single belief to transform something into a religion. What we are talking about now concerns one of the building blocks of religion, namely, the question of the origin of the Cosmos.

Religion is impossible in a culture where the question about origins is an *illegitimate* one. In the Indian traditions, the answers to the question of creation do not count towards the advancement of knowledge. The claim is not that human beings are unable to answer this question. Instead, the suggestion is that these questions are not particularly worthwhile. The claims about the origin of the Cosmos–whether it involves the Golden Embryo, a primal man, or whatever else–are as legitimate as any other claim or even none. If the Indian traditions had considered it a matter of importance to establish the origin of the world, we would not see such divergent accounts. This is the stance that is worth noting from the above examples.

As a further illustration, consider the experience of an association of science teachers in the south-Indian state of Kerala. Overwhelmingly Marxist, this association has been busy carrying science to the people. It believes that India is in the grips of centuries-old prejudices and superstitions. Social change in such an archaic society, they believe, can only be brought about by spreading a scientific attitude among wide segments of the populace. One of the ways in which this association has tried to utilize *Science for Social Revolution* is to organize a series of lectures at the grass-roots level. In summarizing their experience of their lecture campaigns, two authors speak about their first lecture in the following terms:

> In the first lecture...the question on the origin of the universe is presented as an absurd problem. Origin means prior existence and "prior" (i.e. time) cannot exist without matter, it is stated that universe always existed. The presentation gave no place for the creator (Issac and Ekbal 1988: 23).

Notice the curious fact that teachers in the natural sciences think that the origin of the universe is an absurd question, and claim that the world always existed. Intrinsically, no problem is either absurd or sensible but can become so only in relationship to other ideas and opinions we hold. To these Indians, the origin of the universe appears to be an absurd question.

If this is the case, why does such an incredible multiplicity of creation stories exist in the Indian traditions? One of the reasons has to do with the nature of this event. Creation of the world, as told in the creation stories, is neither a unique nor a radical event. It is not unique because several creation stories are attributed to several epochs. As a result, all creation stories turn out to be 'true'. It is not a radical event because creation is not *ex nihilo*, that is to say, it did not come out of nothing. It is, therefore, no creation at all. Consider the following story from the *Visnu Purana*:

> Maitreya: 'Tell me, mighty sage, how, *in the commencement of the kalpa*, Narayana, named Brahma, created all existent things'.

> Parasara: 'At the close of the *past kalpa*, the divine brahma...awoke from his night of sleep...(and) concluding that *within the waters lay the earth, and being desirous to raise it up*, created another form for that purpose; and, as, in *preceding kalpas*, he has assumed the shape of a fish or a tortoise, so, in this, he took the figure of a boar' (Sproul, Ed., 1979: 185; emphasis added).

As Shulman puts it:

> Creation in India is not a unique event at the beginning of time, but an ever-recurring moment, a repetition of something already known. (1980: 75)

Why have Indian intellectuals not found the issue of the origin of Cosmos either interesting or important enough to require systematization? Why have many origin stories proliferated without being subject to censure?

On the Truth of the Stories

The framework of religion is such that its claims have to be true. Furthermore, given both the reflexivity of religion and the kind of beings we humans are, one has to accept the absolute truth of the claims made by religion in order to be religious. With respect to Indian culture, it is a category mistake to ascribe the predicates 'true' or 'false' to its epics and mythologies. It is an ill-formed question to ask, "Do you believe that the *Ramayana* (or whatever) is true?" Two conceptually significant facts can throw some light on how an average Indian looks at the issue.

When we contrast western religious history with that of the East, we notice something significant and striking. In the last three hundred years, the intellectual landscape in the West has been littered with tracts dealing with the truth and historicity of the Bible. Although this intellectual junkyard is a relatively new phenomenon, a space for it was marked out a long, long time ago. This is because it has always been crucial for religion that at least some of its Testament 'stories' be true, and known to be true and indisputable. This attitude, which the western intellectual world is in the grips of even to this day, hardly disturbs or excites their counterparts in India. The questions about the 'truth' or 'falsity' of their holy books are irrelevant within the Indian intellectual tradition.

There are, of course, several 'explanations' for the near absence of such literature in India and the total absence of such an intellectual tradition. One such explanation current in the West argues that this has to do with the absence of a scientific tradition and scientific theorizing in India. However, this explanation does not hold up under scrutiny for the simple reason that religious controversy itself was responsible (to a great extent) for the growth of scientific theorizing in the West. The discussion about the age of the earth, for example, was a controversy within religious discourse itself. The threat of atheism, religious schism, and heresy fuelled the debates about the age of the earth, which was to ultimately provide us with geology, paleontology and so on. In India, by common consent, neither atheism nor 'religious schism' was unknown.

What was unknown and remains unknown to this day is the notion of 'heresy' as understood in the religious traditions of the West. Without 'truth', there can be no heresy either.

Another explanation, which continues along the lines of the former, though less bold in scope, pinpoints the absence of a science of history in India. It's hard to find a single book about India that does not bemoan the absence of historical records. As Arthur Macdonell put it in his *History of Sanskrit Literature*:

> History is the one weak spot in Indian literature. It is, in fact, non-existent. The total lack of the historical sense is so characteristic, that the whole course of Sanskrit literature is darkened by the shadow of this defect, suffering as it does from an entire absence of exact chronology (Brown 1988: 21).

More recently, Paul Hacker formulates the general difficulty in this way:

> There was never any real history writing in India. This applies not only for political history, but also for history of philosophical and religious schools. (in Puttanil 1990: 1)

Instead of entering into polemics with this claim, let's draw another Asian culture into the fray whose science of history has generated admiration in the West, namely, China. The anthropologist Donald Brown speaks of the Chinese historical consciousness in these terms:

> For its combination of depth, comprehensiveness, accuracy, and continuity, Chinese Historical writing has no peer...The Chinese...are so historically minded that for them history takes the place of myth...History was the "queen of the sciences" for the Chinese. (1988: 47).

Now that we've noted that India does not have a science of history, and China has one, let's draw the West into the picture as well. Literally, the first question that the western intellectuals asked when they encountered Buddhism concerned the historical Buddha. If the historicity of the Buddha was a question raised by a culture (the West) that has a science of history, we would expect to find similar questions in the Chinese intellectual tradition as well. After all, Buddhism went out from India, confronted rival 'religious' traditions in China (as described in the standard textbook trivia), and, therefore, the Chinese intellectuals ought to have been interested in doing historical research about the Buddha. To be sure, they do ask the question: 'why did the Bodhidharma come to the East?' However, they ask it not as a historical question, but as a Zen *koan*. Why did the Chinese not analyze the claims of Buddhism the way the West did? Neither anti-Buddhist sentiments nor atheism is alien to China. Why did they not produce tracts along the lines of the European intellectuals?

These are interesting and important questions, and not merely rhetorical ones. They can be answered only after some empirical research. For our purposes though, the answers do not matter as much as the possibility of raising these questions with respect to Chinese culture. Therefore, let's merely note that the absence of this particular kind of questioning is significant. If neither scientific theorizing nor the science of history are responsible for raising questions about the truth or falsity of the claims of the 'holy books', what is? Here is one answer to consider. It is the *attitude* of a particular culture towards its 'holy books' that generates such questions or fails to do so.

This then is the first conceptually significant fact. The absence of a particular genre of enquiry and literature in a culture is indicative of the fact that such a genre is not considered important in that culture. It is an uninteresting exercise to the members of such a culture. This way of formulating the issue may be a bit misleading because it might suggest that the members of such a culture have sat down and deliberated over the issue. The suggestion, rather, is that the intellectual constraints of this culture are such that some lines of enquiry do not occur to them or, where they do, they die out due to lack of intelligibility.

Literature that investigates the truth value of claims made by 'religious texts' is absent in India. This lack indicates that the question of truth is not the right kind of question to ask with respect to these texts. What kind of texts are we talking about? Most of them are stories or mythologies–if we are to restrict ourselves to texts that parallel the Bible. It makes sense to ask whether the story of the Genesis is true, but it is nonsensical to ask whether the story about one of the 'incarnations' of Vishnu is true. It makes sense to ask whether the New Testament references to Jesus Christ are references to a 'historical Jesus'. To ask a parallel question about, say, Rama is to miss the point of what the story is…namely, a *story*. It is not a description of the world, nor is it a knowledge claim.

This, then, is the second conceptually significant fact. In India, an incredible multiplicity of stories state things about the world. These epics (or even, say, the Jataka tales) are not fictions; neither are they facts. To ask whether they are true or false is to exhibit a profound ignorance of the culture whose stories they are. To question their truth status is to assume that they are knowledge items, which they are not. They cannot be knowledge claims because they lack an object, that is, they are not descriptions of objects in the world.

How does an average Indian look at the issue? Let an Indonesian, in discussion with a German writer, tell us:

> When I discovered, or when it was explained to me, that Hinduism is a pedagogical religion, namely, that the best "good deed" of a Hindu consisted of explaining something or the other, I lost my inhibitions and began with questions…
>
> A young Balinese became my primary teacher. One day I asked him if he believed that the history of Prince Rama–one of the holy books of the Hindus–is true.
>
> Without hesitation, he answered it with "Yes".
>
> "So you believe that the Prince Rama lived somewhere and somewhen?"
>
> "I do not know if he lived", he said.
>
> "Then it is a story?"
>
> "Yes, it is a story."
>
> "Then someone wrote this story–I mean: a human being wrote it?"
>
> "Certainly some human being wrote it", he said.
>
> "Then some human being could have also invented it", I answered and felt triumphant, when I thought that I had convinced him.

But he said: "It is quite possible that somebody invented this story. But true it is, in any case."

"Then it is the case that Prince Rama did not live on this earth?"

"What is it that you want to know?" he asked. *"Do you want to know whether the story is true, or merely whether it occurred?"*

"The Christians believe that their God Jesus Christ was also on earth", I said, "in the New Testament, it has been so described by human beings. But the Christians believe that this is the description of the reality. Their God was also really on Earth."

My Balinese friend thought it over and said: "I had been already so informed. I do not understand why it is important that your God was on earth, but it does strike me that the Europeans are not pious. Is that correct?"

"Yes, it is", I said. (Bichsel 1982)

Consider carefully the claims of this young Balinese: (i) Even though the narrative of events could have been invented and written by a human being, his 'holy book' remains true; (ii) He does not know, and is not interested in knowing, whether Rama really lived but this does not affect the truth of the *Ramayana*; (iii) He draws a distinction between whether a story is true and whether it is a chronicle of events on earth; (iv) Finally, it remains his 'holy' book despite the above. He is indifferent to the historical truth and suggests, in the italicized part of the dialogue, that it is not a proper question; even if the invention of a human being and historically untrue, the story is true. Not only is the Indonesian drawing a distinction between a story and a history but also suggesting that the historicity of the *Ramayana* is irrelevant to its truth.

In a way, in the West and elsewhere, we do talk about stories in an analogous fashion. When the Sherlock Holmes Society disputes whether the famed detective ever really said "Elementary, my dear Watson", the dispute is not about whether Sir Arthur Conan Doyle ever wrote such a sentence but whether Sherlock Holmes ever said such a thing. In this sense, we do talk about the truth or falsity of stories (the way the Indonesian does), even when we know that there is no historical truth to them. In the case of this Indonesian, or the Asian, who believes in his 'holy books', the situation is more complicated: in his culture, the *Ramayana* is 'true' though it is not clear what the status of the book is. Perhaps it is fiction perhaps it is not. It is not essential to him that he know whether it is true or not. We can say that Sherlock Holmes did not exist, and still argue that it is true that he lived on Baker Street. When we discuss the truth of fictional objects, we know that we are talking about fictions. The fact that we dispute about the truth of an event in a story is different from an indifference regarding the status of the narrative itself.

How similar is this stance with respect to the Bible? In the last decade, a trend towards a "narrative criticism" with respect to the Bible can be seen in theological circles. Many advocate that we look at the Bible in its entirety as a series of stories; yet others focus on the New Testament in an analogous fashion. Especially under the influence of the 'deconstruction' movement, and of 'post-modern theology', the Greek distinction between *mythos* and *logos* has come under criticism. But this trend is not comparable to the stance in the Indian case.

Whatever the intellectual trend in Biblical scholarship or New Testament theology, we must not forget that they are responses to the historical problems posed by the textual analysis of the Bible. The 'narrative trend' is one answer to the problem of the historicity of Jesus and the truth of the Gospels. Suppose someone were to say the following: Jesus might or might not have existed; he might be The Savior or he might not be; he might have asked Peter to found the Church or he might not have; the Gospels might be the fictitious invention of four people or they might not be. Any of the above possibilities could be true, and their truth or falsity does not affect one's belief in the truth of the Gospels. How would we understand such a person? Probably, the Holy Bible is not 'holy' to him; perhaps he sees the Bible as a moral tract or a story-based philosophical treatise on the human condition. Whether or not such an attitude is justified, it is not enough to make him a Christian.

There is a second point. Even where the Gospel is seen as a story, it becomes an object of investigation as a text. Only as a text can the Bible provide 'knowledge' (of whatever kind). Such an attitude dovetails into the point made earlier that knowledge is primarily

textual in nature in the West. Consequently, even the narrative
trend requires knowledge of the text. Further, it looks at the text of
the Bible as a story without, however, being able to look at stories
in other ways. That is to say, stories are treated as knowledge-
claims of some kind or the other, whether moral, ethical or factual.

The difference, with respect to the Indonesian, lies along these
lines: to him, the story of Rama does impart knowledge *without*
being a knowledge-claim. Stories are 'true' not because they are
fictions and even less because they are historical facts. There is a
dominant metaphor current in Indian culture that may help shed
light on this attitude. Used by the literate and the illiterate alike,
this metaphor is about our relation to the Cosmos: ten blind men,
on feeling ten different parts of an elephant (tusk, tail, ear, etc.),
maintain that an elephant is that part which he happens to be
touching. Such, the wise tell us, is the nature of our disputes about
the world.

Thus, we see an absence of the two conditions that are necessary
for a religion to exist–a creation account, and belief in the truth of
this account. Indian culture could not possibly have religion
because it knows of no unique creation of the Cosmos. The many
origin stories, which do talk about the origins, are neither true nor
false. These mythologies, epics, *puranas* cannot possibly be
construed as knowledge claims about the world, whatever else they
might be. Indian traditions do not have these two necessary
properties of religion.

The Sociological Impossibility

So far, we have examined the situation by looking at some texts
written at different points in time. To speak of societies and
cultures in terms of their religions or worldviews, we have to look
at the issue over a broad period of time as well. Because the
entities under consideration are supposedly belief systems such as
'Hinduism', 'Buddhism', 'Jainism', etc., each of these entities
must be seen to have historical continuity. For any belief system to
have historical continuity, there have to be some *sociological
conditions* that are absolutely necessary for guaranteeing the
identity of these entities. In the absence of these conditions, the
continued existence of a religion or worldview even across two
generations would not be possible. Primarily, these conditions

relate to how a worldview is transmitted across generations. Let's examine these conditions to see whether they are true of Indian culture.

The first condition is that there must be a worldview. If there is a worldview, we can reasonably assume that such a 'Hindu', 'Buddhist', 'Jain' or any other worldview will have been textually codified. Even if they had an 'oral' worldview that was not committed in writing, the last few centuries of empirical work would have brought it to light. Therefore, we are entitled to assume that these worldviews would have been codified. Such codifications, of course, would constitute the 'holy books' or 'scriptures' of these traditions. Quite obviously, not only must these scriptures exist, but they must be known to the 'Hindus', the 'Buddhists', or the 'Jains' as well. Otherwise, there would be no question of transmission.

As we've already seen, 'Hinduism' has no single set (or multiple sets) of authoritative scriptures or texts. Despite everything written about their 'canonical' texts, the same applies to Buddhism and Jainism. Ditto for Shintoism and Taoism. In spite of this, one of the oft-heard claims about the Hindus is that the *Vedas* are their ultimate authority and that these constitute their holy texts. Hindus may talk about 'the message' of the *Vedas* but their knowledge of the *Vedas* is limited, to put it mildly. Let me draw upon two authors, both of whom are British but separated by more than 150 years, prefacing them with my own personal experience.

The first confession has to do with my own upbringing. I was brought up as a very orthodox Brahmin (compared to my other Brahmin friends) and, until I began my work on this book, I did not know what was said in either the *Vedas* or the *Upanishads*. In 1808, Chatfield was expressing the consensus of his time in the following words:

> If...(we consider) the general ignorance of the Brahmins of the present age, the force of their prejudices will be found the more difficult to subdue...

> In confirmation of this opinion of the general ignorance of the Brahmins, it is recorded, that *they cannot even read the books which contain their sacred records*... (Chatfield 1808: 212-13; emphasis added).

To further illustrate the ignorance of the Hindus about the *Vedas*, consider the following story I was told as a young child. Apparently, there was only one manuscript of the Atharva Veda available in India, which the British stole. Having imbibed the knowledge in it, they built their machines and instruments and became rich. To my question as to why we could not ask the British to give our manuscript back, I received answers that satisfied the curiosity of a young child. The British (at times it was the Germans) dumped the manuscript into the sea or they refused to give it back to us and we could not force them because they were very powerful, or some such thing. As I grew up, I never thought about this story any further until I came across a piece of ethnographic work by the British anthropologist Jonathan Parry. Describing the result of his fieldwork in Benares, this is what he had to say:

> In Benares I have often been told–and I have heard variants of the same story elsewhere–that Max Müller stole chunks of *Sama Veda* from India, and it was by studying these that German scientists were able to develop the atom bomb. The *rishis*, or ancient sages, not only knew all about nuclear fission, but as (what we would call) mythology testifies, they also had supersonic aeroplanes and guided missiles (1985: 206).

Such tales exhibit a very deep ignorance on the part of the Hindus (the Brahmins no less, in a city like Benares!) about the content of their 'sacred books'. If such is the ignorance of the Brahmins, the 'priests' of Indian culture, what could we say about the knowledge of other Hindus regarding their 'sacred texts'? The picture is substantially the same. In this sense, the foregoing is enough to show why using texts like the *Vedas* or the *Upanishads* to make claims about Hindu (or Brahmanic) worldviews is a pointless exercise. The same applies to the Buddhists and the Jains.

It's not as though western ethnography of Indian culture is ignorant of this state of affairs. But they describe it in terms of their own cultural assumptions. They distinguish lay Buddhists from *Sangha* Buddhism, or popular Hinduism from philosophical Hinduism, etc. They write books and articles full of such distinctions. This does not tell us anything except the following: texts ought to be central to a religion but they are not so in

Hinduism, Buddhism, etc. We can go either of two ways when confronted with this fact: either Hinduism, Buddhism, etc., are not religions or they are religions and the 'popular' religion is a corrupted version of a purer one that is to be found in secret enclaves and dusty shelves.

One might raise an objection to this argument on two grounds: first, by pointing to the popularity of the *Bhagavad Gita* or the *Ramayana* and the *Mahabharata* among the Hindus; second, by pointing out a similar absence of scriptural knowledge among Jews, Christians, and Muslims. To be sure, the *Bhagavad Gita* is better known among certain layers–but its popularity has to do with western efforts and little to do with the indigenous tradition. Regarding the second objection, my claim is not that a member of a religion must have direct acquaintance with his holy text. Rather, it has to do with the fact that a total ignorance of 'holy texts' is compatible with being a 'Hindu' and even being a Brahmin. There is a contrast between this situation and that of a Jew, a Christian, or a Muslim with respect to their sacred texts. One could not belong to these religions if one (directly or through the mediation of a rabbi, a priest, an imam, or even one's parents) is ignorant of what their scriptures are about.

In either case, the point is this: transmission of a 'Hindu', 'Buddhist', or a 'Jain' worldview requires the existence of such a view in a textual source, and knowledge about it. This sociological condition is not fulfilled in India.

The second sociological condition for the transmission of worldviews relates to the fact that transmission of information across generations undergoes changes. Consequently, if a culture transmits a set of distinct worldviews, it will need to develop mechanisms to limit the extent to which its worldview undergoes transformations. A standard worldview must thus be present–a standard against which transformations are measured. Even if we were to use this notion in the broadest possible sense, i.e., as constraints on interpretation, we would have a hard time identifying any such standard interpretation within the Hindu traditions. The reason for this absence lies in the very nature of these texts. The *Rig Veda* itself, for example, provides us with different creation stories (to restrict ourselves to one idea). If we consider the more widely popular *Puranas*, it is next to impossible to speak of a standard interpretation of any single idea.

Standard interpretations are necessary to transmit worldviews across generations. After all, we are talking of entities like the Hindu, or Brahmanic worldview, the Buddhist and Taoist worldview, and so on. Again, drawing a contrast will highlight the problem. There could not be any Islam, Christianity, or Judaism if there was no transmission of a specific view. If we cannot identify one stable entity (i.e., a standard interpretation), how can we maintain that Buddhism, Taoism, Hinduism are distinct worldviews with a history of 2,000 years or more?

One might be tempted to compare the fragmentation within Christianity, Islam or Judaism with the state of affairs sketched out above, but this does not hold much ground. The reason is simple. Religious schisms involve a conflict of interpretations but not the denial of a limit within which such interpretations can be made. There are definite limits on the interpretations of a Catholic mass; Jesus cannot be interpreted to be the son of the Devil; Idolatry is forbidden; one cannot be a Muslim and say that Muhammad was not a prophet of God; one cannot be a Jew and believe that Jesus was the Messiah, and so on. No such constraints operate for Buddhism, Hinduism, or Jainism. Consequently, we cannot delineate them as worldviews at all.

This brings us to the third sociological condition for the transmission of worldviews. Each individual or each generation interprets a given worldview in some particular way, depending upon the accumulated knowledge and prevailing conventions. Of necessity, therefore, there will be a conflict of interpretations. The conflicts might have to do with the nature of the standard worldview or the direction of its growth. Consequently, in a culture where worldviews are transmitted over generations, there will be a need for resolving these disputes. That is, there must be some kind of authority to settle disputes. An authority is required, because its absence amounts to not having any constraints on interpretation.

The first possibility is a doctrinal authority–a text or a doctrine that sets a purely semantic constraint on the interpretation of a text. Such a text would be the ultimate authority, so to speak. This requires a hierarchy of texts, a sort of theology. Absent from the 'religious' traditions of Asia is precisely such a hierarchy. We could take any text or even none at all, and remain a 'Hindu', 'Brahmin', 'Buddhist' or whatever else. To realize the significance of this point, a citation from an ethnographic work might help. Conducted in Tamil Nadu, India, the author is trying to find out the worldview of the villagers:

> (T)he following creation myth, told to me by an elderly villager in the presence of a number of other villagers *who threw in their own versions, connections and modifications as the narrative unfolded...*

> God (Kat.avul.) was everything. In Him were the five elements of fire, water, earth, and ether [akasam], and wind. These five elements were uniformly spread throughout [the three humors] phlegm [kapam], bile [pittam], and wind [vayu]. They were so evenly distributed that even to say that they were phlegm, bile, and wind would be wrong. Let us say that they were in such a way that one could not tell the difference between them. Let us say they were nonexistent...Even the question as to their existence did not arise. Then something happened. The five elements started to move around as if they were not satisfied, as if they were disturbed. Now, as to who disturbed these elements or why they were disturbed, no one knows.

> At this point, a second villager interrupted the narrator to suggest that the one who caused this mysterious disturbance was Kamam, the god of lust. The narrator found his suggestion unacceptable, because Kama had not even come into existence at that time. But his friend insisted...After considerable debate, it was agreed that it did not make sense to speak of Kamam existing when he was as evenly distributed throughout Kat.avul'.s body as floating atoms... (Daniel 1984: 3-4; emphasis added).

Imagine, if you will, a discussion like this about the 'creation myth' in the Bible, conducted by devout villagers in religious cultures!

This is very typical within Indian culture with respect to the transmission of the epics as well. One of the English translators of the *Mahabharata* speaks about its transmission in these terms:

The text of *The Mahabharata* itself gives us some idea of how we should picture its authorship. In its present form it is recited by the bard Ugrasravas, who recites it after Vaisampayana, who was one of the pupils of Krisna Dvaipayana. In other words, we have right here three generations of reciters through whom the text had been transmitted. One cannot expect that this transmission was a literal one, as it has been in the case of the Veda. A reciter's reputation was based on his skill in bringing the old stories to life again. Successive generations would add, embellish, digress: but also understate what might have been emphasized before...All this creates the impression that what would come down from generation to generation were, first, the summaries, and, second, the technique of spinning out a tale to please the listeners. The reciter was thus also a creative poet, within the idiom of his craft. (van Buitenen 1973: xxiii-iv)

We need to appreciate that changes that occur while telling the story are not as important as the fact that transformations of a text are considered both desirable and necessary.

This brings us to the fourth sociological condition for the transmission of a worldview. What if the conflict involves interpretative difficulties with respect to this textual source? In that case there would need to be some kind of an organizational authority to resolve these difficulties. The problem with any such authority is that it will be manned by human beings and, thus, could always be challenged by other human beings. Therefore, in such a culture, the issue of the legitimacy of the organizational authority, as the ultimate authority, would always be important. Those who challenge its legitimacy would be denounced. In short, there must be a source of excommunication. In the case of Hinduism, it is evident that no such authority exists. The same consideration holds for Taoism. We could say the same for, say, Saivism, Vaisnavism, Buddhism with its *Sangha*, and the Jains.

What happens when two interpretations collide? Does each become a heretic in the eyes of the other? If so, who decides? There exists no organizational authority to recognize someone as a Buddhist or denounce him as a heretic. None of these traditions constitutes a Church. The Buddhist *Sangha* is an association of a group of people who decide to live in one particular way within the Buddhist tradition. They are not the focal points of the laity; they are an association within a community. The members of a community might respect the Buddhist monks, or heed their words where useful, but they have no spiritual power granted to them by virtue of being monks.

Finally, and as the fifth sociological condition for a worldview to be transmitted, there must be some kind of an organization to transmit and propagate the worldviews. This would be the mechanism to ensure that the worldview is not lost or transformed in the process of transmission. Minimally, such an organization must be bigger than a single family; maximally, it could include an entire community that shares the worldview. Otherwise, we could not speak of entities like 'Buddhism' or 'Hinduism' either inter-generationally or intra-generationally.

There is no such source for the communication of a worldview in the Indian traditions. There is no organization to propagate such views. The transmission of these traditions takes place through families and friends. Local characters and customs modify the transmission in innumerable ways. How, then, could we possibly speak of a Brahmin from South India sharing the same worldview as a Brahmin from the North, or a Buddhist in Tibet sharing the same worldview as a Buddhist from China? We simply cannot. Nor could we call them 'Buddhist', unless we specify a standard worldview called 'the Buddhist worldview', which is precisely what the West did. It took a road familiar to it because of its own culture: identification of texts as the unifying element.

These five sociological conditions are necessary to allow the transmission of worldviews across space and time so that they may preserve their identity in the course of their transmission over generations. None of these conditions is fulfilled in India with respect to Hinduism, Buddhism and so on. No matter what the 'facts' are, it is sociologically impossible that the Indian culture could transmit worldviews like 'Hinduism', 'Buddhism', or 'Jainism'. From this, it follows that whatever these traditions might be, they could not possibly be either worldviews or religions.

The above outline establishes the metaphysical and sociological impossibility for the claim that Indian culture could know either religions or worldviews. These arguments have been made without contradicting ethnographic 'facts' but making use of them instead. Based on these arguments we see that Indian culture (or even Asian culture) cannot be described by outlining its worldview. There is no worldview to outline in India.

What, then, have anthropologists been studying all this while? Their claim that religion is a constitutive element of all cultures has been shown to be empirically false. Religion is not a cultural universal. One of the central preoccupations of this work now has an answer. However, it lends greater urgency to the second preoccupation, that is, of making sense of the western intellectuals who have made these claims over the centuries. To carry this task to its successful conclusion, let's pick up the question posed in an earlier section in this chapter. What lends strength and credibility to the feeling that we cannot navigate in this world without having a worldview?

We noted in the first chapter that the manner in which contemporary writers talk about 'religions' in other cultures is an example of inconsistent reasoning. Perhaps a similar inconsistency in arguments about worldviews can help shed light on this matter.

One of the most strongly held beliefs among intellectuals of the western world today concerns the indispensability of worldviews. Among anthropologists, this idea takes on two forms: to study a worldview is to understand the people whose worldview it is. Consequently, to compare cultures is to compare different worldviews. Among other social scientists, including philosophers, there is a very firmly rooted belief that no individual or group could survive in the world if not endowed with a worldview. In its starkest terms, we could formulate this diffuse idea thus: all organisms react depending on representations that they have built up of the world. Without some representation of the world, we cannot survive in the world. Therefore, it is almost evolutionarily necessary that there be worldviews.

Many who subscribe to this general diagnosis of western culture also entertain the following sentiment: there is a crisis in this culture, which is best described as a crisis in its worldview. During the Middle Ages, Christianity provided us with a worldview, which is inadequate for the contemporary world. Thus, one of the most important tasks facing a philosopher or a social theorist is to build an adequate, scientific worldview.

The first thing which ought to strike anyone is the incompatibility between the above two paragraphs. First, a claim is made that no individual could survive without possessing a worldview; next, it is claimed that the old worldview has disintegrated and a new worldview does not (yet) exist. Furthermore, the first claim effectively rules out any possibility of a culture-specific worldview. If each individual builds his own representation of the world, how could you understand the culture of the Dinka, the Hopi Indians, or the Chinese by studying a fragment of a worldview as provided by an informant or two?

One could argue that the scientific revolution inaugurated the disintegration of the religious worldview, and continues to do so to this day. This disintegration, then, has been going on for at least three hundred years now. What has happened in the West during this period? It has colonized the world, accumulated incredible wealth, decimated other cultures and people, exported capitalism, science, technology, democracy, and, as many say, its own worldview to all other parts of the world. Whatever your moral verdict on this state of affairs, these feats mark the flourishing of a culture and not its disintegration.

Let's see if we can determine why evidently gifted and brilliant minds do not appear to see this inconsistency. The notion of 'worldview' seems to be associated with a doctrinal core or refers to a community unified by a doctrinal core. This situation confirms the relationship between religion and worldview although it does not tell us why worldviews are believed to be indispensable. If the term 'worldview' is a secular term for religion then the theological belief that all cultures, peoples, and all individuals have a sense of divinity implanted in them takes on the secularized form that all cultures, peoples, or individuals have a worldview. This is exactly what has happened: the necessity and indispensability of world-views is the secularized version of a theological belief.

Now we can understand why gifted minds do not notice the incompatibilities when advancing such flatly inconsistent ideas. Not only have they taken over a religious idea, but, due to its familiarity, they also believe that it is empirically true. Who needs religious terminology if the same idea can be expressed without being explicitly religious? We can now further understand why claims about the universality of religion find sympathetic echoes in the hearts of even diehard atheists or secular-thinking people: they cannot conceive of peoples without worldviews.

If we hold on to this insight and look afresh at the anthropologists, we can appreciate in what sense they are successors to their Christian (or other religious) ancestors: communities and cultural groups are distinguished along the same lines as were heathens and pagans. They believe that to understand a people or their practices, we have to understand their beliefs. In order to understand beliefs, either they seek information about worldviews, study the texts of a culture, or provide a symbolic interpretation of cultural practices in terms of worldviews!

For the most part, western knowledge of other cultures is based on studying the worldviews of other cultures. If there are cultures which do not have worldviews, what 'knowledge' does the West have of them? What, precisely, are western anthropologists studying when they study nonexistent entities?

The Depth of the Deep Questions

The intuition that 'worldview' is merely a secular equivalent of religion is reinforced by another idea about what worldviews do. Everywhere, human beings ask some 'deep' questions regarding the meaning and purpose of life, and so forth. There are many different answers to these questions. Religion is one such. Worldview could be another.

Religion was also a worldview during, let's say, the Middle Ages. If religion is also a worldview, then any secular worldview must share some common properties with it. Otherwise, we would have a religious worldview and a secular 'something else'. What could distinguish worldviews from each other? It cannot be the fact that they ask or answer different questions. Rather, it is the fact that they give different answers to the same questions. The questions must be general enough to allow for different answers. They must be common across different religions and between religious and secular worldviews. Worldviews are each other's rivals because of their identity and difference: they share a set of questions and a set of answers, and they differ regarding interpretations of both. If this were not the case, they would be indifferent to each other; the questions of one would not be those of the other.

Neither religion nor worldviews can be treated on par with other intellectual products of the human mind like, for example, cosmological, philosophical, or scientific theories and speculations. Neither a religion nor a worldview has come into being as answers to questions that arise independently of having a religion or worldview. They do not solve any cognitive, emotional, or existential problems. Instead, such problems can only be formulated given the existence of a worldview or a religion. The difference between religion's claim to truth, and the cognitive claims of our intellectual products; or the difference between the way we test our theories and the difficulty of testing a worldview, draw attention to the dissimilarities between scientific theories and the status of entities like religions and worldviews. These dissimilarities reinforce the suggestion that worldviews are unlike theories in that the latter come into existence as answers to some problem. By contrast, in entities like religion and worldviews, certain kinds of questions arise.

Universalization of Religion

Thus far, secularization has been described at one level–as a process where beliefs from a specific religion become commonplace and are believed by everyone, from your grocer to your Guru. It is time to expand on what secularization signifies or how it happens.

Religion has to be couched in some or the other doctrine. Universalization of religion implies that religion becomes pristinely simple and its form or structure becomes so well-entrenched that its specific doctrines fade into the background even while their cognitive structure stays in place. The proselytizing drive of some specific religion (in our case Christianity) does not merely mean that it wins converts. It also means that it universalizes itself by becoming increasingly less Christian. Its doctrines spread in two distinct ways. First, by the conversion of people into Christianity. Second, by the widespread acceptance of its account by non-Christians, because the account spreads in a de-

Christianized (or secularized) form. This double aspect of religion enables the universalization of religion.

This double movement is also expressed in the double relation that religions have towards each other: they are intolerant of each other but there is also inter-religious dialogue and the gut-level feeling that 'all religion is one'. Doctrinal differences are both extremely important and, at the same time, the feeling persists that these differences are, at some level, rather unimportant. In those who 'really believe', both feelings are simultaneously present. Hence the urgency for an interfaith dialogue and ecumenism felt by the believers. At the same time, it is impossible to have a real dialogue because tolerance (as a religious, not a secular stance) is simply not possible.

In the West, Christianity universalized itself on a massive scale. The first phase merely universalized a specific religion as it won converts. However, its evolution and development laid the seeds for the universalization of religion–not Christianity. This is because religion can be decked in all sorts of different clothes. The Protestant Reformation sent many hurrying to their tailors and religion could now be clothed in many different ways. What we see after the Reformation is the first phase in the universalization of religion–unrestricted by space, time, culture or ideational clothes. Thinkers from the period of the French Enlightenment may have fought Christianity, attacked its doctrines, and made fun of its beliefs. They were indeed fighting religion–but only to free it from recognizably Christian clothes. Their victory was still the victory of religion–in another set of clothes.

Worldview is that set of clothes. It was brought forth by a specific religion, namely, Christianity. The emergence of something secular-sounding like a worldview might seem to signal a halt to the march of Christianity as a specific religion. However, this does not mean that religion is not being universalized. It does so as a worldview, as something other than and different from Christianity, Judaism and Islam. These religions make the Cosmos into an explanatory intelligible entity. A worldview does exactly the same, but in different ideational clothes. Thus, it is also a religion.

If this argument holds water, let's see how it illumines the situation which has brought us thus far. We can indeed better appreciate why the belief in the universality of religion has such strong roots. Its roots are religious, and religion itself has very deep and very wide roots in western culture. It has to do with the new clothes that religion has assumed over the centuries. Parallel to and alongside proselytization, Christianity has also been secularizing itself. It is not a movement from yesterday, or from the Enlightenment or even from the Protestant Reformation. Religion has constantly expressed this double movement.

Religion constitutes a significant element in the identity of western culture. The belief that religion is one of the constitutive elements of all cultures can be true only because the culture which believes in this is itself constituted by religion. The West has grown into a culture as religion has universalized itself. The West is a culture through the very story of religion itself. To tell such a story is to tell the story of a people in terms of one thread, one aspect, one theme, and of how, in fact, they became a people.

PART IV

The relationship between culture and religion can be understood by examining the structure of the learning process generated by religion. Thus, ethnographic facts about different cultures can be explored in a new light. Each culture has different configurations of learning which result in different ways of going about in the world.

CHAPTER XI

PRELUDE TO A COMPARATIVE
SCIENCE OF CULTURES

Why a "prelude"? It is because a comparative science of cultures can only be possible when there are multiple descriptions given by members of different cultures, using the background of their own cultures. Such a variety of descriptions does not exist at this time since all cultures are described within the framework of the western culture.

The West developed into a distinct cultural entity through, among other things, the double dynamic of religion. This double dynamic consisted in the proselytization of distinctly religious ideas, as well as the spread of these same ideas in a secular guise. The West is the becoming of such a people. To speak of western culture, it is not necessary to first define 'the West'. In his brilliant book on the formation of the western legal tradition, Berman formulates the idea thus:

> The West...is not to be found by recourse to a compass. Geographical boundaries help to locate it, but they shift from time to time. The West is, rather, a cultural term, but with a very strong diachronic dimension. It is not, however, simply an idea, it is a community. It implies both a historical structure and a structured history...
>
> The West, from this perspective, is not Greece, and Rome and Israel but the people of Western Europe *turning* to the Greek and Roman and Hebrew texts for inspiration, and *transforming* those texts in ways that would have astonished their authors. (Berman 1983: 2-3; emphasis in original).

In many ways, the above citation captures the significance of the ideas outlined in this book. Nevertheless, more needs to be done if we wish to understand cultural differences between the West and other cultures. The aspiration in the final part of this book is to develop an overarching hypothesis that can relate culture to religion.

Learning Processes and Cultural Differences

In broad terms, learning is the way an organism makes its environment habitable. When compared to other animals, the human species suffers from disadvantages from several points of view. Such a species, if it has to survive at all, will have to place an enormous premium on its ability to make its environment habitable. The process of learning is crucial to its survival. Evolutionary theory further tells us that reproduction is an inefficient way of guaranteeing human progeny. Coping with groups has been as important as coping with nature in the survival of our species. Human groups, thus, constitute a parallel environment for human beings. Accordingly, we have to learn to live with a group and we have to learn to live in the natural environment.

Generally speaking, human beings are socialized in terms of living with others. The process of socialization involves transmitting knowledge from the reservoir of the group. This reservoir consists of resources such as customs, myths, traditions, etc., which the individual draws upon to learn. The same reservoir places limits on the content and the mechanisms of transmission. Child-rearing practices, formal and informal schooling, etc., are the mechanisms of transmission from one generation to another. These socialization mechanisms have evolved either through deliberation and reflection or through unintended discovery processes. They, in their turn, are limited by the content of transmission.

At the present time we do not know if human beings are genetically compelled to learn in any one particular way. Because of the great diversity of human environments, it is plausible to speak of different kinds of learning processes. Not only have human beings structured their groups differently during the course of history but they also have occupied diverse regions of the earth. The creation of complex societies and forms of social interaction over the centuries; the creation of rich and subtle theories and speculations; the creation of wonderful forms of music, dance, and painting–all of these lend credibility to the idea that they are the results of different kinds of learning processes. Therefore, until such time as there is conclusive evidence with respect to how human learning takes place, we can work with the idea that the human capacity to learn is not limited to any one species-typical learning process.

A human infant must learn how to go about in its natural and social environment. It learns these goings-about from its group. In this way, the individual develops a structured way of going about in the world. The nature and extent of this structuring depends on what the social environment transmits and how it does that. Thus, differences between cultures can be seen as having something to do with the difference in social environments which results in different ways of going about in the world. This makes it plausible to suggest that cultural differences have something to do with the difference in learning processes.

Cultural Differences and Configurations of Learning

There are many kinds of learning processes and each culture has several kinds of learning processes *simultaneously*: the kind that is required to build societies and groups; the kind that creates poetry, music and dance; or the kind required to develop theories and speculations. Members of a culture develop these processes in different degrees and combinations. If we characterize the product of learning as 'knowledge', we can rewrite the above proposal thus: by producing knowledge, human beings manage to live in the world; there are different kinds of knowledge in each culture. This constitutes the reservoir of knowledge present in a culture and teaching involves transmitting this knowledge.

With this in mind, let's see if we can chalk out an approximation of cultural differences:

(1)   The difference between cultures is the presence of several kinds of knowledge in different degrees.

(2)   This reservoir of knowledge puts certain constraints on the content of the transmission as well as on the mechanisms of transmission from one generation to another. Therefore,

cultural differences can be described according to the constraints placed on the learning processes.

(3)   These constraints pattern or structure the goings-about of an individual in the world. That is, there are patterns or structures to our learning activities, as well as to the way we go about in the world.

(4)   As an individual is socialized to go-about, it also learns to structure further goings-about. The varieties of going-about depend upon the different kinds of knowledge present in a culture.

(5)   This process involves a meta-learning, i.e., a learning to learn. An individual not only learns some knowledge but also learns to reproduce this knowledge. That is to say, whatever is used to form or structure learning also brings about this meta-learning by generating the process of learning to learn.

(6)   Because the structuring process configures different kinds of learning, one kind of learning is dominant in such a configuration. Other kinds of learning are subordinate. Such configurations of learning are culture-specific ways of learning. Cultural differences can thus be described in terms of culture-specific ways of learning.

It is worth re-emphasizing that a culturally-specific way of learning does not entail that each culture have only one kind of learning process. The claim is merely that the relationship between the dominant and the subordinate learning processes varies across cultures. A configuration of learning comes into being slowly over a period of time through the coordination of different kinds of learning processes. Because we can study a culture by studying culture-specific ways of learning, it is possible to describe a culture in terms of culture-specific knowledge. Even though the knowledge produced by each learning process is present in all cultures, even though each configuration of learning contains learning processes present in all cultures, knowledge produced by a particular configuration of learning is culture-specific.

With respect to the theme of this essay, here is my suggestion. In the West, a root model of order brings about a configuration of learning. This root model is religion, which configures learning processes by structuring the experience of the world in a particular way. Typically, this specific way of learning involves 'knowing about'. It produces a species of culture-specific knowledge, namely, theoretical knowledge, that we call the sciences.

Religion as the Root Model of Order

As we have seen, religion claims that the world is explanatorily intelligible. It does not merely claim this; it makes the world into such an entity by itself being an exemplification of the order that the Cosmos is supposed to be. Religion generates an attitude and an orientation; it puts constraints on the intellectual and practical energies of a culture; it generates a feeling of relevance and importance. It is able to do this because it is the ultimate example of an explanation. The structure of its description mirrors the structure of the object described. Because of this relation, religion is the model of the order the world is supposed to be. In this sense, it is the basic model which inspires other explanations, including scientific explanations.

Religion generates a culturally-specific way of learning. Here, going about in the world requires knowledge about the world. Successful navigation in the world requires knowing what there is in the world. This orientation comes about because religion claims that the Cosmos expresses God's purposes. To act in the world requires knowing what those purposes are. Therefore, knowledge about the world–knowing what there is in the world–is a prerequisite for properly going about in the world.

Knowing what there is in the world means seeking to decipher God's Will, as it is expressed in the world. His Will is revealed in the phenomena and is also their hidden regulator. Discovering these regularities focuses the intellectual and practical energies of this culture. Actions in the world are 'proper' insofar as 'knowledge about' an action guides the actions. To be a friend or a father, one must know what it is to be a friend or a father; to build a good society, one must first know what a good society is; to build human relationships, one must know what they are, etc. This type of a rational action is the execution of a rational decision, which is the result of rational deliberation using rational criteria about rationally-gathered information.

Human goings-about in the world begin to mirror the Divine in many ways. God's will and His actions are different from each other but difficult to distinguish. Human intentions and human actions appear to share the same fate. In such a culture, human actions are described according to their intentional states, or as an expression of beliefs. The very identity (or existence) of actions depends upon specifying the agent and his intentions. 'Knowing about' becomes the dominant way of learning and is extended to all other goings-about in the world. Because all human actions are thought to be expressions of beliefs, knowledge about other cultures means having knowledge about the beliefs of these cultures. Thus, a culture-specific way of learning is also expressed in the way a culture seeks to understand other cultures.

Then there is God's message that does several things in this culture. As a message, because oral, it is not only a source of knowledge but also the form of knowledge. All knowledge is sayable. If something is knowledge, it can be said. Otherwise, it is a hunch, an intuition, or perhaps a skill. However, the main thing is that knowledge is what can be said. Even though this message is oral, it is constantly accessible as a text. Stories, sagas, or myths become texts, studying which one can find out what they are saying. This interpretative orientation can be carried as far as one likes: actions can be interpreted in terms of beliefs or in terms of symbols; cultures can be interpreted in terms of their worldviews; and, further, one can even see cultures as texts and oneself as the interpreter. The possibilities are endless.

In such a culture, inter-individual problems get resolved by talking about them. Sophisticated psychological jargon ends up as clichés in daily language. Art, architecture, and poetry become subordinate modes, as they, too, are embodiments of ideas; they too tell us about the world. The artist tells us about his perception of what there is in the world; he expresses 'abstract' ideas; he does 'conceptual' art and, through his chosen medium, enters into debates with contemporaries. Art is thinking-about; art makes you think-about too. The distance between a critic of art and an artist begins to narrow. What counts are one's ideas irrespective of whether one can paint or sculpt.

This way of learning makes 'knowledge about' the only form of knowledge. Knowledge about what? Of what there is. What is there? An explanatorily intelligible entity. The Cosmos becomes a place where you can ask certain kinds of questions. One such pertains to 'meaning'; the other seeks explanations. As the root model of order, religion enables one to pose the 'meaning problems': does the Cosmos have a meaning? What is the meaning of man? What is the meaning of life? The foundation of these questions can and does vary: it used to be the Bible, now it could be biology; it used to be the infinite God, today it is our finitude, etc.

The gradual emergence of religion as the root model of order is, among other things, what made the West into a culture. The universalization of religion exhibits a two-fold dynamic: proselytization by the Christian communities and the secularization of religion as the root model of order. Seeking 'knowledge about', as the dominant learning process, generates theoretical knowledge: the natural sciences–a species of knowledge that grew out of a religious culture.

A Dialogue Concerning Religion

Since I have suggested several times that the development of science is related to religion, it is time to expand upon this topic. A good way to examine the stages involved in the kind of experience that religion structures is to return to the example of the 'primitive' man. Let's reconsider this issue in light of what has been said about the Biblical structuring of the experience of the world, and the suggestion that religion is the root model of order in the West.

If religion shapes the basic experience of the world-as-an-order, how can we describe such an experience? We can distinguish three conceptually distinct moments in this experience by taking our 'primitive' man as an example. To begin with, he has a naïve experience of order. This naïve experience is merely that of the regularities of his world: seasonal, astronomical, natural, and biological. Let's further suppose that he comes across unanticipated or unexpected events off and on. Now his world consists of two groups of events: the familiar and the unfamiliar. Regular encounters with the unfamiliar transform them into the familiar, even if they remain unexpected. Thus he would have gone to his grave, had he not had the good fortune of meeting a member from a religious culture, say, a certain Mr. David Hume by name.

"Look here, old fellow", as an imaginary *Dialogue Concerning the Necessity of Religion* might have gone, "why do you think there was thunder when the sky was cloudless, and there is no rain on the plains?" Our primitive scratches his head, looks up at the blue sky, blinks in puzzlement, and admits that it never really struck him to ask this question. "I forgive you for this lapse, not being Scottish and all that", continues Mr. Hume, "but tell me, old chap, why is the sky blue, why don't pigs have wings, or even why your father died the other day?" Our primitive gapes at the extraordinary sharpness of the interrogator and replies that things have always been this way ever since he was a young boy. The sky is blue when there are no clouds; many people he has known have died; and as to why pigs don't have wings, well, there's this story his grandmother told him...

"Yes, yes, I know all that", interrupts Mr. Hume impatiently. "But why, my dear fellow, why?" Without waiting for an answer, Mr. Hume goes on: "Thunder strikes from a cloudless sky, the sky is blue, people die, pigs do not have wings...and you don't even know why. There is no rhyme or reason to any of these things. In fact..." Pausing ominously for a moment, Mr. Hume lowers his voice to a dramatic whisper. "Don't you see, old chap, the world is a chaos. Things just happen..."

In other words, the second conceptual moment must deny the naïve experience of order, and focus on the unexpected, unanticipated, and the unfamiliar. It must then reinterpret the familiar in terms of the unfamiliar. At this point, the world does begin to appear chaotic in light of the account that has just re-described the world.

The third conceptual moment then reintroduces order into this chaotic world. This too is part of an account. The ordering force is invisible; it is hidden below the surface. It is not an empirical given, but one which manifests itself in the form of the 'order' the world appears to have. As David Hume put it:

> The order of the universe proves an omnipotent mind; that is, a mind whose will is *constantly attended* with the obedience of

every creature and being. (Hume 1740: 633, n. 1; emphasis in original).

These, then, are the conceptual moments involved in the experience of the world-as-an-order in a religious culture: the bracketing away of a naïve experience of order, the postulation of chaotic phenomena, and the rediscovery of an underlying force to account for the apparent phenomenal order. Hume's description of the origin of religion is not an account of how religions came into being, but an expression of his own culture's experience of the world. It involves the postulation of a hidden force to reduce the 'chaos' the world is. Precisely this account makes the world appear chaotic in the first place. Such an experience of the world requires that the experience be structured by an account. It has to be an account, linguistic in nature, because both 'chaos' and the underlying 'order' are theoretical notions and not part of a naïve experience of the world.

In this sense, these explanations about the origin of religion are actually the results of the development of religion. Religion makes the world into an explanatorily intelligible entity, and it does so as an account. In other words, religion structures the experience of the world so that, in the absence of deeper underlying laws, the phenomenal world seems chaotic. Human beings have never experienced a chaotic world independent of a belief in the experience of the world-as-an order. Yet those who belong to a religious culture are convinced that such is the case. Consequently, they attribute an experience of chaos to the 'primitive' man who supposedly orders his world by postulating an invisible set of powers to regulate the chaos.

Science and the Root Model of Order

One of the familiar stories regarding the growth of scientific thinking in the West is about the conflict between the Church and Science. While there is a great deal of truth to this, the basic thrust of the narrative can be put in a different light. This conflict is not due to any inherent antagonism between science and religion. Religion was a necessary condition for the development of scientific thinking. Many thinkers have perceived the important role religion has played in the growth of the sciences. Their arguments, however, are different from the thesis I am developing here.

First, religion related phenomena to each other: the Cosmos to the individual; actions to beliefs; individuals to society, and provided the ground for all of these in one single postulate–the God of the Bible was the fountainhead of everything. In fact, in its conflict with the philosophical schools of the Greco-Roman period, one of the virtues of the Christian doctrine was its simplicity.

Second, this doctrine provided an explanatory link between phenomena otherwise unconnected, by appealing to an invisible ordering force. The dissemination of this belief among all layers of the population for more than a thousand years is absolutely unique to religion. The typical belief that grounded the basic attitude of the West for centuries was the explanatory intelligibility of the Cosmos.

Third, this intelligibility was not evident to the senses, but required a search for the underlying explanatory units. In other words, what we call a scientific attitude today is continuous with the religious attitude. Religion formed it, nurtured it, and gave birth to science as a result. Religion, then, provides us with the most fundamental model of what it is for something to be an explanation. It links parts of the world to each other by postulating necessary and intelligible connections between them. This is the reason why the natural sciences emerged in religious cultures: among the Jews, Christians, and the Muslims. And why they failed to emerge in, say, China.

Of course, this is not sufficient to explain the extraordinary growth of the sciences. This is merely to identify one of the conditions for their emergence in the West. To make this claim stick, several other questions need to be answered: what about the sciences in Antiquity? How are we to understand the conflict between science and religion? How about the development of the science of language and ritual in India? More empirical research needs to be done before these questions can be answered adequately. Nevertheless, we can try to develop one thread of an answer as it is relevant to some of these questions.

Religion and Science

For the growth of the sciences, it was necessary that there be a fertile cognitive soil where speculations and theories could take root and grow. In Antiquity, to be sure, we do see the emergence of the sciences (geometry, hydrostatics, etc.). However, their growth was restricted by the extremely limited social group within which they arose. What religion did was to generalize the attitude required for the growth of the sciences. It severed the link that had tied the sciences to an elite social group. Now the sciences could develop, expand, and flourish in the cognitive soil prepared for them. That is to say, religion transformed science into a social process by slowly universalizing itself. It developed a way of learning through which science could emerge and it enabled its emergence by making the Will of the Sovereign constant, and His works trustworthy, in an absolutely perfect way.

The dynamic of religion also helps us to understand the conflict between religion and science. As religion spread through its proselytizing drive, it also began to secularize itself: through the crystallization of the root model of order. This very secularization of religion, however, limited its proselytizing aspect. Consequently, a religion is limited by itself, i.e., in its character as religion. Hence, in the initial stages, we witness hostility against the growth of scientific theories. These theories challenged the doctrines of a specific religion. Until then, only rival religions had posed such challenges. The consequence of this challenge by scientific theories was that Christianity ended up treating them as rivals.

The 'knowledge' that religion is can never be claimed by finite human beings. Our knowledge is hypothetical and tentative, whereas religion lays claim to the truth. As human beings, we can only have a perspectival relationship with the world. Growth of theoretical knowledge implies knowledge of increasingly more slices of the world. The more we slice the world, the more we know how to slice, which leads to more slicing. Specialization increases in leaps and bounds. Increase in knowledge can only take the form of increased specialization. This view has an important bearing with respect to the relation between human knowledge and 'the truth' that religion is. Any kind of human knowledge is indifferent to 'the truth'. As human beings slice the world up in many different ways, and the knowledge of these slices combine and recombine in different ways, human knowledge moves away from–neither against, nor for, but totally indifferent to–religious knowledge.

At first sight, theoretical knowledge appears unlimited. However, this statement requires qualification. First, only knowledge can draw the limits to knowledge (ignorance is not the limit of knowledge). Second, since the dominant way of learning subordinates other knowledge-producing processes, other modes of knowledge cannot draw that limit either. Hence, it appears as though there are no limits to this configuration of learning. There are, however, limits. The heathens and pagans limit religion; other cultures limit any particular culture; the boundary to knowledge is drawn by knowledge and within knowledge. Our knowledge about the world itself draws a limit, by pointing out other configurations of learning present in cultures elsewhere. Other kinds of knowledge, that are products of other configurations of learning, are as much knowledge as theoretical knowledge is. Let's, therefore, pick an alternate configuration of learning and show how such a configuration can also generate knowledge. The example, again, will be India.

Conceptualizing Cultural Differences

We can regard configurations of learning as cultural answers to the biological problem of our survival. That is, they answer the question: 'How to live?' One answer to this question, as examined above, is to find out what there is in the world. Another answer can be derived by finding out how to go about in the world. Both the question and the answer become performative in nature. In this case, a practical or performative learning process will dominate the configuration of learning. As a culturally-specific way of learning, it would also give identity to a culture.

Its way of going-about solves the problem of 'how to live' not by building a worldview but by developing an ability to try to live the best one can. Its way of learning involves *how to live*. This is not done by imparting knowledge about the world but by imparting practical knowledge. If the Indian traditions impart this knowledge to their members, this culture itself must be an embodiment of this 'how to' knowledge.

Since the dominant unit of teaching in such a culture does not impart knowledge about the world, i.e., it does not tell you much about what the world is like, such units of knowledge cannot be considered explanatory in nature. Neither can they be considered to be true or false. Stories, for example, are neither true nor false, nor are they explanatory. Moreover, if this way of learning is specific to a culture, then its dominant mode of learning must be deeply connected to practices. Goings-about in the world must themselves be experienced in performative terms.

An Alternate Configuration of Learning

Let's try to envisage a culture-specific way of going-about where performative knowledge (seen as a 'how to' ability) dominates. This is a purely hypothetical construction, generated under the constraints imposed by a particular kind of knowledge, i.e., theoretical knowledge.

First, the domain of such knowledge will have to do with building and sustaining groups and societies; creating and sustaining inter-individual relationships. More broadly put, the domain of practical knowledge is the social environment.

Second, if this knowledge is the dominant one in a culture, the social environment must exhibit an extraordinary degree of stability and cohesion, integration and differentiation, complexity and dynamism. Individual members should be able to reproduce such an environment without knowing the rules of its reproduction.

Third, performative knowledge must subordinate other kinds of knowledge. That is to say, the object of 'thinking about' must be the 'activities' of going-about; the purpose of 'thinking about' is to improve these activities.

Fourth, theoretical speculations must be formulated in recognizably performative terms.

Fifth, in a configuration of learning where practical or performative learning dominates, the entity that structures the configuration must itself be a structured set of goings-about in the world.

Sixth, this structured set of goings-about, which structures the learning processes, must also generate a meta-learning, or a way of learning to learn.

Seventh, if this configuration of learning has to be stable, the structure of the entity that forms this configuration of learning should be seen as a possible answer to the problem of survival.

These seven parameters will enable us to think more concretely about this different configuration of learning. What kind of an entity is it that could structure a configuration of learning where performative learning dominates? If we conceive of our actions in the world in terms of kinds: teaching, or acting as a father, or doing logic, etc., this entity would be a structured set of generic actions that belongs to no specific kind of going-about in the world.

It would be helpful to look at what this entity has to do to structure actions. We can do so by drawing a parallel between this entity and religion on one hand, and looking at the way we talk about actions on the other. In a religious configuration, actions are differentiated according to the intentional states of an actor. That is, actions are what an actor does; what he believes to be doing; what he hopes (desires, anticipates, etc.) to achieve thereby. Minimally, we need at least two things to identify an action—an actor and his intentions. This is because in this way of going about in the world, actions are expressions of belief-states. Because belief-states are always someone's belief states, we need an actor. By contrast, in our alternate configuration of learning, this is not the case. Actions do not instantiate belief-states; they are generic actions that are agent-less, hence they are goal-less too. Therefore, the entity that structures the goings-about of individuals whose learning is predominantly performative must be a set of actions without agents, without goals and without meaning.

This way of formulating the description already shows that we are reaching the limits of our ability to conceptualize an alternate configuration of learning, while remaining within the framework of the one we are using. We are not discussing human actions as they are conceptualized in the western configuration of learning. We are trying to think about another configuration of learning which structures human goings-about differently. People think, dream, and hope in every culture. People reason everywhere too.

One way to talk about the relation between thought and action is to say that 'actions are intentional'. However, there are other ways of expressing the relation between action and thought, including one where thought merely limits action.

Religion has generated a way of going about in the world that is recognizably religious. Similarly, the entity that produces performative knowledge must also generate a way of going-about which is recognizably practical. This entity is a structured set of generic actions; it could be described as non-intentional, agent-less, and goal-less. This entity is ritual.

Ritual, like religion, brings about a culturally-specific way of going about in the world. Learning to do rituals is performative; the way in which members of this culture go about in the world is itself recognizably ritualized. Finally, the configuration of learning generated by ritual is stable because the ritual structure is a recursive structure. A recursive structure is one that allows the sequencing and combining of smaller units into larger wholes. It is not task-specific. Thus, the structure allows for different permutations and combinations applicable in a variety of contexts. Performative or practical knowledge is the ability to act recursively in the world. The social environment created in such a culture will itself exhibit the properties of recursive systems. The history of this culture, the coming-to-be of a people, just like the way it is with the West, is the story of the emergence, crystallization, and development of a recursively structured learning configuration.

Because rituals are what they are due to their structure, they are 'meaningless' actions. However, we must be careful in assuming what is 'meaningless' about rituals. It will not do to fall back on the common description of rituals within the West which is that they are "mechanical, repetitive, and stereotyped". We would only describe a recursive structure as being "repetitive" when we do not recognize it as a structure. It seems "stereotyped" because configurations of actions appear to return constantly. It seems "mechanical", because it appears difficult to specify it in terms of intentional states. Remember, in the common-sense psychology of the West, even opening a door is seen as an intentional act. In exactly the same intentional psychology, rituals appear "mechanical" and it is difficult to fit them under an intentional description. The point (or the goal) of ritual does not appear to be evident.

At this point, theoreticians of the West step in wearing ridiculous hats. Of course, there is a purpose to rituals, they claim. Its function, you guessed it, is to reduce anxiety and tension; to act as a cementing bond of the community (*'re-ligare'* perhaps), and so on. Perhaps ritual does do some or all of these things, but, surely, this is a bit silly. The same is also said of religion, of dancing in Africa, of anything one does not know much about, which is just about everything regarding human beings: war does it, sex does it, ideology does it, worldviews do it, magic does it, religions do it, so, why not rituals?

Further, there is a tendency to draw a relation between rituals and something else to make sense of the claim that rituals are meaningless. Rituals enact a myth, it is claimed; or they are symbolic actions, which signify important events; or whatever else takes one's fancy. The motivation is the same in these cases: to show that rituals may appear meaningless, but they are not. Why ever not? Because all our actions are believed to be meaningful, it is difficult to conceive of an action that is not. If every mechanical action is a ritual, there would be difficulty in distinguishing an obsessive or pathological action from a ritualistic one. To Freud, this was no problem: both religion and ritual were neurotic behaviors.

The way in which the West characterizes ritual shows an acknowledgement of the fact that rituals are somehow different from intentional activities of human beings. Because of this, there is the acknowledgement that we may perform rituals believing whatever we may want to believe. The persistent idea is that rituals appeal to a 'need for rituals' the way 'religious experience' appeals to a 'need for a religious experience'. They are acts pure and simple, acts as such. To act, that is, independent of the meaning of these actions. As Lewis puts it:

> What is clear and explicit about ritual is how to do it–rather than its meaning. (1982: 19).

Such a meaningless set of actions, in a culture where meaning questions predominate, appear best given up. After all, performing meaningless actions knowingly is irrational or pathological.

In a culture where ritual forms a configuration of learning, the way its members go about in the world will itself be recognizably ritualistic. The entire social process itself would look ritualized,

> from the way the emperor opens the doors of the temple of Heaven on great ceremonial occasions right down to the way one entertains the humblest guest and serves him tea. (Smith, H. 1972:10).

In China, Japan, and India, people have reflected on rituals much more extensively than in the West. They have suggested that a correct performance of rituals is an absolute presupposition for the continued existence of society. Because rituals generate a way of learning whose domain is that of building societies, the insight about the 'cohesive' function of the rituals is preserved. A random example from Chinese culture, as the *Book of Rites* (the *Li Chi*) puts it:

> Ceremonies are the bond that holds multitudes together, and if the bond be removed, those multitudes fall into confusion. (Citation by Radcliffe-Brown in Schneider, Ed., 1964: 67.)

This is not merely the opinion of the early writers. Modern writers share the same impression. As Watson formulates his opinion on the subject:

> By enforcing orthopraxy (correct practice) rather than orthodoxy (correct belief)...it (was) possible to incorporate people from many different ethnic or regional backgrounds, with varying beliefs and attitudes, into an overarching social system we now call China. (1988: 10-11).

And further:

> If anything is central to the creation and maintenance of a unified Chinese culture, it is the standardization of ritual...What we accept today as 'Chinese' is in large part the product of a centuries-long process of standardization (*ibid.* 3-4).

While Watson believes that this makes China unique, Staal repeats the same sentiment with respect to India. Assuming that both ancient and modern scholars share the intuition that rituals were somehow responsible for the creation and reproduction of societies, our problem is to explain this intuition.

Performative knowledge is responsible for the creation and reproduction of societies, whether in the East or in the West. However, my suggestion is that neither religion nor ritual is the cohesive bond, which enables the creation of communities. Rather, ritual generates a configuration of learning, whose *dominant* learning process builds societies. Religion generates another configuration of learning whose *subordinate* learning process builds societies. Adherence to a worldview does not create a community any more than adherence to some ritual creates societies. Empirical histories of religions in fact show the opposite: religion divides communities; it does not unite them. As for the idea that rituals unite societies by being present across a culture, recall what Weightman said of Hinduism:

> (no) practice can be held to be essential to Hinduism. It is…possible to find groups of Hindus whose respective faiths have almost nothing in common with one another, and it is also impossible to identify any universal belief or practice that is common to all Hindus. (1984: 191-192).

It must be obvious what has gone wrong. Many correctly identify that religion dominates one culture and ritual the other. Because both are societies too, they conclude that both religion and ritual are cohesive bonds. My proposal is attractive because it captures the insights of these thinkers, while shedding light on their confusions at the same time. In the process, without violating the 'facts' at our disposal, avenues for further research open up. If intolerance is necessary for religion, how can it create communities? Since rituals are performed by individuals at home, how can a community come into being? It makes more sense to consider that both ritual and religion generate configurations of learning whose learning processes build societies, rather than to claim that ritual and religion themselves build societies.

If performative knowledge is a product of this alternate configuration of learning, then it must also leave its mark on other walks of life in such a culture. Three areas can illustrate this point: the experience of going about in the world, speculative thinking, and the problem of the meaning of life.

In western culture, we experience ourselves as agents. Our hopes, desires, and frustrations appear to guide our activities. Deep down, the belief is that we are 'selves' or 'persons' with ambitions, longings, and projects. What would happen to such an experience in a culture where ritual structured our activities? Since ritual actions are 'agent-less', the configuration of learning brought forth by ritual must engender an absence of the experience of self, agency or personhood; or create a weak sense of self at the minimum. Is this the case?

Agehananda Bharati, an anthropologist, puts it thus:

> None of the scholastics of the Hindu tradition was concerned with the empirical self in any manner resembling that of the psychologists, anthropologists, sociologists, and even poets in the west. All Hindu traditions talk about the self either in order to reject its ontological status...or to assimilate it to a theological and metaphysical construct, which is a Self with a capital 'S'. When any of the Hindu traditions speak about what might look like the individual, like an empirical self, it is not to analyze but to denigrate it...The self as the basis of such important human achievements as scholarship, artistic skill, technological invention, etc. is totally ignored in the Indian philosophical texts.

> One might think that such abstruse thoughts could only have been relevant or exciting to an intellectual or religious elite...that would not affect Hindu India at large. Common sense and intelligent intuition might suggest that the non-scholarly Hindu had a down-to-earth notion of something very much like the subject-matter of an 'empirical self'. Such an intuition, however, would be wrong. Hindu thoughts and perceptions, Hindu values–*all* Hindu values–have been thoroughly informed by these...concepts. (1985: 189).

And again:

> Hindu concepts of self and Buddhist concepts of self and non-self...share family resemblances so strong that they cannot be juxtaposed except by radical contrast to western

notions…Western notions of self are systematically unrelated
to Indian notions, Hindu, Buddhist, and Jaina (*ibid.* 204).

Shweder and Bourne, two psychologists, speaking about the
differences in the concept of 'person' between the Americans and
the Indians, say:

> It is by reference to "contexts and cases" that Oriyas (in
> Orissa, India) describe the personalities of their friends,
> neighbours, and workmates. These personal accounts…are
> concrete and relational…The concrete-relational way of
> thinking about other persons differs from the abstract style of
> our American informants. Americans tell you what is true of a
> person's behavior (e.g., he is friendly, arrogant, and
> intelligent) while tending to overlook the behavioral
> context…(T)he striking tendency of Oriyas (is) to be more
> concrete and relational than Americans. (1982: 172-73).

Alan Roland, a practicing psychoanalyst, tries to show the same
thing. Contrasting the "familial self" of the Indians and the
Japanese to the "individualized self " of the Americans, he says of
the former:

> (T)he experiential sense of self is of a "we-self" that is felt to
> be highly relational in different social contexts. (The)
> narcissistic configurations of we-self regard that denote self-
> esteem (derive) from strong identification with the reputation
> and honor of the family and other groups…from nonverbal
> mirroring throughout life…(A) socially contextual ego-
> ideal…carefully observes traditionally defined reciprocal
> responsibilities and obligations, and a public self (that looks
> after) the social etiquette of diverse hierarchical relationships,
> in complexly varying interpersonal contexts and situations…
> These inner psychological organizations, structures, and
> processes of the familial self underlie the great variety of
> group character throughout the Indian subcontinent… (1988:
> 8).

Speculations about the universe would also take on a characteristic
tinge. The *karmic* doctrine could be seen as an attempt to
thematize rituals in this way. One of the creation stories from the
Rig Veda speaks of the world in these terms: the gods created the
world by sacrificing the primal man. By sacrificing, they were
sacrificing to sacrifice. This is a description of the world in terms
of ritual. The act of creation was a performative rite; the

emergence of the world is a ritual; the act of performing a ritual is a ritual; and ritual is all there is to the world.

When speculations about the world and human beings are formulated in action terms, one of the conceptual problems is about the actor-action relationship. In fact, this problem would be seen as important in a culture where the sense of self is either absent or weak. The reason need not be the feeling that action without an agent is impossible. It could well be to do with actions themselves; whether 'something' acts; whether this something is acted upon by the action; whether action-less agents could also exist as much as agent-less actions, etc. These different answers partially distinguish Indian traditions from one another. Let's look at the Buddhist polemical formulation of the issue:

> The view that movement is identical with the mover is not proper. The view that the mover is different from the motion is not proper. If the movement were to be identical with the mover, it would follow that there is identity of agent and action. If the discrimination is made that the mover is different from motion, then there would be movement without the mover, and mover without the movement. (2, 18-20; Kalupahana, Trans., 1986: 128-129).

Therefore,

> An agent proceeds depending upon action and action proceeds depending upon the agent. We do not perceive any other way of establishing them. Following this method of rejection of agent and action, one should understand grasping. The remaining existents should be critically examined in terms of the concepts of action and agent. (8, 12-13; *ibid.* 186-187)

The agent and his action come into being simultaneously, said some among the Buddhists. Some others held that it was not an empirical agent but the *atman*, who did not act but was nevertheless the only agent. This is present in everything, has all properties and no properties, and so on and so forth. In the *Brihadaranyaka Upanishad*, for instance, there are descriptions of this *atman*. He dwells in the earth, the water, fire, sky, air, heaven, sun, space, moon and stars, ether, darkness, light, all beings, breath, tongue, eye, ear, mind, skin, knowledge, etc. How does he dwell in all these things? What is he? Here is an example of a verse:

> He who dwells in the seed, and within the seed, whom the seed does not know, whose body the seed is, and who pulls the seed within, he is thy Self, the puller within, the immortal; unseen, but seeing; unheard, but hearing; unperceived, but perceiving; unknown but knowing. There is no other seer but he, there is no other hearer but he, there is no other knower but he. This is thy Self, the ruler within, the immortal. (III, 7, 23: Müller, Ed., 1879: 136)

This *atman* does some interesting things:

> And as a caterpillar, after having reached the end of a blade of grass, and after having made another approach (to another blade), draws itself together towards it, thus does this Self, after having thrown off this body and dispelled all ignorance, and after making another approach (to another body), draw himself together towards it. And as a goldsmith, taking a piece of gold, turns it into another, newer and more beautiful shape, so does this Self, after having thrown off this body...makes unto himself another newer and more beautiful shape...That Self is indeed Brahman, consisting of knowledge, mind, life, sight, hearing, earth, water, wind, ether, light and no light, desire and no desire, anger and no anger, right or wrong, and all things. (IV, 4, IV-V: *ibid.* 175-176).

There is at least one way in which even the idea of rebirth becomes possible evidence for the suggestions I am putting forward. It becomes possible to talk about the significance or the meaning of actions without taking recourse to intentional states. That is, by determining an action with respect to what went before and what comes after. If the self is only weakly experienced, then the significance of the self would lie in its relationship to its predecessors and to its successors. The question about the meaning and purpose of the life of some person is intelligible only by referring to what went before this life and what comes after this life. Life would be an unbroken movement of lives; by the same token, there could be neither a unique or a radical beginning, nor a unique or a radical end to a person.

I am not interested in either defending or criticizing these positions. Before undertaking either, we need to understand them.

All I am trying to do now is to tie some known 'facts' about Indian culture as possible evidence for my proposals. The evidence would look like this if India indeed has a different configuration of learning generated by a set of actions.

A Difference That Makes a Difference

I have attempted to conceptualize cultural differences in terms of configurations of learning, while remaining within a culturally-specific way of going about in the world. In anthropology, this problem is examined in terms of 'relativism' and 'universalism'. "How can we ever be certain that we have truly understood other cultures?" asks one; "But then", says the other, "when can we be certain that we have really and truly understood ourselves?" "Because everything that is said is within our own cultural framework, we can never understand the other" is the general objection. When so many intelligent people passionately discuss a theme, it tends to suggest that there's a genuine issue there somewhere. However, the way in which these disputes take place indicates a greater likelihood that this is a pseudo-debate. I would like to trace one facet of this problem as it is relevant to the theme of this essay.

Consider two mothers with sick children. One goes to an image of Ganesha and the other to that of St. Anthony. How can we assume that both behaviors are members of the same class? Let's examine this question by generalizing it as a problem that confronts any student of religion.

Despite their differences, several observances, such as pilgrimages or fasting, appear common across both India (Asia) and the West. Consider, for example, devotional movements like the *Bhakti* movement in India. If we look at the attitudes, orientations, and thoughts expressed in devotional songs we cannot but be struck by their closeness to attitudes, orientations, and thoughts considered characteristically 'religious' in the West. How can we understand the closeness between, say, *Bhakti* and the characteristically religious feeling in the West, if India (Asia) does not indeed know of religions?

The first point to consider is that merely noting a similarity between two entities does not tell us much. It is always possible to draw a similarity relationship between any two objects in the world in one way or another. I could say that a tree is similar to a laptop because both contain carbon. This is not a particularly interesting observation. Things can have something in common in one particular description of the world and not in another. Facts can have multiple implications. These general points, made in excruciating detail throughout this essay, are not meant to be answers to the questions raised above but merely to neutralize their force.

As a substantive answer to this question, let's begin with the following observation: the question "what distinguishes cultures from one another?" constitutes the most fundamental preoccupation of every anthropologist. In spite of this, anthropological theory has not formulated it as a problem. In fact, ethnological field work and theoretical anthropology go their different ways precisely around this question. While doing field work, the ethnologist focuses upon details and differences; while attempting to build a theory, the anthropologist is on the lookout for a grand unifying theory of human culture. This internal opposition seems to exist within all anthropologists. Consequently, it does not come as a surprise to see groups polarized around the issue of the relative importance of theory and fieldwork in anthropological practice.

An ethnologist might give a very precise answer to the question, "what are the differences between the *Holi* festival in North India and the New Year celebrations in Sicily?" However, his fieldwork results do not answer the question whether these differences constitute cultural differences. A theoretical anthropologist merely sees similarities. New Year celebrations are part of each culture, or so he might reason, and thus arrive at the question: why is the New Year celebration a necessary component of human culture?

Even though the above characterization may be crude, it will suffice to illustrate the point that mere fieldwork does not suffice. We need a theory about cultural differences in order to build a theory of human culture. The theory I am developing here enables us to sift through differences. It shows that a mode of learning dominant in one culture works as a subordinate mode in other cultures. The relationships between the dominant and subordinate processes of learning, among other things, give shape to a culture.

In this sense, religion or worldview is absent in Indian (Asian) culture. However, this does not imply that the elements present in a religion are absent altogether. The presence of elements in cultures, which resemble each other very closely, does not tell us much in and by itself. These elements could be the products of different processes. Both a fortress and a cathedral make use of some basic elements: wood, cement, bricks, iron, or stones. We can either focus on these elements, or study the structure. Depending on the focus of our research, we could argue that all the elements of one culture are present in the other or we could say what their differences are. That is, we can either regard culture as a set of elements, or we can see it as a structured way of going about in the world.

The first approach, postulates a set of elements (the religious phenomena) and accounts for the differences among cultures by characterizing the different relationships between the elements. This approach has not been particularly productive. This is because it does not establish whether Ganesha and God are members of the same class or belong to different classes. In other words, as repeatedly pointed out, the discussion does not go beyond problems of classification.

The second approach, as developed here, attempts to characterize religion as a structured and structuring unity, and sees cultural differences as differences in patterns of life. In the first stages of building a theory, the theoretical claims are highly abstract. Often called the method of 'idealization', it moves through successive concretizations in the process of studying the empirical phenomenon in question. The more the descriptions begin to approximate the phenomenon in question, the more concrete they become. My description of religion and ritual is abstract. It is capable of capturing some, but not all, of the details.

In a culture where performative knowledge dominates, worldviews may try to emerge but the cultural soil does not nourish them. Very soon any such attempt falls apart and is subordinated to the dominant mode of learning. It survives only as a fragment of a speculation of a finite slice of the world. Ideas that could grow into a worldview do not do so in such an environment. Consequently, what we recognize in India (Asia)–when looking from the West– are fragments and pieces. Not of Indian (Asian) worldviews, note this well, but of those which are a part of worldviews in the West. These pieces are a part of a different pattern in India (Asia); they enter into different relationships with other parts; and they have an entirely different hue as a result.

Just to get this idea across, a contrasting description might be of help. In the West, where the 'symbolic' dominates the performative, the latter itself becomes the symbolic (ritual is a symbol). In India, where the relation goes the other way, the symbol itself is performative (symbol is a ritual). Perhaps we can get an even better grip on the issue if we examine the way each culture looks (and has looked) at the other with respect to learning itself.

An Encounter of Cultures

Reconsider the evidence from the Indian traditions presented in the previous section. The 'law' of *karma*, the belief about the *atman* and reincarnation, appear to describe the worldview or religion of the Indians. Yet I am presenting them as evidence for the absence of a worldview or religion in India. There is nothing puzzling about this state of affairs. It merely confirms what I've tried to argue. Each culture contains many building blocks: theories, social groups, music, etc. Among other things, a culture is a configuration of learning. Religion has generated a configuration of learning in the West by universalizing itself. The way this culture looks at others is partially determined by the way it has become a culture: namely, through religion and worldview. Consequently, in this culture, understanding another culture involves describing the other in terms of its worldview. The 'other' is seen as the 'other worldview' in this culture. This can be seen as both the weakness and strength of western culture.

Let's us begin with its strength. A worldview can explain a perspective but a perspective cannot explain a worldview. If we know what there is in the world and what the world is like, we can generate descriptions of multiple perspectives. Religion is the explanatorily intelligible account of the entire cosmos. Nothing falls outside it.

The same strength is also its weakness. That is to say, the divinity of the message is the weakness of the message: its recipients are limited beings, with finite abilities, so that their ability to understand the message is itself finite. One cannot speak with certainty about this divine knowledge. This strength and weakness of religion also characterize western culture. Much like religion, which constitutes one element of its identity, the West is limited by itself.

Consider the typically western way of posing this question: why do Indians have the worldview they have? Why do they talk in terms of the *atman* or *karma*? Their answers to such questions exhibit the conceptual weakness of western culture. These are seen as different beliefs, belonging to different worldviews, and this is how cultural differences are conceptualized in western culture.

To appreciate this as a conceptual weakness, look at what Christianity did. The 'others' were pale and erring variants of itself. If indeed God came to the Arabian Desert several times and gave religion to a people, "why did God do so" is a question that cannot be answered. Its exact correlate is our inability to answer the question why different cultures have different 'worldviews'. The West sees the differences between cultures only in its terms, i.e., as having another (different) worldview. It cannot conceptualize them in any other way.

The pagan cultures have their strengths and weaknesses too. A religion or a worldview, the explanatorily intelligible account of the Cosmos, ends up becoming a mere perspective in their hands. Not having received the message from the true God, they look at such messages from a human perspective. Having worldviews is not how a human being goes about in the world. It is merely a way of going about. Some cultures may claim to have the worldview; the pagans acknowledge this possibility and merely say that it is not their way of going about.

A Contrasting Description

Keeping the logic of this situation in mind, let's review the contact between the West and Asia. One culture is so obsessed with chaos and order that it channels all its intellectual energies towards discovering the order buried underneath the postulated chaos. This culture produces philosophers, theologians, and scientists. Theories are destined to break away from practical life because they neglect to consider any experiential order. Not only do these theories have less and less to do with experiential units, but they also run counter to practical life. The idea is that given a good set of principles, good rules, and good statutes, the emergence of a good society and a good human being will be logical consequences. As the intellectual energies of this culture focus on locating the rational bases of social and human life, the transmission of practical or performative knowledge is arrested and becomes secondary. The practical life and interactions of a people correspondingly become impoverished. Theories grow rich and sophisticated, whereas daily life becomes barren and poor.

Then, there was (is?) another culture. All its intellectual energies went towards creating, sustaining, and continuously modifying a social or practical order. The order in society could be seen and experienced. Practical actions became sophisticated patterns of interaction. Theoretical disquisitions about some imagined order were neither essential nor much encouraged. A peculiar kind of theoretical poverty emerged as a result. These two cultures met in the most unfortunate of circumstances. One was willing to learn, the other thought that it could only teach. In any case, the gift was made:

> It is, I believe, no exaggeration to say that all the historical information that has been collected to form all the books written in the Sanskrit language is less valuable than what may be found in the most paltry abridgements used at preparatory schools in England. In every branch of physical or moral philosophy the relative position of these two nations is nearly the same...
>
> The question before us is merely whether...we shall teach languages [Sanskrit and Arabic] in which, by universal confession, there are no books on any subject which deserve to be compared to our own; whether, when we can teach European science, we shall teach systems which, by universal confession, whenever they differ from those of Europe, differ for the worse; and whether, when we can patronize true philosophy and sound history, we shall countenance, at the public expense, medical doctrines which would disgrace an English farrier–astronomy, which would move laughter in girls at an English public school–history, abounding with kings thirty feet high, and reigns thirty thousand years long–and

geography, made up of seas of treacle and butter (cited in Keay 1981: 77).

This is Sir Babbington Macaulay in his famous minutes concerning the need for a British education system in India. I am using the word 'gift' advisedly, because, in India, theoretical knowledge is not a product of learning. It is not so much a result of effort put in by an individual, as it is a gift given by the teacher. Acquisition of knowledge requires a peculiar kind of receptivity on the part of the pupil–a readiness to receive the gift from a teacher. Being a pupil in this culture implies preparing oneself to receive.

The attitude towards scientific knowledge in India, which is received mostly through western science, appeared as something utterly mysterious. Choudhuri calls this the 'schoolboy conception of science', transmitted in the Indian centers of learning:

> A good scientist must be a genius, intellectually much superior to the (student's) best professors. He is fully equipped with all the technical tools, which may possibly be necessary for any kind of research he may wish to undertake. He usually spends his time pondering over the fundamental issues of his discipline and when this divinely inspired individual happens to have a brilliant idea, he works it out in a straightforward way without much trouble, like a smart schoolboy solving his test problems (1985: 489).

In a culture like Asia, where performative knowledge dominates over the theoretical, the above cultural contact raises the following question: how to do science? Given what this culture is, the question has a practical answer. Hundreds of thousands of its members take to learning how to do science; to learn about science; to learn about the culture that has produced science. That is to say, this culture begins to mutate. Its specific way of going about in the world begins to shift, evolve and change shape. A new way of going about begins to emerge.

However, a cultural way of going-about is not a shirt to change at will. The sciences are the product of a different way of going about in the world. Asia encountered the sciences from within its way of going-about. In its old way of going-about, theory was subordinated. Consequently, the relationship between the elements in the configuration begins to shift. Yet it shifts within its culture-specific way of going about in the world. What is happening in Asia, what has been going on for the last 150 years or more, is the emergence of an altered configuration of learning. Asian cultures are doing a massive experiment in shifting and altering the relationship between different learning processes until a newer, more stable configuration comes into being. From the outside it does look as though they are taking on a worldview. That is exactly what they are not doing. Their old ways are changing, but they are changing in conformity with their own way of going about in the world. Doing sciences is a practical or performative problem to them. Asia might be becoming 'westernized', but it is happening in an Asian way.

The contrast cannot be sharper from the other side. While one culture is busy learning to evolve a new way of going about in the world, the other is smug and satisfied as though it does have God's truth. With this observation, this story has not reached its resting phase. My hope is that this proposal has at least drawn attention to a hitherto unsuspected dynamic. Asia might be becoming 'westernized'; but it is happening in an Asian way.

Traditio, Knowledge, and Religious Culture

Christianity was born in a pagan milieu. Thus, it was influenced both by its own characteristics as a religion and the milieu it operated in. It absorbed several aspects of pagan intellectual culture. The point to note is not that it took over some doctrines, but rather what it made of them. The predisposition of Judaism, Christianity, and, at a later stage, Islam, to assimilate Greek philosophical thought has to do with the nature of religion. The doctrines they took over went on to elaborate and flesh out a worldview. Neither the Greek nor the Roman cults had felt inclined to integrate their philosophical doctrines with *religio* the way Judaism or Christianity did. Philosophizing was one kind of activity, whereas cults and their ceremonies were another kind of activity. These cults did not feel impelled to spin out their theology as a response to philosophical attitudes and positions. Both Judaism and Christianity felt compelled to do what Roman *religio* did not do. These two religions could have followed the example of the cults, but they did not. This is an additional reason why Judaism and Christianity are religions and the Roman *religio* was not.

Roman *religio* can be regarded more in terms of performative knowledge than in terms of the worldview that religion is. As a collection of ceremonies, festivals, civic functions, and rituals, *religio* was not merely transmitted from generation to generation, but it was also experienced as something crucial to social interaction. Performative knowledge (whose exemplification is in rituals) is required to build societies and sustain social interactions. This is the 'how to live' ability mentioned earlier. To speak of traditions is to speak of accumulated performative knowledge and the mechanisms of transmission of such knowledge. Roman *religio* was very close to this performative knowledge and it was practiced because this practical knowledge was *traditio*.

What belongs to *traditio* or performative knowledge? When speaking of tradition, the point is not about enumerating its contents. Tradition merely transmits the practical knowledge of living together. This is why philosophers, especially during the Roman Empire, strenuously argued against having to found traditional practices on rational arguments. Their argument was that it was neither necessary nor possible to base practices on theoretical arguments. It was not necessary because practical knowledge itself was knowledge, and human practices do not require a foundation in reason. It was not possible, because the kind of certainty one falsely attributed to reason was illusory. Actions need not be guided by anything other than tradition and custom, which are themselves a species of knowledge, transmitted from generation to generation.

Such an attitude, it has often been charged, is conservative. In which way though? Practical knowledge essentially conserves; it is accumulated knowledge of and for living with other human beings. This charge of conservatism is hardly a critique but a very trivial consequence of the fact that human beings do not change dramatically every other day. A culture dominated by theoretical knowledge misunderstands such 'conservatism'. Such critics see this as acquiescence to old ideas, or the slavish submission to authority. Because of their notion that human action is an execution of an idea or a belief, it appears impossible for them to conceive of knowledge that is not theory or belief, but practical in nature.

The arguments of the Greco-Roman skeptics with those who tried to give a foundation to human praxis in reason were twofold: praxis itself is knowledge and therefore needed no foundation in reason; and, in any case, theoretical knowledge is ill-equipped to take over the role of practical knowledge. They argued against those who championed the cause of only one kind of knowledge by showing that we could not know anything with certainty. Hence, if we believed that we needed to know in order to act, we could not act at all.

Within western culture, the skeptical argument against theoretical knowledge is misunderstood. The skeptical position in defense of performative knowledge is seen to lead, of all things, to inaction. The Greco-Roman skeptic says, I do not need to 'know about' actions in order to act; the 'modern' skeptic says that because he does not 'know about' actions, he cannot act. Listen to Hume, the 'modern' skeptic.

> A Pyrrhonian…must acknowledge, if he will acknowledge anything, that all human life must perish if his principles universally and steadily to prevail. All discourse, all action would immediately cease; and men remain in total lethargy, till the necessities of nature, unsatisfied, put an end to their miserable existence (Hume 1777: 160).

The Greco-Roman skeptic argued for practical knowledge in order to act–as a separate kind of knowledge that is not based on theoretical reason. Hume could not understand them any more than his successors could. To both, skepticism merely posed a challenge about the impossibility of ever being certain about anything.

To sum up, *traditio* is best conceived as a variant of performative knowledge and *religio* did not require any theoretical justification. What Christianity did, something that Judaism had done much earlier, was to try to absorb practical or performative knowledge into the theoretical, and to see human activity as the execution of an idea or a plan.

The Dynamic of Religion

The Christianization of the West was a gradual and differentiated process. For instance, it retained some elements of the pre-Christian Germanic culture and eliminated some others. My characterization of religion enables us to come to grips with this differentiation by speaking about (i) the evangelizing process and (ii) the secularization process. Both are linked in the process of the universalization of Christianity.

Firstly, there is a differential degree of evangelization; secondly, there is a differentiated spread of the attitudes brought forth by evangelization. The emphasis on 'knowledge about' and the 'meaning questions' spread differentially along with the spread of this religion. Communities and individuals, who were barely Christian, began to shift and change their attitudes and questions. The process of the secularization of Christianity followed the process of evangelization. Three events in my narrative indicate the extent to which this process of universalization had spread. The popular nature of the Protestant Reformation indicates how rooted the Christian doctrines were; the Enlightenment indicates the extent to which the secularization of religious ideas had taken place; and the development of the sciences shows how a configuration of learning had already taken on a recognizable form.

The process of secularization, as contrasted with that of evangelization, gives us a clue about the kind of issues that people in the West confront. People accept questions and adopt attitudes that a religion has brought forth. This does not mean that they need to accept or even be familiar with the doctrines of this religion. Nevertheless, a religious attitude has spread. The secularization of Christianity consisted in making the Cosmos an object of experience without being dependent on its religious account. It is like possessing the structure of an account without accepting any particular interpretation of its variables. If the West did not have religion or worldview, its members would not have the attitudes they have now. To ask meaning questions in the Cosmos requires that some theory has made the Cosmos into such a place. Therefore, the belief is completely theoretical. Without such a theory, without using the resources of such a theory, we could never formulate these kinds of questions.

Idolatry and the Sin of the Secular

The process by which themes from a religion become low-level facts about human beings constitutes the dynamic of religion. That is, religion itself is a process and a movement. The question I had posed earlier was the following: could we demonstrate the double dynamic of religion and also show that this very dynamic constitutes religion? Let's tackle this question by looking at it from the perspective of idolatry.

Recall the suggestion that worship is the means through which the Cosmos retains its explanatory intelligibility. This idea is applicable not merely to the individual believer but also to the religious dynamic itself. Religion reproduces itself through worship. Note that this is different from both proselytization and secularization which refer to the expansive dynamic of religion. We are now talking about the daily or simple reproduction of religion, i.e., how believers continue to sustain their faith. This reproduction of religion, at the same time, reproduces the boundary between the religious world and the secular world. If we step back in time and visit the Roman Empire during the early days of Christianity, we observe Christian religious communities living within pagan society. The Christian communities continue to survive as religious communities by praying, worshipping God, following the liturgy, etc. Worship and prayer separate the believers from the non-believers, Christians from the pagans, and the religious world from the secular world. Both the induction of people into the Christian community and their exclusion from it would have to be drawn in terms of worship.

'Worship' and 'idolatry' are twin aspects of the same process: the first refers to the reproduction of the community of believers; the second refers to the reproduction of the boundary drawn by the community of believers. A congregation also segregates. But idolatry does not just demarcate the believers from the non-believers; it also domesticates and absorbs the other. Religion does not merely set apart; it also expands by *denying otherness to the other*. 'Idolatry' belongs to that arsenal of concepts which are crucial for the mechanism of the spread of religion.

Christianity confronted a problem when it expanded within the pagan world. From all the practices in pagan society, it needed to determine which were truly pagan practices and which merely those performed by the pagans. Which practices were 'idolatrous' and which 'civic'? As is to be expected, this question has its twin: *What is to be a Christian?* The trichotomy which had existed before, of Christian (or sacred), secular (or civic), and pagan (or profane) vanished, to be replaced by a simple dichotomy: sacred or profane, or, simply, Christian and pagan. About what kind of practices are we talking?

> Like honouring the martyr on his feast day by getting drunk; attending circus games and enjoying spectacles; banquets, giving presents, etc., during the New Year (i.e. the first of January); honouring an important person (like the emperor) by holding races and games; 'secular' festivals and banquets; attending shows in the theatres and hippodromes...the list is practically endless. (Markus 1990: 134).

If the pagan world is pagan because of pagan practices, the practices are pagan because they are idolatrous, and idolatry is Devil worship, what must a Christian do in order to remain one? Tertullian found the shows in the theatres to be an expression of idolatry; Augustine found them more neutral. Christians thought that celebrating the New Year was not wrong; Churchmen like Ambrose and Jerome were unanimous in attacking it virulently. The former said,

> we commit no sacrilege, these are only games...it is the gladness over the new, rejoicing over the start of a new year; it is not the falsehood of the [pagan] past, nor the sin of idolatry... (*ibid.* 104).

But the bishops thought otherwise:

> "he who would play with the Devil cannot rejoice with Christ" (*ibid.* 104-105).

Christian emperors repealed prohibitions imposed by the local Christian authorities on festivals and theatrical shows as long as decency, modesty and chaste manners were preserved; the Christian authorities had thought that all of these were associated with pagan rites. What one ate, how one dressed, what jewelry one wore, these too were matters for theological reflection. Pope Nicholas I (858-67), for example, was asked about such matters by the recently converted Bulgars. Some of their queries received categorical answers:

> necklaces given to the sick for healing are 'demonic phylacteries' and their users are condemned by 'apostolic

anathema'; the death penalty for negligent sentries is contrary
to the example–a significant choice!–of Saul's ferocity abjured
by St Paul on his conversion; but their king's habit of dining
alone was 'not against faith, though it offends good manners',
so in this matter they were offered 'not commands, but
persuasion'. But when it came to anxiety as to whether
Bulgarian women might wear trousers, not even advice was
offered, for this was a matter of indifference (supervacuum):
'for what we desire to change is not your outward clothing but
the manners (mores) of the inner man'. Here is a spectrum of
practices, from what the pope considered as indifferent to what
he regarded as supremely relevant (*ibid.* 6).

In other words, as Christianity expanded within the pagan world,
the pagans now confronted this religious world as well. They were
the 'other'. But what kind of 'otherness' could there be to an
account that makes everything explanatorily intelligible? Since
nothing falls outside its orbit, the mechanism of effacing the
otherness of the other must come into play. As Christianity gained
political recognition and economic power, the fate of the pagan
world was sealed. It had to be absorbed into the Christian world.

The pagan world was the *totality* of all pagan practices, including
those that we would today call secular. By making a distinction
between the sacred and the secular, Christianity brought about a
contraction of this secular, pagan world. Markus, in his brilliant
book, calls this process the 'desecularisation' of the Roman world.

As Christian discourse shrank to the scriptural, so the world of
which it spoke shrank to the sacred. The secular became
marginalised, merged in or absorbed by the sacred, both in
discourse and in the social structure and institutions.
Corresponding to the 'epistemological excision' of the secular
from the Christian discourse a 'de-secularisation' of its society
took place on a variety of levels (*ibid.* 226).

'Idolatry' is a religious concept, rooted in the Christian theology. It
looks outward into the non-Christian world and enables the
assimilation of the secular world into the Christian world. The
'desecularizing' process in the Roman world, as Markus remarks,

is not simply the gradual collapse of 'secular' culture and
institutions; nor is it...the progressively wider and deeper
'christianisation' of Roman society and culture.

> Accompanying these…was a change in the nature of Christianity itself: a contraction in the scope that Christianity…allowed to the 'secular'…one of the forms in which this change in the nature of Christianity manifested itself was in the tendency to absorb what had previously been 'secular', indifferent from a religious point of view, into the realm of the 'sacred'; to force the sphere of the 'secular' to contract, turning it either into 'Christian', or dismissing it as 'pagan' or 'idolatrous' (*ibid.*16).

What was the nature of these practices that made them pagan and not Christian? Idolatry and Devil worship, naturally. "What is it to be Christian?" was not a question which could be solved by enumerating the properties of a 'true' Christian. This question was and is raised incessantly. This should indicate that it is an issue about the *relation* between the religious and the secular world and not about any criteria for membership in the Christian world.

As western Christianity expanded, the civic, pagan world contracted and was marginalized in the process. The concept of idolatry drew the boundaries. After being neutralized of its sin, a pagan or civic practice would be admitted into the Christian world. It is thus that a 'secular' world was to emerge, but within the Christian world. It is a Christian-secular world that came into being, as generated by a Christian-religious world. That is why the secular world is in the grips of a religious world.

The problem that the Semitic religions have with respect to idolatry is not merely theological. The immense importance attached to fighting it does not derive merely from the commandments of God. The virulent and vehement attacks are sustained by the very nature of the religious dynamic–to absorb the pagan, civic world into itself and generate another world, a 'secular' world, but as defined by the religious world.

If this process is indeed a description of the dynamic of religion, we can better understand how members from this culture would experience cultures elsewhere. There is the typical missionary experience: the other culture is idolatrous. However, another equally typical experience is important to us today. To the early Christians, it was evident that they lived in a world dominated by false religion, which permeated all walks of life. Contrast this experience with a modern-day description of the same pagan world:

> While there is...an abundance of evidence that the Romans were even obsessively convinced of the need to placate the gods, belief in the gods seems to have had little effect on their conduct...If it were not for the descriptions of ritual a reader might conclude that the Romans of the late republic lived in *as secular a world as our own*... (Liebeshuetz: 1979: 3; emphasis added).

Does this mean that the Christians of the early pagan world were merely hallucinating for nearly five hundred years when they saw Roman practices as religious and not secular practices? Not quite. The early Christians experienced pagan Rome in the same way that our contemporary secular world experiences other cultures. Since our secular world is dominated by the religious world, religion must be seen to dominate all walks of life. Let's refer to a modern-day writer on Asia:

> There can never be a clear-cut understanding of the East on the part of the West until Westerners realise that all Asian thought is religiously conditioned... I can think of no single department of human activity in Asian lands that is not encompassed by religious concepts (Abbot Sumangalo 1972: 19-20).

If you replace 'religious' with 'secular', you are closer to Liebeshuetz's description of Ancient Rome. You are also closer to understanding the nature of Asian cultures. In other words, the western experience of other cultures today (as evidenced by the above citation) is no different from that of the early Christians. It is not called 'idolatrous', to be sure, but that is because the 'secular' world of ours is also a de-Christianized religious world.

We can begin to appreciate why people in the West believe that religion is a constitutive element of all cultures. It's because their culture is constituted by religion. Going about in this culture requires 'knowing about'. This includes knowing about what other cultures 'know about' the world. This is the reason why it creates religions and worldviews in other cultures. Religion is necessary, so says this culture, because all human beings need to know about the world in order to go about in the world. But this is one culture's way of going about in the world. Religion has brought forth one configuration of learning; other things have brought forth other configurations of learning elsewhere. I have argued that religion is not a cultural universal but that one can explain why the West thinks so. Both have to do with religion: what religion is to *this* culture, namely, its constitutive element. Need more be said?

CHAPTER XII

AT THE END OF A JOURNEY

Now that we have reached the end of this journey, it is time to assess the nature of the arguments put forward. The western intelligentsia and western-trained intellectuals hold firmly that religion is a cultural universal. This belief is both part of the commonsense and a claim in the literature on the subject. The proponents of this idea represent a consensus that cuts across many different fields in the social and human sciences, from anthropology through sociology to human socio-biology. The belief in the universality of religion does not merely imply that there are believers in different parts of the globe. When people say that religion is a cultural universal, they do not just say, for instance, that there are Christian communities in all cultures. The claim does not mean that every human being has a religion either. These theorists do notice the existence of atheism, agnosticism, or indifference to religious matters. They also notice that secular ideologies play a dominant role in the social life of most countries in the West.

When people claim that religion is a *universal*, it means that religion is native to human cultures. That is to say, all cultures must have an indigenous religion. The claim that religion is a *cultural* universal means that religion is constitutive of human cultures. That is, religion lends identity to a culture, or that it is indispensable to a culture. Again, it is important to note that both scholars and non-professionals hold this belief. When socio-biologists and cognitive neuroscientists propose speculative hypotheses about the genetic or neural basis of religion; or when the Europeans try to understand the immigrant communities in their midst by talking about Islam; the presupposition is that cultures can be described at least partially by relating religion to culture.

The burden of this essay is two-fold: to demonstrate that religion is not a cultural universal and to clarify at the same time why people think that it is. The merit of the essay consists in the fact that it captures both points of focus. It does not put forward *ad hoc* explanations, and the arguments are open to empirical and logical control. Together with their problem-solving potential, these two aspects lend credibility to the arguments. The entire essay constructs one argument and develops two themes: is religion a cultural universal? Why do people think it is?

On one hand, contemporary authors appear unsure that what they're talking about is, "properly speaking", a religion. On the other hand, after recording this observation, they proceed to give an account of these 'religions'. My arguments show that there is an inconsistency in their reasoning and I question why these authors have not seen it. In an effort to render these authors consistent, I examine the possible theoretical and empirical grounds for this belief. An explicit examination of whether the belief about the universality of religion is a result of empirical enquiries shows that it is not so. This lays the groundwork for looking into the theoretical grounds for this belief.

By contrasting Roman *religio* with the religion of the Jews and the Christians, I suggest that we should seek the origin of our problem in the emergence of the Christian world. When European culture encounters other cultures elsewhere in the world for the second time, in the sixteenth century, Indian culture is the 'other' now. Empirical investigations into the universality of religion will have to begin here, if anywhere. The travel reports of this period assume that religion exists in India too, except that it is the religion of the heathens. The schism within Christianity, between the Protestants and the Catholics, now determines how the question of religion is approached. The drama from Roman times about the opposition between 'false' religion and the 'true' one is restaged once again with a new cast of characters. The Enlightenment thinkers are among this new cast. I argue that they do not merely reproduce Protestant themes, but do so with vigor. They merely extend Christian themes in a secular guise.

I try to show where the Indian religions came to be made up and plot the trajectory of the manufacturing process. It begins in Paris, the cultural centre of Enlightenment Europe. The process then shifts to London, the administrative and political centre of colonial India. The British administrators lay the foundation for 'the Oriental Renaissance'. The product is finished and reaches wholesale distribution centers under the expert guidance of the Germans, especially the German Romantics. This process suggests that the creation of religions in India must be understood in terms of the conceptual compulsion of a culture.

I show how some anthropological 'facts' are merely secularized claims from the Bible. I then proceed to build a case for the charge that the secular world is, in fact, a secularized religious world. The belief about the universality of religion is a theological idea, and its persistence indicates the secularization of religious themes. I show why the West believes in the universality of religion. It's in the very nature of religion to generate the belief that religion is a cultural universal. By showing how religion has been a constitutive element of the West, I suggest how to thematize cultural differences. I specify how cultures differ from each other by relating learning processes to cultural differences.

This essay does not pretend to provide a theory about religion. It is merely the first phase in such a process. It is a partial description of a people and their culture as provided by someone from another culture. Despite this, the description is not mere ethnography. Nor does it merely plead the case that people from different cultures provide different descriptions of the world. It does more; better put, it is forced to do more. It shows that the belief in the universality of religion is false. Because this belief is pervasive, it is not enough that I appeal to pluralism in descriptions and rest content with that. More is required on my part. That 'more' is simply this: to provide you with good reasons why my description is more acceptable than the received wisdom of the last three hundred years.

My proposals are cognitively productive. Many new problems have come to the fore; solution to each problem has generated new questions. If science is a problem-solving activity, then surely, my approach is scientific. The competing theories are both barren and unproductive. More than two hundred years of theoretical and empirical enquiry has not gone beyond the question: 'why does religion exist in all cultures?' Because it is 'God-given' says one camp; because it is 'man-made' says the other. The question is the same, and the answers do not generate any new problems for enquiry. This does not bring us any further in our quest for an understanding of the subject.

Scientific theories can be judged in terms of their explanatory power. Based on this criterion, this essay does not disappoint. It is able to bring together beliefs about religion with the nature of the entity that religion is. It connects these with the experience of the 'self' and relates social organizations to ritual. Consequently, the hypotheses are promising; they indicate how theory-formation should proceed. This is more than can be said about the existing theories or ethnographic descriptions.

The history of the natural sciences has taught us that many scientific theories which we once believed to be true have turned out to be false. Consequently, it would be nothing short of a miracle if all my claims turn out to be true. Because of this, it is important to know how to treat my claims. Theories can be examined by linking them to the context of discovery or the context of justification. That is, what are the relevant socio-psychological contexts in the origin of a theory, and how to appraise a theory? Why accept a theory at all? The ideas in this essay require further exploration and development before it can become a theory. Such explorations must involve a collective effort.

How, then, can I persuade you to take my claims seriously? One strategy to demonstrate the truth of my hypothesis would be to compare my proposal with others that exist in the marketplace. I have tried to do this. It appears to be cognitively productive and heuristically fertile. It promises to deliver an empirically testable theory. In each of these aspects, it fares better than its rivals do. Therefore, shall we try to see what it can present us?

Maximally, it presents a reasonable case for the interesting nature of the endeavor. More, it cannot do. This is because the battle it must fight is not against any well-articulated theory, but against a deeply entrenched idea that is a hydra-headed monster. This idea prevents the emergence of an understanding and appreciation of other cultures. The last statement is controversial for more reasons than one. In the concluding section of the book, I would like to look at one such reason.

The problem, as inherited from the field of anthropology, involves the question of ever being able to describe the other. How is it possible to break out of one's own conceptual framework to describe the otherness of the other? Is it possible to describe the other without using one's own categories? Even if we use the categories of the other, the problem of translation guarantees that we end up describing a variant of our own experience of the world. Hence, it is not possible to describe the other. This is a dilemma for all cultures. They cannot describe the otherness of the other. The other is beyond language.

But this is not as insurmountable a problem as the field of anthropology makes it out to be. We project our categories upon other cultures. Thus, what we describe as the other is merely a variant of ourselves. Assume that the only way we could ever describe the other is by projecting our own categories. In that case, let members from other cultures project their own categories upon the social world too. This way we would have multiple descriptions. When we have such multiple descriptions, we can ask the question: how must the different social worlds be that allow multiple descriptions? The answer to this question will be the beginning of a comparative science of cultures. It is comparative in the sense that it begins–from its very inception–by taking multiple descriptions as the facts it must account for.

In this book, I have tried to demonstrate what the projection of a particular culture's categories on the other actually amounts to. I have identified two phases. In the first, there is a secularization of theological themes. This generates some facts. In the subsequent phase, the theories that develop retain these theological facts and try to explain these facts. That is to say, religious themes are generalized, which generates facts that lead to the development of further theories to account for these facts.

Theology was the first theory of religion. Secular theories merely transformed theological facts and made these into their objects of study. However, these facts remain themes from theology–for instance, the 'fact' that all cultures have religion. In other words,

European intellectuals did not project their own categories in the process of understanding other religions. They took over those from theology. My opponents may come up with the charge that my portrayal is trapped in my own categories. This does not matter. The dispute is not about what human beings are capable or incapable of knowing. It is about empirical investigation.

Let's examine the claim that it is impossible to describe the otherness of the other. Consider the two cultures I have talked about: India and the West. Because we are talking about the 'other' in anthropological terms, it means that (a) Indian culture is the other of the West; (b) The West is the other of Indian culture. If we grant that people from different cultures experience the world differently, and that their descriptions reflect this difference, it means that: (c) the otherness of India, as westerners experience it, depends on western culture; (d) the otherness of the West, as Indians experience it, depends on Indian culture. Therefore, it follows that if these cultures are different, so are their experiences of each other.

From the above, there is no way to logically infer that it is impossible to describe otherness. It is a matter of empirical research into whether each of these cultures succeeds or fails in describing this otherness. It is a logical fallacy to claim that otherness cannot be described. Maybe it can; maybe it cannot. This is an empirical issue about two cultures, not a point about the capacity or incapacity of human beings to know something.

Of course, you could challenge the truth-value of the assumptions I have made. It might be the case that cultures do not experience the world differently; it might also be the case that their descriptions do not reflect their experiences. But again, this is an empirical issue about two cultures, not a point about human beings' ability to know something.

Western culture has brought forth anthropology and ethnography, as we know them. Each culture (as the West has described it) is the other of western culture in exactly the same way. The otherness in western descriptions is merely anotherness. Western descriptions erase otherness. This means that the Indian or the African cultures–as the West has described them–are the other of each other and of the West in exactly the same way. We do have a problem of the 'other' on our hands if the West is the Cosmos of all cultures and if cultures do not differ from each other in different ways but only in the way the West imagines it to be the case.

However, if the West is but one culture in a universe of cultures; if it is typical to the way in which the West has looked at itself and the others then it is not a problem at all. In fact, this is how I have tried to make sense of western culture: why does the otherness disappear from western descriptions of other cultures? Why is the sheen of all other cultures reduced to a monochromatic dullness? I have answered these problems partially, but not by blaming the big bad wolf–religion. After all, it is my argument that religion has produced both western culture and science. What I have tried to do is something other than apportion blame. I have argued that the otherness of western culture, when viewed against the background of mine, lies in its transformation of the other into another.

I have provided a description of the mechanism of transforming the other into another. This constitutes the otherness of western culture. My description of the West is located within my experiential world. An objective description would suggest that the West has the truth about the world. From my experiential world, this description merely has the following significance: this is typical of western culture; it is the western way of going about in the world and not mine.

In other words, I have located my description of western culture in an experiential context. However, the task involves an explication of the experiential context as well. Completion of this task requires further theorizing. We have to describe Indian culture as it sees itself. This is a task for the future; the flag-waving with respect to ritual hints in a possible direction. However, the pre-requisite is that we break out of the shackles of a descriptive straightjacket that is centuries old.

We can describe the other in such a way that the other recognizes itself in the description provided. Our descriptions must be constrained by the notions of rationality, scientificity, and objectivity. This is theory-generation under constraints and it is never a finished job. Such a description is hypothetical; it is partial; it merely describes one kind of difference–and even that at a very high level of abstraction. All scientific theories face analogous problems. How can we generate an alternate theory, when imprisoned by the received theory? In the case of a science of cultures, the job is easier and less mysterious. There are different cultures and, therefore, different partial descriptions of the other are possible. Hence, we can generate different theories. Theories could compete with each other, whatever the epistemic status of the facts might be.

What have I done in this book then? I hope to have shown why the question about the existence of religion is cognitively interesting. It is not a definitional question. It requires developing a theory about religion, culture, and their mutual interrelationship. I do not know the extent to which I have persuaded you to take my ideas seriously; at least I hope to have made it plausible why I think a serious discussion about this issue requires a rethinking of the entire problem. The ideas proposed in this essay could turn out to be wrong, but that is hardly the problem. There is wrong, and there is wrong. It is better to be wrong in an interesting way than to recycle barren ideas that everyone wrongly believes to be right.

With these remarks, I have reached the end of this essay. Even though the journey is far from complete, there is this feeling that at least some distance has been covered. Perhaps this is the best that we can say about any essay, any journey, and not merely this one.

REFERENCES

ABBOT SUMANGALO, 1972
"Common Denominators of Asian Thought." In John Bowman, (Ed.), *Comparative Religion*. Leiden: E.J. Brill, 19-34.

AGEHANANDA BHARATI, 1985
"The Self in Hindu Thought and Action." In Anthony J. Marsella, George Devos, and Francis L. K. Hsu, (Eds.), *Culture and Self: Asian and Western Perspectives*. London: Unwin, 185-230.

ALMOND, PHILIP, C., 1988
The British Discovery of Buddhism. Cambridge: Cambridge University Press.

ALSTON, WILLIAM, P., 1967
"Religion." In Paul Edwards, (Ed.), *The Encyclopedia of Philosophy*, Vol. 7. New York: MacMillan Publishing Company, 140-145.

APOSTEL, LEO, 1981
"Mysticism, Ritual and Atheism." In Apostel, Pinxten, Thibau, and Vandamme, (Eds.), *Religious Atheism*? Gent: Story Scientia, 7-55.

ATHENAGORAS
A Plea for the Christians. In Rev. Alexander Roberts and James Donaldson, (Eds.), *The Ante-Nicene Fathers: Translations of the Writings of the Fathers down to A.D. 325, Vol. 2, Fathers of the Second Century*. American reprint of the Edinburgh edition (n.d.). Michigan: Wm. B. Eerdmans Publishing Company, 1978.

AUGUSTINE
Of True Religion. Translated by J. H. S. Burleigh.
Chicago: Henry Regnery Company, 1968.

BADGER, GEORGE PERCY (ED.), n.d.
*The Travels of Ludovico Di Varthema in Egypt, Syria,
Arabia Deserta and Arabia Felix, in Persia, India and
Ethiopia*, A. D. 1503 to 1508. Translated into English in
1863 by J. WINTER JONES. The Hakluyt Society, Series
II, Vol. XXXII. Reprinted: New York: Burt Franklin,
Publisher.

BARROW, R. H. (TRANS.), 1973
*Prefect and Emperor: The Relationes of Symmachus. A.D.
384*. Oxford: The Clarendon Press.

BENZ, ERNEST, 1959
"On understanding Non-Christian Religions." In Mircea
Eliade and Joseph M. Kitagawa, (Eds.), *The History of
Religions: Essays in Methodology*. Chicago: The
University of Chicago Press, 115-131.

BERMAN, HAROLD, J., 1983
*Law and Revolution: The Formation of the Western Legal
Tradition*. Cambridge, Massachusetts: Harvard University
Press.

BICHSEL, PETER, 1982
*Der Leser, Das Erzählen: Frankfurter Poetik-
Vorlesungen*. Darmstadt und Neuwied: Hermann
Luchterhand Verlag.

BODIN, JEAN, 1857
Colloquium of the Seven about Secrets of the Sublime.
Translated by Marion Kuntz. Princeton: Princeton
University Press, 1975.

BROWN, DONALD, E.
1988   Hierarchy, History, and Human Nature: The
Social origins of Historical Consciousness. Tucson: The
University of Arizona Press.

CALAND, W. (ED.), 1926
   Ziegenbalg's Malabarische Heidenthum. Amsterdam:
   Koninklijke Akademie van Wetenschappen.

CALVIN, JOHN
   Institutes of the Christian Religion. Translated by Henry
   Beveridge in two volumes. Michigan: William B.
   Eerdmans Publishing Company, 1983.

CAMERON, AVERIL, 1991
   *Christianity and the Rhetoric of Empire: The Development
   of Christian Discourse. Sather Classical Lectures,* Vol. 55.
   Berkeley: University of California Press.

CHATFIELD, ROBERT, 1808
   *An Historical Review of the Commercial, Political and
   Moral State of Hindoostan.* Reprinted as *Social, Political,
   Historical and Commercial Review of Hindoostan from the
   Earliest Period to the Present Time.* Delhi: Bimla
   Publishing House, 1983.

CHOUDHURI, ARNAB RAI, 1985
   "Practising Western Science Outside the West: Personal
   Observations on the Indian Science." *Social Studies of
   Science,* 15, 475-505.

CICERO
   De Natura Deorum. Translated by H. Rackham. The Loeb
   Classical Library. London: William Heinemann Ltd.,
   1933, 1979.

CLAUSEN, CHRISTOPHER, 1975
   "Victorian Buddhism and the Origin of Comparative
   Religion." *Religion,* 5(1), 1-15.

COHEN, MORRIS, R., 1946
   "Baseball as a National Religion." In Louis Schneuder,
   (Ed.), *Religion, Culture and Society: A Reader in the
   Sociology of Religion.* London: John Wiley and Sons,
   1964, 36-38.

CROOKE, WILLIAM, 1913
"Hinduism." In James Hastings, (Ed.), *Encyclopedia of Religion and Ethics*, Vol. 6. New York: Charles Scribner's, 686-715.

DAMES, MANSEL LONGWORTH (ED.)
1812a *The Book of Duarte Barbosa: An Account of the Countries Bordering on the Indian Ocean and their Inhabitants written by Duarte Barbosa, and Completed about the year 1518 A. D. Vol. 1.* London: The Hakluyt Society, Series II, Vol. XLIV, 1918.

1812b *The Book of Duarte Barbosa: An Account of the Countries Bordering on the Indian Ocean and their Inhabitants written by Duarte Barbosa, and Completed about the year 1518 A. D. Vol. 2.* London: The Hakluyt Society, Series II, Vol. XLIX, 1921.

DANDEKAR, R. N., 1969
"Hinduism." In E. Jouco Bleeker and Geo Widengren, (Eds.), *Historia Religionum: Handbook for the History of Religions, Vol. 2*, Religions of the Present. Leiden: E. J. Brill, 237-345.

DANIEL, VALENTINE, E., 1984
Fluid Signs: Being a Person the Tamil Way. Berkeley: University of California Press.

DAVIDSON, DONALD, 1963
"Action, Reasons, and Causes." *The Journal of Philosophy*, 60, 685-700. Reprinted in Steven Davis, (Ed.), *Causal Theories of Mind: Action, Knowledge, Memory, Perception, and Reference.* Berlin: Walter de Gruyter, 1983, 58-72.

DAVIES, BRIAN, 1982
An Introduction to the Philosophy of Religion. New edition. Oxford: Oxford University Press, 1993.

DE BISSCHOPPEN VAN BELGIË, 1987
Geloofsboek. Tielt: Lannoo.

DROBIN, ULF, 1982
"Psychology, Philosophy, Theology, Epistemology: Some Reflections." *Scripta Instituti Donneriani Aboensis*, XI, 263-274.

DUBOIS, ABBÉ, 1816
Hindu Manners, Customs and Ceremonies. Third Edition. Delhi: Oxford University Press, 1906, 1985.

DUFF, ALEXANDER, 1839
India and India Missions: Including Sketches of the Gigantic System of Hinduism Both in Theory and Practice. Delhi: Swati Publications, 1988.

DURKHEIM, EMILE, 1912
The Elementary Forms of Religious Life. In W. S. F. Pickering, (Ed.), *Durkheim on Religion*. London: Routledge and Kegan Paul, 1975.

EILBERG-SCHWARTZ, HOWARD, 1990
The Savage in Judaism: An Anthropology of Israelite Religion and Ancient Judaism. Bloomington: Indiana University Press.

ELIADE, MIRCEA, 1959
Cosmos and History: The Myth of Eternal Return. New York: Harper Torchbooks.

1961   *The Sacred and the Profane: The Nature of Religion*. New York: Harcourt, Brace, and Co.

1969   The Quest: History and Meaning in Religion. Chicago: The University of Chicago Press.

ELISON, GEORGE, 1973
Deus Destroyed: The Image of Christianity in Early Modern Japan. Council on East Asian Studies, Harvard University, 1988.

EMBREE, AINSLIE, T. (ED.), 1988
Sources of the Indian Tradition, Vol. 1, From the Beginning to 1800. Second Edition. New York: Columbia University Press.

EUSEBIUS
Praeparatio Evangelica. Translated by E. H. Gifford. Oxford, 1903. *The History of the Church*. Translated by G. A. Williamson. Harmondsworth: Penguin Books, 1965.

EVANS-PRITCHARD, E. E., 1965
Theories of Primitive Religion. Oxford: Oxford University Press.

FINLEY, SIR MOSES, 1985
"Foreword" to P. E. Easterling and J. V. Muir, (Eds.), *Greek Religion and Society*. Cambridge: Cambridge University Press, xiii-xx.

GAY, PETER, 1973
The Enlightenment: An Interpretation, Vol. 1, The Rise of Modern Paganism. London: Wildwood House.

GAZZANIGA, MICHAEL, J., 1985
The Social Brain: Discovering the Networks of the Mind. New York: Basic Books.

GEERTZ, CLIFFORD, 1966
"Religion as a Cultural System." In Michael Banton, (Ed.), *Anthropological Approaches to the Study of Religion*. London: Tavistock Publications, 1-46.

GIBBON, EDWARD, 1776
The Decline and Fall of the Roman Empire. In Great Books of the Western World, Vol. 40, London: Encyclopædia Britannica, 1952.

GILL, SAM, 1987
Native American Religious Action: A Performance Approach to Religion. Columbia: University of South Carolina Press.

GLOVER, T. R., 1909
The Conflict of Religions in the Early Roman Empire. London: Methuen and Co.

GOULD, JOHN, 1985
"Making Sense of Greek Religion." In P. E. Easterling and J. V. Muir, (Eds.), *Greek Religion and Society.* Cambridge: Cambridge University Press, 1-33.

HARRISON, PETER, 1990
'Religion' and the Religions in the English Enlightenment. Cambridge: Cambridge University Press.

HERMAN, A. L., 1983
An Introduction to Buddhist Thought: A Philosophic History of Indian Buddhism. Lanham: University Press of America.

HICK, JOHN, 1989
An Interpretation of Religion: Human Responses to the Transcendent. New Haven: Yale University Press.

HODGEN, MARGARET, T., 1964
Early Anthropology in the Sixteenth and Seventeenth Centuries. Philadelphia: The University of Pennsylvania Press.

HUME, DAVID, 1740
A Treatise of Human Nature. Selby-Brigge Edition. Second edition edited by P. H. Nidditch. Oxford: Clarendon Press, 1978.

1757   *The Natural History of Religion.* In Thomas Hill Green and Thomas Hodge Grose, (Eds.), *The Philosophical Works of David Hume.* Reprint of the 1882 London Edition, Vol. 4. Aalen: Scientia Verlag, 1964.

1777   *Enquiries Concerning Human Understanding and the Principles of Morals.* Selby-Brigge Edition. Second edition edited by P. H. Nidditch. Oxford: Clarendon Press, 1975.

ISSAC, THOMAS, T. M., AND EKBAL, B., 1988
Science for Social Revolution: The Experience of Kerala Sastra Sahitya Parishat. Trichur: Kerala Sastra Sahitya Parishat.

JAMES, E. O., 1969
"Prehistoric Religion." In E. ouco Bleeker and Geo
Wildengren, (Eds.), *Historia Religionum: Handbook for
the History of Religions, Vol. 1, Religions of the Past.*
Leiden: E. J. Brill, 23-39.

JAMES, WILLIAM, 1902
The Varieties of Religious Experience. New York: The
New American Library, 1958.

KALUPAHANA, DAVID, J. (TRANS.), 1986
Nagarjuna: The Philosophy of the Middle Way. New
York: State University of New York Press.

KEAY, JOHN, 1981
India Discovered. London: Collins, 1988.

KLEIN, RICHARD, G., 1989
*The Human Career: Human Biological and Cultural
Origins.* Chicago: The University of Chicago Press.

KUPER, ADAM, 1988
*The Invention of Primitive Society: Transformations of an
Illusion.* London: Routledge.

LACH, DONALD, F., 1965
*Asia in the Making of Europe, Vol. 1, The Century of
Discovery.* Chicago: The University of Chicago Press.

LACTANTIUS
The Divine Institutes. Translated by Sister Mary Francis
McDonald. *The Fathers of the Church, Vol. 49.*
Washington, D. C.: The Catholic University of America
Press.

LAUDAN, LARRY, 1990
*Science and Relativism: Some Key Controversies in the
Philosophy of Science.* Chicago: The University of
Chicago Press.

LEWIS, DAVID, 1978
"Truth in Fiction." *American Philosophical Quarterly*, 15, 37-46. Reprinted together with Postscripts" in his *Philosophical Papers, Vol. 1*. Oxford: Oxford University Press, 1983, 261-280.

1986   *On the Plurality of Worlds*. Oxford: Basil Blackwell.

LEWIS, GILBERT, 1982
Day of Shining Red: An Essay on Understanding Ritual. Cambridge: Cambridge University Press.

LIEBESCHUETZ, J. H. W. G., 1979
Continuity and Change in Roman Religion. Oxford: Clarendon Press

LING, TREVOR (ED.), 1981
The Buddha's Philosophy of Man: Early Indian Buddhist Dialogues. London: Everyman's Library.

LOTT, ERIC, J., 1988
Vision, Tradition, Interpretation: Theology, Religion, and the Study of Religion. Berlin: Mouton de Gruyter.

MACINTYRE, ALASDAIR, 1981
After Virtue. Second Edition. Notre Dame: University of Notre Dame Press, 1984.

MARKHAM, C. (ED.), 1877
Book of the Knowledge of all the Kingdoms, Lands, and Lordships that are there in the World, and the Arms and Devices of Each Land and Lordship, Or of the Kings and Lords who Possess them. Written by a Spanish Franciscan in the Middle of the XIV Century. London: The Hakluyt Society, Series II, Vol. XXIX, 1912.

MARKUS, ROBERT, 1990
The End of Ancient Christianity. Cambridge: Cambridge University Press.

MARSHALL, P. J. (ED.), 1970
    *The British Discovery of Hinduism in the Eighteenth
    Century*. Cambridge: Cambridge University Press.

MASSARELLA, DEREK, 1990
    *A World Elsewhere: Europe's Encounter with Japan in the
    Sixteenth and Seventeenth Centuries*. New Haven: Yale
    University Press.

MASSIE, J. W., 1840
    Continental India, 2 Volumes. Delhi: B. R. Publishing
    Company, 1985.

MAW, MARTIN, 1990
    *Visions of India: Fulfilment Theory, The Aryan Race
    Theory, and the Work of British Protestant Missionaries in
    Victorian India*. Bern: Peter Lang Verlag.

MORRIS, BRIAN, 1987
    Anthropological Studies of Religion. Cambridge:
    Cambridge University Press.

MÜLLER, MAX (ED.), 1879
    The Upanishads. 2 Volumes. New York: Dover
    Publications, 1962.

NEILL, STEPHEN, 1984
    *A History of Christianity in India, Vol. 1, The Beginnings
    to A. D. 1707*. Cambridge: Cambridge University Press.

O'FLAHERTY, WENDY DONIGER (ED.), 1975
    Hindu Myths. Harmondsworth: Penguin Books.

    1981   *The Rig Veda*. Harmondsworth: Penguin Books.

O'TOOLE, ROGER, 1984
    Religion: Classic Sociological Approaches. Toronto:
    McGraw-Hill Ryerson Limited.

OLTHUIS, JAMES, H., 1989
    "On Worldviews." In Paul A. Marshall, *et. alii.*, (Eds.),
    1989, 26-40.

ORIGEN
   Contra Celsum. Translated by Henry Chadwick.
   Cambridge: Cambridge University Press, 1965.

OTTO, RUDOLF, 1917
   The Idea of the Holy. Oxford: Oxford University Press,
   1923, 1950.

PAILIN, DAVID, A., 1971
   "Some Eighteenth Century Attitudes to `Other Religions'."
   Religion, 1(2), 83-108.

   1984   *Attitudes to Other Religions: Comparative
   Religion in Seventeenth and Eighteenth-century Britain.*
   Manchester: Manchester University Press.

PARRY, JONATHAN, 1985
   "The Brahmanical Tradition and the Technology of the
   Intellect." In Joanna Overing, (Ed.), *Reason and Morality*.
   London: Tavistock Publications, 200-225.

PIATIGORSKY, A., 1985
   "Some Phenomenological Observations on the Study of
   Indian Religion." In Richard Burghart and Audrey Cantile,
   (Eds.), *Indian Religion*. London: Curzon Press, 208-258.

PREUS, SAMUEL, J., 1987
   *Explaining Religion: Criticism and Theory from Bodin to
   Freud.* New Haven: Yale University Press.

PROUDFOOT, WAYNE, 1985
   Religious Experience. Berkeley: University of California
   Press.

PUTTANIL, THOMAS, 1990
   *A Comparative Study on the Theological Methodology of
   Irenaeus of Lyon and Sankaracharya.* Bern: Peter Lang
   Verlag.

RADCLIFFE-BROWN, A. R., 1952
   "Religion and Society." In Louis Schneider, (Ed.),
   *Religion, Culture, and Society: A Reader in the Sociology
   of Religion.* London: John Wiley and Sons, 1964.

RAITT, THOMAS, M., 1987
"The Ritual Meaning of Corn Pollen Among the Navajo Indians." *Religious Studies*, 23, 523-30.

RIST, J. M., 1972
Epicurus: An Introduction. Cambridge: Cambridge University Press.

ROGERIUS, ABRAHAMUS, D., 1651
De Open-Deure tot het Verborgen Heydendom ofte Waerachtigh vertoogh van het Leven ende Zeden, mitsgaaders de Religie, ende Godsdienst der Bramines, op de Cust Chormandel, ende de Landen daar ontrent. Leiden. Reprinted by De Linschoten-Vereeniging, Vol. X, 's-Gravenhage: Martinus Nijhoff, 1915.

ROLAND, ALAN, 1988
In Search of Self in India and Japan. Princeton: Princeton University Press.

RUSSELL, BERTRAND, AND COPELSTON, F. C., 1948
"The existence of God–A Debate." In Paul Edwards and Arthur Pap, (Eds.), *A Modern Introduction to Philosophy: Readings from Classical and Contemporary Sources.* Third Edition. New York: The Free Press, 1973, 473-490.

SCHIPPER, KRISTOFER, 1982
Tao: De Levende Religie van China. Amsterdam: Meulenhoff, 1988.

SCHLEIERMACHER, FRIEDRICH., 1799
On Religion: Speeches to its Cultured Despisers. Translated by RICHARD CROUTER. Cambridge: Cambridge University Press, 1988.

SCHNEIDER, LOUIS (ED.), 1964
Religion, Culture and Society: A Reader in the Sociology of Religion. London: John Wiley and Sons.

SCHWAB, RAYMOND, 1950
The Oriental Renaissance: Europe's Rediscovery of India and the East 1680-1880. New York: Columbia University Press, 1984.

SCHWEINITZ, JR., KARL DE, 1984
"John Stuart Mill and India." *Research in the History of Economic Thought and Methodology*, 2, 47-61.

SHARPE, ERIC, J., 1965
Not to Destroy but to Fulfil: The Contribution of J. N. Farquhar to the Protestant Missionary Thought in India before 1914. Uppsala: Swedish Institute of Missionary Research.

1990   *Nathan Söderblom and the Study of Religion*. Chapel Hill: The University of North Carolina Press.

SHULMAN, DAVID DEAN, 1980
Tamil Temple Myths: Sacrifice and Divine Marriage in the South Indian Saiva Tradition. Princeton: Princeton University Press.

SHWEDER, RICHARD, A. and BOURNE, EDMUND, J., 1982
"Does the Concept of the Person Vary Cross-culturally?" In R.A. Shweder and R.A. Levine, (Eds.), *Culture Theory: Essays on Mind, Self, and Emotion*. Cambridge: Cambridge University Press, 1984.

SMITH, HUSTON, 1972
"Accents of the World Religions." In John Bowman, (Ed.), *Comparative Religion*. Leiden: E.J. Brill, 1-18.

SMITH, WILFRED CANTWELL, 1962
The Meaning and End of Religion. London: SPCK, 1978.

SÖDERBLOM, NATHAN, 1913
"Holiness." In James Hastings, (Ed.), *Encyclopedia of Religion and Ethics, Vol. 6*. New York: Charles Scribner's, 731-741.

SOUTHWOLD, MARTIN, 1978
"Buddhism and the Definition of Religion." *Man* (n.s.), 13, 362-379.

SPIRO, MELFORD, E., 1966
"Religion: Problems of Definition and Explanation." In Michael Banton, (Ed.), *Anthropological Approaches to the Study of Religion*. London: Tavistock Publications, 85-126.

SPROUL, BARBARA, C. (ED.), 1979
Primal Myths: Creating the World. New York: Harper and Row.

STAAL, FRITS, 1986a
Over Zin en Onzin in filosofie, Religie en Wetenschap. Amsterdam: Meulenhoff.

1986b *The Fidelity of the Oral Traditions and the Origins of Science*. Mededelingen der Koninklijke Nederlandse Akademie van Wetenschappen, Afdeling Letterkunde. Nieuwe Reeks 49(8). Amsterdam: North Holland Publishing Company.

1988 "De Godsdiensten van het oosten zijn niet oosters en ook geen godsdiensten." In his *Een Wijsgeer in het Oosten*. Amsterdam: Meulenhoff.

1989 *Rules Without Meaning: Ritual, Mantras, and the Human Sciences*. New York: Peter Lang Verlag.

STANIFORTH, MAXWELL, (TRANS.)
Early Christian Writers: The Apostolic Fathers. Harmondsworth: Penguin Books, 1968.

STRABO
The Geography of Strabo. Translated by H. L. Jones. The Loeb Classical Library. London: William Heinemann Ltd., 1930.

TERTULLIAN
The Prescription Against the Heretics. In Rev. Alexander Roberts and James Donaldson, (Eds.), *The Ante-Nicene Fathers: Translations of the Writings of the Fathers down to A.D. 325, Vol. 3, Latin Christianity: Its Founder, Tertullian*. American reprint of the Edinburgh edition

(n.d.). Michigan: Wm. B. Eerdmans Publishing Company, 1978.

THEOPHILUS OF ANTIOCH
   Theophilus to Autolycus. In Rev. Rev. Alexander Roberts and James Donaldson, (Eds.), *The Ante-Nicene Fathers: Translations of the Writings of the Fathers down to A.D. 325, Vol. 2, Fathers of the Second Century*. American reprint of the Edinburgh edition (n.d.). Michigan: Wm. B. Eerdmans Publishing Company, 1978.

TILLICH, PAUL, 1958
   "The Lost Dimension in Religion." In William Williamson, (Ed.), 1985, 41-47.

TYLOR, SIR EDWARD, B., 1873
   Primitive Culture, Vol. 2, Religion in the Primitive Culture. New York: Harper Torch Books, 1958.

URWICK, W., 1885
   India 100 years Ago: The Beauty of Old India Illustrated. London: Bracken Books, 1985.

VAN BUITENEN, J. A. B., 1973
   "Introduction" to The Mahabharata, Vol. 1, The Book of the Beginning. Chicago: The University of Chicago Press, xiii-xliv.

VAN BAAL, J., 1971
   Symbols For Communication: An Introduction to the Anthropology of Religion. Assen: Van Gorcum.

   1981   *Man's Quest for Partnership*. Assen: Van Gorcum.

VERHELST, THIERRY, 1985
   Cultures, Religions and Development in India: Interviews Conducted and recorded by Thierry Verhelst, 14 to 23-1-1985. A.P.H.D. working group on Religions and Cultures. Brussels: Broederlijk Delen, Mimeo.

VERNON, GLEN, M., 1962
Sociology of Religion. New York: McGraw-Hill Book Company.

WARDER, A. K., 1971
Outline of Indian Philosophy. Delhi: Motilal Banarasidas.

1980   *A History of Buddhism*. Second Revised Edition. Delhi: Motilal Banarasidas.

WATSON, JAMES, L., 1988
"The Structure of Chinese Funerary Rites: Elementary forms, Ritual Sequence, and the Primacy of Performance." In James L. Watson, and Evelyn S. Rawski, (Eds.), *Death Ritual in Late Imperial and Modern China*. Berkeley: University of California Press.

WEBER, MAX, 1958
The Religion of India: The Sociology of Hinduism and Buddhism. Hans G.Gerth and Don Martindale, (Eds.). New York: The Free Press, 1967.

WEIGHTMAN, SIMON, 1984
"Hinduism." In John R. Hinnells, (Ed.), *A Handbook of Living Religions*. Harmondsworth: Penguin Books, 191-236.

WIEDEMANN, THOMAS, 1990
"Polytheism, Monotheism, and Religious Co-existence: Paganism and Christianity in the Roman Empire." In Ian Hamnet, (Ed.), 1990, 64-78.

WILKEN, ROBERT, L., 1984
The Christians as the Romans Saw Them. New Haven: Yale University Press.

WILLIAMSON, WILLIAM, B., 1985
Decisions in Philosophy of Religion. Buffalo: Prometheus Books.

WILLSON, LESLIE, A., 1964
   A Mythical Image: The Ideal of India in the German Romanticism. North Carolina: Duke University Press.

YOUNG, RICHARD FOX, 1981
   Resistant Hinduism: Sanskrit Sources on Anti-Christian Apologetics in Early Nineteenth-Century India. Leiden: E. J. Brill.